The Short Oxford History of the British Isles

General Editor: Paul Langford

# The Sixteenth Century

Edited by Patrick Collinson

**Figure 1** The frontispiece to Michael Drayton's 'chorographical' poem of
12,000 lines, *Polyolbion* (1612), sometimes described as William Camden's
*Britannia* in verse, and extolling 'Albions glorious Ile', 'my England'. The
fecund figure of Albion sits on the rock of Great Britain, wrapped in the map
of England. She is flanked by Brutus the Trojan, Julius Caesar, Hengist the
Saxon, and William the Conqueror, but it is Albion herself who is enthroned.

The Short Oxford History
of the British Isles

General Editor: Paul Langford

# The Sixteenth Century

## 1485–1603

Edited by Patrick Collinson

OXFORD
UNIVERSITY PRESS

# OXFORD
### UNIVERSITY PRESS

Great Clarendon Street, Oxford OX2 6DP

Oxford University Press is a department of the University of Oxford.
It furthers the University's objective of excellence in research, scholarship,
and education by publishing worldwide in

Oxford New York

Athens Auckland Bangkok Bogotá Buenos Aires Cape Town
Chennai Dar es Salaam Delhi Florence Hong Kong Istanbul Karachi
Kolkata Kuala Lumpur Madrid Melbourne Mexico City Mumbai Nairobi
Paris São Paulo Shanghai Singapore Taipei Tokyo Toronto Warsaw

with associated companies in Berlin Ibadan

Oxford is a registered trade mark of Oxford University Press
in the UK and in certain other countries

Published in the United States
by Oxford University Press Inc., New York

British Library Cataloguing in Publication Data

Data available

Library of Congress Cataloging in Publication Data

Data applied for
ISBN 0–19–820767–0 (hbk)
ISBN 0–19–820766–2 (pbk)

1 3 5 7 9 10 8 6 4 2

Typeset in Minion
by RefineCatch Limited, Bungay, Suffolk
Printed in Great Britain by
T.J. International, Padstow, Cornwall

# General Editor's Preface

It is a truism that historical writing is itself culturally determined, reflecting intellectual fashions, political preoccupations, and moral values at the time it is written. In the case of British history this has resulted in a great diversity of perspectives both on the content of what is narrated and the geopolitical framework in which it is placed. In recent times the process of redefinition has positively accelerated under the pressure of contemporary change. Some of it has come from within Britain during a period of recurrent racial tension in England and reviving nationalism in Scotland, Wales, and Northern Ireland. But much of it also comes from beyond. There has been a powerful surge of interest in the politics of national identity in response to the break-up of some of the world's great empires, both colonial and continental. The search for new sovereignties, not least in Europe itself, has contributed to a questioning of long-standing political boundaries. Such shifting of the tectonic plates of history is to be expected but for Britain especially, with what is perceived (not very accurately) to be a long period of relative stability lasting from the late seventeenth century to the mid-twentieth century, it has had a particular resonance.

Much controversy and still more confusion arise from the lack of clarity about the subject matter that figures in insular historiography. Historians of England are often accused of ignoring the history of Britain as a whole, while using the terms as if they are synonymous. Historians of Britain are similarly charged with taking Ireland's inclusion for granted without engaging directly with it. And for those who believe they are writing more specifically the history of Ireland, of Wales, or of Scotland, there is the unending tension between so-called metropolis and periphery, and the dilemmas offered by wider contexts, not only British and Irish but European and indeed extra-European. Some of these difficulties arise from the fluctuating fortunes and changing boundaries of the British state as organized from London. But even if the rulers of what is now called England had never taken an interest in dominion beyond its borders, the economic and cultural relationships between the various parts of the British Isles would still have generated many historiographical problems.

This series is based on the premiss that whatever the complexities and ambiguities created by this state of affairs, it makes sense to offer an overview, conducted by leading scholars whose research is on the leading edge of their discipline. That overview extends to the whole of the British Isles. The expression is not uncontroversial, especially to many in Ireland, for whom the very word 'British' implies an unacceptable politics of dominion. Yet there is no other formulation that can encapsulate the shared experience of 'these islands', to use another term much employed in Ireland and increasingly heard in Britain, but rather unhelpful to other inhabitants of the planet.

In short we use the words 'British Isles' solely and simply as a geographical expression. No set agenda is implied. It would indeed be difficult to identify one that could stand scrutiny. What constitutes a concept such as 'British history' or 'four nations history' remains the subject of acute disagreement, and varies much depending on the period under discussion. The editors and contributors of this series have been asked only to convey the findings of the most authoritative scholarship, and to flavour them with their own interpretative originality and distinctiveness. In the process we hope to provide not only a stimulating digest of more than two thousand years of history, but also a sense of the intense vitality that continues to mark historical research into the past of all parts of Britain and Ireland.

*Lincoln College*
*Oxford*

PAUL LANGFORD

# Contents

**Conclusion**                                                   217
*Patrick Collinson*

# List of Illustrations

# Genealogy and List of Maps

# List of Contributors

**SIMON ADAMS** is Senior Lecturer in History at the University of Strathclyde. His publications include *Household Accounts of Robert Dudley, Earl of Leicester* (1995) and *Leicester and the Court: Essays on Elizabethan Politics* (forthcoming, 2002). *Elizabeth I* (English Monarchs Series) and *The Road to Nonsuch: England and the Netherlands 1575–1585* are in progress.

**PATRICK COLLINSON** is Regius Professor of Modern History, Emeritus, in the University of Cambridge, and a Fellow of Trinity College. He previously held chairs at the Universities of Sydney, Kent at Canterbury, and Sheffield. He is a Fellow of the British Academy and of the Australian Academy of Humanities. He has written extensively on the religious, social, and political history of the sixteenth century, his books including *The Religion of Protestants: the Church in English Society 1559–1625* (1982) and *The Birthpangs of Protestant England: Religious and Cultural Change in the Sixteenth and Seventeenth Centuries* (1998).

**STEVEN G. ELLIS** is Professor of History at the National University of Ireland, Galway. His many publications on British and Irish history include *Ireland in the Age of the Tudors 1447–1603: English Expansion and the End of Gaelic rule* (1998), and *Tudor Frontiers and Noble Power: The Making of the British State* (1995).

**JOHN GUY** is Professor of Modern History at the University of St Andrews. His many publications on early-modern British history and the history of political thought include *Tudor England* (1988), *The Tudors: A Very Short Introduction* (2000), and *Thomas More* (2000). He is a freelance presenter and historical consultant for BBC2 television.

**DIARMAID MACCULLOCH** is a Fellow of St Cross College and Professor of the History of the Church at Oxford University; he is a Fellow of the British Academy, and co-edits the *Journal of Ecclesiastical History*. His biography *Thomas Cranmer: A Life* (1996) won the Whitbread Biography, Duff Cooper, and James Tait Black Prizes; his latest book is *Tudor Church Militant: Edward VI and the Protestant Reformation* (1999).

J. A. SHARPE is a Professor at the History Department of the University of York. He has published extensively on the history of crime and punishment, and latterly witchcraft, in early modern England. He is also the author of *Early Modern England: A Social History 1550–1760* (1997). His current research interests are the operation of the legal system in the early modern Isle of Man, and the history of violence in England between 1600 and 1800.

GREG WALKER is Professor of Early-Modern Literature and Culture at the University of Leicester. He has published widely on the literary and cultural history of the late-medieval and Renaissance periods, including, most recently, *The Politics of Performance in Early Renaissance Drama* (1998) and *Medieval Drama: An Anthology*.

**Figure 2** Hans Holbein's drawn portrait of Thomas Cromwell ('Lord Cromwell'). In workaday dress, without frills and finery, and regardless of whether Cromwell can be personally credited with a 'Revolution in Government', this image conveys more powerfully than any of the painted portraits of the age the human energy released in Tudor England.

# Introduction

## Patrick Collinson

For much of the twentieth century, history enjoyed a privileged position in sixth-form and university syllabuses. And in England history meant primarily English history, which more often than not included that old faithful, 'Tudors and Stuarts'. In Scotland, the subject taught was, naturally, Scottish history. It is a not uncommon experience for a product of an English education to find, in conversation with a Scot, striking differences in what they think happened in their interrelated pasts, not least in the sixteenth century. Ireland, too, had its own nationalist historians. As for anything which could be called British history, it hardly existed, so that in 1975 the distinguished historian John Pocock was able to publish an article with the title 'British History: A Plea for a New Subject'.[1] But is British history a subject, or rather, when did it become one?

It was events in the seventeenth century which forced historians to take Pocock's plea seriously. The British Isles then constituted a multiple monarchy, the three still distinct kingdoms of England (with the Principality of Wales), Scotland, and Ireland all subject to the same Stewart king. But for events first in Scotland and then in Ireland there might have been no English Civil War. Indeed, that may be in itself a misnomer, since in the 1640s and 1650s there was large-scale conflict in all the constituent parts of the British Isles, Scottish armies were engaged in England and the English in Ireland, so that some historians prefer to speak of the War of the Three Kingdoms, a term already current (in Gaelic) in late seventeenth-century Ireland. Professor Conrad Russell called his history of the events leading to those wars *The Fall of the British Monarchies 1637–1642* (1991). An appropriate

---

[1] *Journal of Modern History*, 47 (1975), 601–28.

metaphor might be a game of billiards or snooker, events in the three kingdoms so many balls bouncing off one another and occasionally falling into pockets.

But that is not to say that 'Britain' or 'Britishness' existed in any very tangible or meaningful form in the seventeenth century, still less in the sixteenth. In what one reviewer called her 'dashingly readable' *Britons* (1992), Professor Linda Colley located 'the forging of the British nation' in a long eighteenth century which began with the Act of Union of 1707 joining Scotland to England and Wales, followed by a century of almost unrelenting wars with France (38 years of active hostilities between 1702 and 1815) which she believes had most to do with 'the invention of Britishness'. However, Colley's book was no sooner published than it was followed by a period of unprecedented uncertainty and soul-searching about the British question, which continues. Britishness is threatened without by progressive integration into the European Union, within by a process of devolutionary disintegration, and its character is inevitably affected by increasing ethnic diversity. With the revival of a Scottish Parliament after three centuries, and the invention of a quasi-parliamentary Assembly in Wales, the idea of a single British identity, or nation, has become newly problematical. To be sure, for many English people, and for Americans, 'Britain' and 'England' have always been virtually synonymous. But what, in these altered circumstances, *is* England, which is governed through the Parliament of the United Kingdom and which, at the time of writing (2000) has no separate parliamentary representation of its own, either national or regional; and what is Englishness?

Historians live in their own times, not in the past, and the contributors to this volume have been sensitive to this unstable, evolving backcloth of contemporary events. They have written a history of the British Isles in the sixteenth century where a generation ago they would probably have been writing the history of Tudor England. In the chapters which follow, Wales, Scotland, and Ireland all receive more attention than they would have been accorded in the past. But it is not so clear that this is a history of Britain in the sixteenth century, for arguably there was no such history, or place, except in the imagination, for example the imagination of the antiquary William Camden whose *Britannia* was published in 1586. However nine volumes in the 'Penguin History of Britain', tell the story from AD 100 to 1990. The volume covering the sixteenth century, by Susan Brigden, includes a great deal of Irish history, but scarcely a mention of Scotland, presumably on the grounds that Ireland was ruled from England, Scotland not.

One contributor to this book, Steven G. Ellis, who teaches in a university in the far west of Ireland, is especially conscious that to envisage history from a vantage point in London and the cultivated and civilized southern and midland counties of England, and with a vision extending no farther than the river Trent, is a serious distortion of sixteenth-century reality. The greater part of the British Isles consisted of thinly populated, upland regions, where animal husbandry rather than arable farming was the mainstay of existence, and which had their own means of maintaining, or failing to maintain, some sort of order. The Tudor monarchy, or state, exerted itself, with indifferent success, to control these (from its centrist point of view but not theirs) peripheral borderlands, fluctuating between the policy known in twentieth-century West Africa as 'indirect rule' through local bigwigs and direct control and colonization, which in the case of Ireland would eventually entail conquest. Ellis, to a greater extent than the other contributors, finds that he really is writing British history, since the problems of the far north of England and of Ireland, problems, that is, for the Tudor state, were very similar and invited similar policy responses. But, ironically, it was only in that south-eastern, centrist perspective that they could have appeared similar. Northern English magnates and Irish chieftains literally did not speak the same language.

The contributors are not under any illusion that the British Isles in the sixteenth century were hermetically sealed off from the rest of Europe, or had a self-contained history. Simon Adams opens his chapter on 'Britain, Europe, and the world' with the affirmation: 'There are few greater myths in British history than "our island story".' It is arguable that the constituent parts of the British Isles had more to do with the politics, culture, and trade of one region or another of continental Europe than with each other. (And much depends upon what we mean by 'parts'. In the sixteenth century what are now Northern Ireland and the Western Isles of Scotland constituted one Gaelic world, connected rather than separated by the narrow waters of the North Channel.) Scotland was a subject for foreign policy specialists, like the Protector Somerset in the mid-sixteenth century and his apprentice, William Cecil, who believed in its incorporation into an English scheme of things, by fair means or foul. Ireland was a different kettle of fish. What George Bernard Shaw called 'John Bull's other island' was a lordship and, under Henry VIII, a newly declared kingdom 'annexed' to England. It was a fatal nexus for both parties to this unequal conjunction: fatal for Ireland, which was reduced to the status of a colonial society and preparing for its own terrible seventeenth century when it would lose, in ten years, 41 per cent of its population, not, as in the nineteenth century, to famine and migration but to civil war and the plagues attendant upon war; fatal, then as for centuries to come, for the reputations of representatives of the English Crown, both civil and military.

Any sense of national identity is bound to draw upon the past, or rather upon that collective, selective memory of the past which is history. And English identity has always been especially nourished by the history of the sixteenth century. It has not been easy, as a student, to avoid altogether 'the Tudors'. For generations, the subject was encountered in two historical classics, S. T. Bindoff's *Tudor England* (1950) and G. R. Elton's *England under the Tudors* (1955). Neither book, incidentally, allows much room for Scotland or Ireland, Bindoff's index noting, under Scotland, 'English intervention in' and 'immigration from'. And Bindoff devoted just twenty-five words to Wales.

Bindoff's tone was, for the time, typically upbeat. It was under the 'able guidance' of its Tudor monarchs, 'no wiser or mightier ever adorned the English throne', that 'England rose magnificently to great occasions and experienced something of a Golden Age' which has always 'captivated the popular imagination'. Dating his preface 'Empire Day, 1950', the even more exuberant A. L. Rowse published his *The England of Elizabeth* in the same year as *Tudor England*, only ten years after the summer of 1940, claiming that at that time of peril, 'people turned for inspiration to that earlier hour, and were renewed and went on.' (Did they?) That earlier hour was the Elizabethan hour, and especially the Armada Year, 1588. 'Perhaps it was in that electric, charged moment that our people suddenly reached maturity and became aware of themselves as a people, first saw themselves in the mirror of their destiny, half glimpsed the extraordinary fate that lay ahead of them across the seas and in the world.'[2] A similar point had

---

[2] Publisher's blurb to S. T. Bindoff, *Tudor England* (London, 1950); A. L. Rowse, *The England of Elizabeth* (London, 1950), 17–18.

already been made in Laurence Olivier's film version of Shakespeare's *Henry V* (1944). Sir John Neale had contributed significantly to the glorification of the late Tudor age in his hugely successful biography of *Queen Elizabeth* (1934), which went through umpteen editions and was translated into six other languages. Following the lead of the man he called 'the greatest of modern English historians' (a judgement which now looks distinctly odd), Bindoff called Elizabeth 'the superb and matchless flower'.[3] This at least partly invented sixteenth century was placed at the threshold of Britain's global greatness, which itself is now a thing of the past, so that no one is any longer likely to write in such extravagant terms. But there is no doubt that the sixteenth century continues to captivate the popular imagination, thanks above all to five individuals: Henry VIII and Elizabeth I, who are never absent from our TV screens for long, Sir Thomas More, Sir Francis Drake, and the everlasting Shakespeare.

But what should a history of the sixteenth century consist of? As Elton pointed out in 1955, all history writing involves awkward choices and some aspects of the story must be made more equal than others. For Elton the subject had a spinal cord, which was political. 'To me it seems that what matters most in the story is the condition, reconstruction, and gradual moulding of a state—the history of a nation and its leaders in political action and therefore the history of government in the widest sense.'[4] Economic, social, literary, military matters received less attention. 'This could not be helped.' Elsewhere in his writings, Elton made clear that he did not disagree with an earlier occupant of his chair who had defined history as 'past politics'.[5] Swimming deliberately against the tide of the more fashionable social history, he wrote that 'historians who can muster no interest for the active political lives of past societies have no sense of history at all.'[6] As Dr Johnson might have said, the historian who is tired of politics is tired of life—and of history itself.

So it was that all those generations of school and university students were taught by Elton that the most important things which happened in the sixteenth century happened in the 1530s, the decade

[3] Bindoff, *Tudor England*, 306–7.
[4] G. R. Elton, *England under the Tudors* (London, 1955), p. vi.
[5] Attributed to Sir John Seeley, but also to E. A. Freeman and to Herbert B. Adams. All were late nineteenth-century historians.
[6] G. R. Elton, *Political History, Principles and Practice* (London, 1970), 4.

dominated by Thomas Cromwell, who Elton believed to have been one of the most creative statesmen in the whole of English history. For it was then that the late medieval state which Henry VII had strengthened and stabilized was transformed into something more recognizably modern. Thanks to the decision to declare unilateral independence from Rome, the result of Henry VIII's marital difficulties, this was a state defined as fully sovereign within itself, under one king and supreme religious head and one law. Elton believed this state to have been moving towards self-perpetuating and bureaucratic governmental departments which were no longer dependent on the vagaries of personal monarchy, well able to withstand the historical accidents of a royal minority and the rule of two women, which followed the death of Henry VIII. It is only a slight exaggeration to say that Elton almost reduced the history of the sixteenth century to the creative deeds of one man in one decade.

In these Cromwellian years, Wales was fully incorporated in what amounted to a Union of England and Wales, and the writing was on the wall for other semi-independent franchises. But it was in the following decade, in what looks like a departure from Cromwellian unionism, that the long dependent island of Ireland was declared a no less dependent kingdom, albeit a kingdom without a crown, whose kings were never to visit it in person except in 1689. To the 1540s, also, belongs an aggressive diplomacy applied to the Scottish question, soon employing the rhetoric of a greater Britain as a desirable consummation of the long troubled history of the northern and southern parts of the island. And that, too, was not Cromwell's policy.

Elton's *Tudor Revolution in Government*, the title of his first book, published in 1953, has not stood the test of time, or the onslaughts of his critics, especially a number of former pupils who in 1986 published *Revolution Reassessed*. But such has been the deep impress which Elton made on the sixteenth century that it was on his own chosen ground of government and administration, especially in the 1530s, that revisionism and reassessment have occurred. The points at issue were still Elton's points. When John Guy, one of the contributors to this volume, came to publish his own *Tudor England* in 1988, he explained that he too was bound to be selective and had conceived of his book as essentially a political (and religious) narrative, the chapters on economy and society serving as 'context'. As for Elton's 'revolution', Guy's judgement was that it was perhaps feasible if the period in which it was supposed to have happened were to be extended to the death of Elizabeth in 1603: 'though whether the word "revolution" is appropriate—as opposed to "readjustment" or straightforward "change"—is a matter of judgement'. Guy has more recently called the 'revolution in government' debate 'old hat', and those who wish to be informed about it or to learn about such administrative departments of state as the Court of Augmentations or the Court of First Fruits and Tenths will have to go back to the writings of Elton and his critics.[7] There is almost nothing about these matters in this book—which is not to deny their importance for the history of governmental institutions.

Bindoff's *Tudor England* had rather different priorities. In spite of his admiration for the Tudor monarchs, this was more a history of the English people, written with evident sympathy, even admiration, for the 'honest, sober, sturdy folk' who rose in rebellion in the North in 1536, the so-called 'Pilgrimage of Grace', in East Anglia in 1549 ('Kett's Rebellion'), and in the Rebellion of the Northern Earls in 1569, which was also a demonstration by several thousand peasants. At the heart of the book was its longest chapter, called 'Commonwealth and Commotion', dealing with the economic and social troubles which distracted the minority reign of Edward VI, and which were factors contributory to what some historians have called the 'Mid-Tudor Crisis': a story of sheep, wool, cloth, prices, the impact of these things on the rural, agrarian scene, of the radical critique by preachers and pamphleteers of the antisocial evil of 'covetousness', and of direct and even violent action by the common people, especially in the countryside. 'In the history of the Englishman's getting and spending the fifteen-forties are as pregnant with change as are the fifteen-thirties in the history of his governance and creed', years 'of central and crucial importance'.[8]

Behind the pages of Bindoff lay thirty or forty years of study of the economic history of a period of drastic change marked, according to your point of view, by rapacious landlords, enclosing and rack-renting; or by another so-called 'revolution', this time of prices, the first significant inflation experienced in England for centuries; or by

[7] John Guy, *Tudor England* (Oxford, 1988), 157; John Guy (ed.), *The Tudor Monarchy* (London, 1997), 4.
[8] S. T. Bindoff, 'Ket's Rebellion 1549', in Joel Hurstfield (ed.), *The Historical Association Book of the Tudors* (London, 1973), 94; Bindoff, *Tudor England*, 209–10.

an increase of population after two centuries of stagnation, following the mid-fourteenth-century Black Death. This subject was almost created by the great R. H. Tawney (denounced by Elton as 'a very good man and a very bad historian'[9]) in the most deeply researched of all his works, *The Agrarian Problem in the Sixteenth Century* (1912), a book born of the conviction that the bottom line in any pre-industrial society must be the distribution and exploitation of the land. The subject was carried forward for many years in the University of London, where from 1924 students were taught from the three volumes of *Tudor Economic Documents*, edited by Tawney and the distinguished medieval economic historian, Eileen Power.

So it was that Bindoff was able to bring together two rather different approaches to the sixteenth century, and to give it a shape different from Elton's. But there was not to be another book quite like it. Tawney's (and to some extent the much more conservative Bindoff's) social history had a socialist edge, far removed from Elton's outlook and most forcefully stated in an economic history of the early sixteenth century by that great historian of the English landscape, W. G. Hoskins, *The Age of Plunder* (1976). Hoskins suggested that the whole of English history since 1066 had been one of plunder by the governing class, and when he quoted Thomas More in *Utopia* to the effect that all so-called commonwealths were really conspiracies of rich men, he could not resist the comment: 'This profound truth remains undiluted in twentieth-century Britain, and is equally disguised from public debate.'[10]

But by this time a new economic history, and a new social history, was gathering pace, lacking in Hoskins's indignation, ever more technically proficient, and vastly expanding the areas of enquiry to cover: fundamentally, population ('historical demography' was a new and independent subject), but also such topics as crime, witchcraft, education and literacy, childhood and youth, and, above all, women, a subject on which Bindoff had had almost nothing to say. Reviewing these immense achievements, Professor Keith Wrightson has written: 'A "new social history" has appeared, a history in which a deliberate effort has been made to recover the experience of the mass of the

---

[9] G. R. Elton, *Return to Essentials* (Cambridge, 1991), 86–7.
[10] W. G. Hoskins, *The Age of Plunder* (London, 1976), 121.

English people, to rediscover them as members of a distinct and vigorous culture and to understand their part in the making of their history."[11]

But there was a price to be paid, one of fragmentation, or at least bifurcation. The economic and social history of the period became a distinct subject, in many universities separately taught and examined. The history of religion in sixteenth-century England, conventionally labelled as the history of the English Reformation (and Counter-Reformation), although closely connected to the history of the state and of political processes, so that both Elton and Guy were bound to give it generous measure, has also threatened to become a free-standing subject with its own scholarly literature, simply because of the intensity of the research devoted to it by literally hundreds of historians, especially those working at a local level.

The time has come to put the Humpty Dumpty of the sixteenth century together again and to reintegrate political and social history, for all politics are played out in a social context, and everything which happens in society is in some sense political. Social and economic historians will continue to work their way through their own exacting agenda, much of which is outlined in Jim Sharpe's contribution to this collection. And there will always be scope for the Eltonian study of the institutions which made up, for Elton, the Tudor 'constitution'. It is time, for example, for some brave souls to make a greater impact on the utterly voluminous and hard to access records of the central courts of justice: no mystery that they have been left to last!

But it is now clear that for the purpose of a fully rounded account of Tudor politics, Elton's preoccupation with the 'public', 'official', 'bureaucratic' departments of government was far too restrictive. As long ago as the 1970s, David Starkey established that much of the political energy of this society was expressed and exerted informally, in the royal household, which is to say, at Court. Elton's rigid distinction between 'courtiers' (by implication merely ornamental) and 'councillors' was quite unrealistic. They were usually the same people. But what is more, we now acknowledge that the political life of Tudor England was multilayered, a carpet, as it were, with a very thick pile. Even small towns and rural parishes had their politics, often

[11] Keith Wrightson, *English Society 1580–1680* (London, 1982), 11–12.

self-contained, but also relating to the wider scene, localities interacting with the centre, in ways which will invite much more research, and which will be paralleled in the work of new generations of Scottish historians.

The religious history of these islands through a century of destructive but also reforming and defining religious change is so large and important a subject that it demands separate treatment, which it receives in this volume from Diarmaid MacCulloch, who evenhandedly covers not just the time-honoured subject 'The English Reformation' but religious change throughout the British Isles. But such was the central place of religious belief and practice in the sixteenth century that having taken it out for close examination in his own specialized laboratory, the religious historian must reinsert it into the whole fabric of society. The mechanisms of church government, recorded in England in the copious archives of bishops' and archdeacons' courts and in Scotland in the minutes of 'kirk sessions', will continue to engage their own more or less specialized ecclesiastical historians. But these records teem with rich social detail, and above all with the language in which denizens of the sixteenth century expressed themselves and interacted. One only has to turn a few hundred folios of the evidence given in the Norwich ecclesiastical court to come across the Norfolk vicar who was said to have two illegitimate children living in the parish, and whose wife called him 'Scot bastard bearer' and scratched his face; or the Suffolk parson who allegedly boasted that he had had the use of all the wives in the village 'saving four', and who was said to spend his days drinking and playing cards in beer houses with 'tinkers, mariners and rovers'.[12] (These were not necessarily 'typical' East Anglian clergymen of their time, or they would not have found themselves in court.)

What has been added to the varieties of Tudor history offered by Elton on the one hand and Bindoff on the other is greater sensitivity to the mentalities, the thinking and the language of English men and women in the sixteenth century. Here we are much indebted to historians of ideas and the intellect, whose subject used to be called 'Political Thought', but which is now given a wider scope. That has led to the creation of what is almost a new subject for study: Tudor

---

[12] These East Anglian clerics will be found in Norfolk Record Office, DEP 22–3, fos. 209 seq., DEP 21, fos. 400 seq.

'Political Culture', in which ideas, and the articulation of ideas in language, and especially the formalized language of rhetoric, have a central part to play.

'Rhetoric' is today a relatively unfamiliar and pejorative term which may require comment. Standard forms of rhetoric included parliamentary speeches, sermons, correspondence, including diplomatic correspondence, and the courtly language of compliment and criticism, all subject to the rules of the game, which were learned at the higher levels of a sixteenth-century education. The form of any discourse was as important, for those both uttering and on the receiving end, as content, and rhetorical forms must be understood before one can hope to penetrate the intentions of the speaker or writer. Both form and much of the content were derived from the classical literatures of Greece and Rome, in which any educated person was more at home than all but a handful of academics and Classics teachers today. To make this point concrete: the Roman senator and orator Cicero, and the historian Tacitus, neither of whom will be found in the indexes to Bindoff's and Elton's books, had long-running afterlives in the sixteenth century, not only expressing but actually shaping its politics. If Thomas More had not read his Tacitus, he would not have given us his history of the reign of Richard III, which means that Shakespeare would not have written his play on the same subject, or, at least, not the same play.

All educated persons in the sixteenth century learned from the same textbooks and followed the same rules in what they said and wrote. All were children of the classically oriented Renaissance. But there agreement ceased. The religious revolution of the Reformation, and the vigorous Counter-Reformation reaction against it, which under Mary had the backing of the English state but under Elizabeth was a proscribed religion of active and passive resistance to the state, fractured a society which at the beginning of the sixteenth century was to a large extent united in its religious faith, one of the most Catholic countries in Europe. In Scotland Protestantism was an overturning, revolutionary force redefining the nation, and so it would remain for a full century to come. In Ireland it was a violent, and unsuccessful, imposition. Throughout the British Isles, religious difference fuelled ideological conflicts which make up a large part of the intellectual history of the century: Catholics against Protestants, Nonconformist Puritans and Presbyterians against the religious orders and forms imposed by monarchs and bishops. Yet it is not really appropriate to apply to this age the words of the poet John Donne: 'All coherence gone'. These profound religious differences were contained within the same moral universe, and belief in Divine Providence as determining all of human life appears to have been nearly universal.

There is no reason why the often violently contested culture of politics should be restricted to the spoken and written word. The pageantry of triumphal royal entries and processions, royal progresses, portraiture, architecture, costume, the to us arcane and inaccessible symbolic language of heraldry ('coats of arms') which was everywhere to be seen: all were, in the language of anthropology, political signifiers. It was at York, in the early days of the reign of the first Tudor, that someone thought of the logo of a red rose superimposed on the white, the famous Tudor rose which would soon fill every vacant surface in Henry VIII's magnificent completion of King's College Chapel in Cambridge, in its entirety a potent political statement. When, at the end of the century, the richest woman in England, Bess of Hardwicke, countess of Shrewsbury, built the grandest and most beautiful of all Elizabethan prodigy houses, this too was a political statement, for her granddaughter, Lady Arbella Stewart, had a plausible claim to succeed to the throne. Not only did Bess set her initials 'ES' (Elizabeth Shrewsbury) in stone on the battlements of Hardwicke Hall, where they can still be seen from the M1; in the great state room at the top of the house she also positioned those same initials within the royal motto: DIEU EST MON DROIT. Nothing had been written, but the Privy Council still sent a party up to Derbyshire to investigate. The most studied institution in sixteenth-century England, Parliament, cannot be fully understood without reference to what one historian has called the ritual and gesture of accommodation, which in a sense was what a parliament was all about. It was important that, some way into the famous 'Golden Speech' which she delivered to her last Parliament, a speech which was all about accommodation, Elizabeth told the Commons, who had all been kneeling, to stand up, 'for I shall yet trouble you with longer speech'.[13] To be sure, since neither we nor the TV cameras were there, it is only rarely that we can observe such rituals. But we should be aware that

---

[13] J. E. Neale, *Elizabeth I and her Parliaments 1584–1601* (London, 1957), 389.

the bare written word of journals and parliamentary diaries is just that.

These are so many details of the cultural world of the Renaissance in Britain, the useful if very elastic expression explored here by Greg Walker. It is significant that his is not the last chapter in the book, which it would have been in the old days, when Elton's equivalent chapter came just before the end, dealing with the arts, poetry, and drama, as if they were so many appendices to the main plot.

As Professor Walker amply demonstrates, one of the most promising developments in what we may call the reconstruction, or reinvention, of the sixteenth century, has been the insight that if many of the historian's 'documents' are also 'texts' (rhetoric), with often slippery meanings, the 'texts' studied by literary scholars, such as Edmund Spenser's poems or Shakespeare's plays, can also serve as documents. Another scholar has made the important observation that what we call 'literature' and the English nation were interactive and interdependent, both in the course of being invented, not finished, stable entities. And so with the other nations inhabiting the British Isles. For the English, Ireland was an imaginary place, demonized in Spenser's *View of the State of Ireland*, a fictional landscape in his *Faerie Queene*, greatest of the English literary masterpieces of the age but written entirely in Ireland, from which Spenser was forced to flee when, in 1598, real life caught up with the poet and his Irish estate was destroyed in the Tyrone Rebellion.

This was an age in which most politicians were also what we should call authors, and when almost all educated persons wrote poetry, often for a privately or publicly political purpose. When the musician and playwright Thomas Whythorne needed to detach himself from his many female admirers, he did so by composing verses and leaving them on their dressing tables. When Elizabeth's courtiers wanted to persuade her to marry and so secure the succession to the throne, they conveyed the message indirectly, in the fiction of plays, which the queen knew very well were directed at her, but which she was more inclined to tolerate than parliamentary speeches on the subject. These, in the words of one of Greg Walker's book titles, were *Plays of Persuasion* (1991). And when Sir Philip Sidney wanted to express his pent-up political frustration, faced by a queen and a monarchical system throughout Europe which always made the wrong decisions, or, which was almost worse, in the case of Elizabeth was chronically indecisive, he did it in the encoded language of a romance, *Arcadia*. As for Shakespeare, who wrote so many plays about Roman and English politics, his politics remain so elusive that there is no reason why the question whether he had any should not be discussed for ever. We have come a long way since A. F. Pollard, who dominated Tudor history before Bindoff or Elton were born or thought of, wrote, in 1910, that 'no period of English literature has less to do with politics than that during which English letters reached their zenith'—the sixteenth century.[14] It no longer makes sense to study the history of the sixteenth century without reference to the literature, or the literature without knowledge of the history.

So the ambitions of today's Tudor historians are almost limitless, in the jargon of the trade 'holistic'. There is clearly some danger of sharing the fate of Icarus, who flew too close to the sun and came a cropper. A history which attempted to be a history of everything would in the end tell us nothing, or at least would make no sense. In this book, just as in the earlier accounts of the subject by Bindoff, Elton, and Guy, we have been selective. What we have written is what we, living when and where we do, think worth covering in 80,000 words on the history of the British Isles in the sixteenth century.

[14] A. F. Pollard, *The History of England from the Accession of Edward VI to the Death of Elizabeth* (London, 1910), 440.

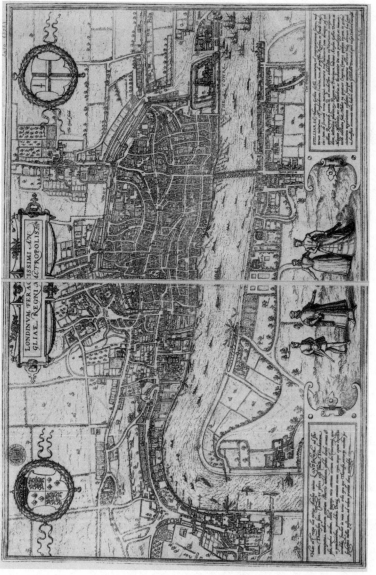

**Figure 3** London in the first half of Elizabeth's reign; although the metropolitan area had not yet spread beyond the city walls, London was by far the biggest urban centre in the British Isles, with a population rising from about 120,000 in 1550 to some 200,000 in 1600.

# 1

# Economy and society

## J. A. Sharpe

For the few sixteenth-century visitors whose opinions have come down to us, the British Isles were clearly regarded as being something rather exotic if a little bit backward. England and Scotland had long been locked into European diplomacy, and Ireland, like these two countries, had equally long been a welcoming recipient of cultural and intellectual influences from the continent. But observers from more sophisticated places, like Castille, the Southern Netherlands, or Northern Italy, while finding much to comment upon favourably, were aware that they were in a peripheral area, still relatively under-developed by the most advanced continental standards. The idea that this area would one day be the location of the world's first industrial nation, or that it would lie at the centre of the most extensive empire the world has ever seen, would have seemed improbable to foreign observers in 1500, and hardly less so to those arriving a century later. Many of the Spaniards who accompanied Philip II to England when he came to marry Mary Tudor in 1554 commented on the strangeness of the land in which they found themselves 'I had always heard that the marvels described in books of chivalry fell far short of what was to be seen here', wrote one.[1] The perceived geographical and cultural marginality of these islands was demonstrated in 1474 when the duke of Milan, Galeazzo Maria Sforza, was contemplating a marriage alliance with the Stewarts. He eventually decided against the plan, as

[1] *Calendar of Letters, Despatches and State Papers Relating to the Negotiations between England and Spain*, xiii. *Philip and Mary, July 1554–November 1558*, ed. Royall Tyler (London, 1954), 61.

it would be an act of parental cruelty to send his daughter to a place 'so far off as Scotland would be.'[2]

Then as now, travellers' accounts of foreign lands, especially those written by diplomats, should be treated with caution. The Spanish diplomat Pedro de Ayala's description of Scotland of 1498 was written to produce as favourable an impression of the country as possible in the context of a peculiar phase in Spanish foreign policy. The *Italian Description of England*, written at about the same time and frequently quoted by historians of the Tudor period, was similarly a somewhat biased source. And (to take another much quoted work) Edmund Spenser's *A View of the Present State of Ireland*, written in the mid-1590s, was essentially a justification for imperialism, and laced with notions of English cultural and racial superiority. Such accounts are vivid and still entertaining, but they cannot serve as more than a very imperfect basis for the historian setting out to analyse the economy and society of the period. To do this, impressionistic accounts must be set alongside the finding of detailed and sometimes labourious research on archival sources: on parish registers, wills, customs accounts, taxation records, the archives of criminal and civil courts, on family papers and a host of other forms of documentation. Historians of the British Isles in the sixteenth century have completed an impressive amount of work on such materials. Gaps in the records, and the archives that remain as yet unexplored, mean that any account of the social and economic history of the British Isles must as yet remain in many respects tentative: but enough research has been completed to make at least a partial reconstruction possible.

## The underlying structures

Any such reconstruction must acknowledge, and attempt not to be defeated by, the sheer complexity of the subject. There is no single social or economic history of the British Isles: rather, there is a mosaic of individual histories of varied economies and societies, some of

[2] Quoted in Jenny Wormald, *Court, Kirk and Community: Scotland 1470–1625* (London, 1981), 4.

which interlocked and interacted, some of which operated effectively enough without knowledge of or contact with many of the others. Most people in the British Isles in the sixteenth century lived out their lives in a very local context. In many regions (notably most of Scotland, Gaelic Ireland, and much of Wales) the really important social ties were those of lordship, friendship, and kinship, and these operate most effectively within a narrow geographical context. Most economic activity was regional, concentrating, once the needs of subsistence had been met, on the local market. The lack of economic integration both within and between the component parts of the British Isles mirrored the lack of political integration. Much of Ireland in 1500 lay outside any central control, in England the monarchy (admittedly working from a sound basis) was still pushing continually towards a more integrated governmental system, while sixteenth-century Scotland was essentially a fragmented and decentralized society, a patchwork of localities upon which the Edinburgh government usually impinged only infrequently and lightly. Yet there was a wider world, in which people operated and of which those who did not move outside their locality were aware. One of the biggest problems for historians of this period is to balance their sensitivity towards its localism with evidence of the interplay between the locality and the regional, national, and indeed international contexts. Thus, on the one hand, we must acknowledge that intense localism of Scottish society which we have noted, but set against it such evidence of geographical mobility as that furnished by the four Scotsmen who turned up in Moscow in 1507 trying to sell their expertise as artillery specialists.

Scotland, indeed, possessed one of the most important and most frequently acknowledged regional splits in the British Isles, that between the Highlands and the Lowlands. Neither zone was without its own internal divisions. The south-eastern Highlands were more feudalized, and stood in contrast to what many contemporaries, including James VI, regarded as the real problem area: the Isles (until 1496 a separate lordship) and the western Highland mainland. In general, however, contemporary commentators, both lowland Scots and foreigners, regarded the Highlands and their inhabitants as backward, uncouth, and rebellious. Thus, the Scottish historian and clerical academic John Major, in his *History of Greater Britain*, published in 1521, could claim that just as among the Scots we find two distinct tongues, so we likewise find two different ways of life and conduct. For some are born in the forests and mountains of the north, and these we call men of the Highland, but the others men of the Lowland. By foreigners the former are called wild Scots, the latter householding Scots . . . in dress, in the manner of their outward life, and in good morals, for example, these come behind the householding Scots—yet they are not less, but rather much more, prompt to fight; and this, both because they dwell rather towards the north, and because, born as they are in the mountains, and dwellers in forests, their very nature is more combative. It is, however, with the householding Scots that the government and direction of the kingdom is to be found, inasmuch as they understand better, or at least less ill than the others, the nature of a civil polity.[3]

Many of the comments made by lowland Scots about highlanders carry those same assumptions of cultural superiority that are familiar in English writings of the period about the Irish. Indeed one lowlander, the poet Alexander Montgomerie, went so far as to declare that God had created the first highlander from a horse turd.

Yet, when we make due allowance for the ideological assumptions which underlay such comments, it is clear that the Highlands were different. Some parts were, as we have noted, feudalized, and some noblemen in the area, notably the dukes of Atholl, look very much like commonplace feudal landholders. Highland society in general, however, was organized into that most celebrated of Scottish institutions, the clan. Clans loom large in popular notions about the Scottish past, yet there is much about their historical reality which remains unclear. They were essentially a product of combined elements of feudalism, kinship, and various local associations. The kinship was often fictive. The clan patronymic might be extended to those wishing to come under the clan chief's protection, while it was not unusual in the Highlands to employ that late feudal contract, a bond of manrent, to extend the clan and bring in new members on a basis of clientage and local affinity. It was, of course, the protection offered by the clan chief that formed the basis of his authority, this authority upheld by the sometimes lavish hospitality that a clan chief would offer clan members, his role in arbitrating disputes between clan members, and the eulogies composed by the Gaelic bards which all clan chiefs regarded as an essential part of their entourage. But the

---

[3] *A Source Book of Scottish History*, ii. *1424 to 1567*, ed. William Croft Dickinson, Gordon Donaldson, and Isabel A. Milne, 2nd edn. (London, 1958), 8–9.

paternal ethos of the clan did not make the chiefs impervious to the dictates of economic management. Highland farming was organized largely on a joint tenure system, and an intermediary was needed between tenants and their lord. This usually came in the form of the tacksman, frequently a relative of the lord, who performed a managerial function on his behalf. The tacksman was responsible for organizing agricultural production, collecting rents and other feudal dues, and, when occasion demanded, ensuring that military service was done by the tenants.

If the Lowlands were different, the differences were sometimes of degree rather than absolute. True, 'Scots' (a language which, in its written form at least, seems much like English) was spoken there rather than Gaelic, the king had greater authority, a developed urban sector existed, and, after the Reformation, the Kirk had a much greater hold. But there too the nobility was dominant and kinship remained an important cement of social life. Outside of kinship, relations were still conceived of in essentially feudal terms. Lordship was, as in the Highlands, reinforced by bonds of manrent, in effect contracts by lords promising mutual support or, more fequently, between lords and men promising to protect and serve one another. Some 800 of these bonds were made between c.1450 and 1603. And the Lowlands contained their very own problem area in the form of the Borders, which were seen by the Edinburgh government (like royal administrators in England) as an especially troublesome zone. The border traditions of raiding, cattle rustling, feuding, and occasional larger manifestations of disorder became increasingly irritating to central government in Scotland, not least late in the century, when the knowledge that James VI was likely to be Elizabeth I's successor made the maintenance of good relations with the English a matter of prime importance.

Thus, in parts of Scotland social and economic life might be disrupted by endemic but essentially small-scale violence and disorder. In Ireland the sixteenth century was a time marked by periods of sustained disorder and severe and damaging warfare. Even in relatively peaceful periods, cattle raiding and feuding were endemic among the Irish nobility. These activities often took the form of a traditional aristocratic sport or a demonstration of masculine prowess rather than large-scale or prolonged mayhem, yet they were disruptive of normal economic life. English authority, in the early part of the century exercised through the earls of Kildare, continued in the Pale, but in Gaelic Ireland the dominant social group was the Irish nobility: the O'Neills, O'Donnells, Burkes, O'Briens, MacCarthys, earls of Desmond, earls of Ormond, MacMurroughs, and a host of lesser lordlings. From the 1530s a more aggressive policy by the English regime meant that these nobles found themselves having to redefine their relationship with what was becoming recognizable as central authority: they, and Irish society as a whole, were affected as the English crown in Ireland moved from being a sometimes ineffective feudal overlord to conceiving itself as an imperial power. This process, and the noble revolts it understandably provoked, involved warfare, and warfare in Ireland, certainly by the late sixteenth century, was a vicious affair of punitive raids, atrocity and counter-atrocity, and scorched earth policies. In particular the Nine Years War, which came to its conclusion in 1603, left Ulster devastated, with some of its towns, notably Armagh, in ruins.

If society in Scotland was divided into two zones by topography, in Ireland the same situation obtained due to the patterns of medieval Anglo-Norman conquest. In the Pale, southern Wexford, and the hinterlands of such towns as Carlow, Cork, Waterford, and Limerick, an essentially English style of agriculture was practised, with manors, three-field systems, nucleated settlements, and the occasional enclosure. The extension of what Tudor administrators would have regarded as 'civilized' forms of agriculture through 'plantation', the settlement of English or Scottish colonists, was essentially a part of seventeenth-century Irish history. Yet the first plans for such a policy were put forward in the early 1550s by the then Lord Deputy, Sir James Crofts, as a means of forming a buffer zone around the Pale, and by the early seventeenth century there was a plantation of about 12,000 English settlers in Munster. Even before then Richard Boyle, 1st earl of Cork, had put into motion his plans to remodel the countryside around Limerick on an English pattern.

For Gaelic Irish society was, as English observers were wont to comment, very different. The first difference was topographical, for the land outside of English control tended to contain much dense woodland and upland or bog areas where pastoral farming was the norm: recent research has modified the picture somewhat, yet it remains clear that in Gaelic Irish society wealth was measured in cattle, and dairy products played a large part in the diet. Gaelic society was founded on the *tuath*, an area of land, sometimes extending to 400 square miles, ruled over by a lord yet belonging to a kinship group. Patterns of landholding and inheritance varied between these units of land. Generally, however, inheritance under Gaelic law was governed by *tanistry*, whereby land was, on the death of the lord, passed on to his successor by an elective process supervised by the 'eldest and worthiest' of his surviving kinsmen. The system involved collective landholding, partible inheritance, little by way of fixed tenures, and was clearly well adjusted to a society which enjoyed a strong sense of kinship and which was based on a pastoral agriculture heavily dependent upon transhumance. Gaelic landholding and inheritance customs, as well as the pastoral agriculture which underpinned them, were decried as major symbols of Irish backwardness by English observers, devoted as they were to notions of private property, primogeniture, and fixed tenancies. But throughout the sixteenth century this traditional society persisted, dominated, as we have suggested, by the Irish aristocracy. The military nature of this society was emphasized by the fortified towerhouses in which the lords lived, Gaelic culture was kept alive by bards, and Gaelic law upheld by *brehon* judges. Yet whatever the strength of traditional culture, the economy in Gaelic Ireland was backward and still very dependent on barter and payment in kind. Thus, when Margaret Tobin married late in the century she brought with her a dowry of eighty cows, twenty-four stud mares, five riding horses, a pair of backgammon tables, unspecified household goods, and a harp.

English influence was creating more marked developments in the economy and society of Wales, but here the changes marked the end of a lengthy process, were less disruptive, and were welcomed by many influential Welsh. The full integration of Wales into the English administrative system in 1536, for the economic and social historian symbolizes the fact that, after due attention is paid to local variations, the broad trends in Welsh society and economy were parallel to those obtaining in England. Wales was essentially an underdeveloped pre-industrial society having much in common with upland England, its population mainly involved in agriculture, and such industry as there was based on the processing of agricultural products. Farming in Wales, as in all regions of the British Isles, was dictated by topography. Some 60 per cent of the total acreage of Wales lies above 500 feet, about a quarter over 1,000 feet, and both contemporary observers and later historians have been conscious of the presence of upland and lowland zones in Wales as a whole and in many individual counties. In the upland areas farming was mainly pastoral, with a woollen industry which sold most of its products through Shrewsbury. In lowland areas, a mixed farming was practised, and the sometimes rich land and the proximity of ports in South Wales meant that in the circumstances of the later sixteenth century farming became more commercial and more profitable. If the Welsh gentry saw political advantages in the integration of Wales into England in the 1530s, the economic developments which set in from mid-century meant that many of them, or their descendants, were also to derive considerable material benefits.

England itself was similarly divided into upland and lowland zones, although, as elsewhere, there were a number of sub-regions within these broad divisions. Again as elsewhere, pastoral farming was widely practised in the upland zone, while mixed or arable farming predominated in lower lying areas. The east Midlands, south-eastern England, and East Anglia, regions of fertile soil, were home to the most advanced arable farming in the British Isles, while taxation returns in the 1520s revealed that Kent, Norfolk, Essex and Suffolk were the richest English counties. Over the sixteenth century agriculture in this region, largely in response to the stimulus of the ever-growing London market, became more commercial, and what was to become the distinctive English rural social structure of landlord, large tenant farmer, and agricultural labourer was clearly present by 1600. There were numerous modifications of field systems, but in many areas the traditional three-field system still operated, often with adjustments to meet the needs of a continually commercializing agriculture. The main English industry in the period was the production of wool or woollen cloth, and hence sheep were widely kept, possibly outnumbering the human inhabitants of the country by three to one. The most important of the human inhabitants were, of course, the nobility, in 1500 only recently emerged from the aristocratic bloodletting and political instability of the Wars of the Roses. The upper stratum of this group rapidly set about re-establishing their fortunes, as did that broad class of lesser landowners, the gentry.

Yet if England, in common with nearly all of Europe, was dominated by noble landowners, it also enjoyed at least a small urban sector, with perhaps 5 per cent of the population living in towns in 1500.

Only one of these towns, however, was a large one: London. One of the main facts of English social and economic life in the sixteenth century was the growth of London, whose population increased from 50,000 in 1500 to 100,000 in 1570 to 200,000 by the end of the century. By that date London dwarfed other English towns. Norwich, with some 13,000 inhabitants by the late sixteenth century, was the second largest, followed by Bristol and Newcastle, both of which had populations in excess of 10,000. Urban social structures varied, while many of the smaller urban centres, among them most of England's 760 market towns, can hardly have been distinguishable from large villages. In larger centres the basic pattern was one of a relatively small urban elite enjoying power over the bulk of the population. It is at least easy to trace the inequalities of wealth. Taxation returns from Coventry in 1522 reveal that 699 persons were untaxed on grounds of poverty, 176 were taxed at less than £2, and 222 at between £2 and £4. At the other end of the scale one person was taxed at between £500 and £999, and two were taxed at over £1,000. These last two were taxed at £2,333 between them, while the 176 persons who were taxed at less than £2 paid £151 between them. Most towns enjoyed the presence of a large group of craftsmen and tradesmen of middling fortunes, many of them, at the beginning of the century at least, enjoying the advantages of guild membership. But the relatively high mortality rate in towns meant that a constant stream of immigrants was needed to maintain population. Many of these were poor, coming to towns in search of work, and usually finding themselves at the bottom of the social structure, living in hovels in the suburbs which, much to the disquiet of town authorities, grew up immediately outside the walls of many urban centres

Scotland, Ireland, Wales, and England each had their own distinctive experiences over the sixteenth century, but their respective economic and social histories do invite some points of comparison. The most striking of these is the dominance of the landed orders, the nobility and those representatives of the *nobilitas minor* who were known as gentry in England and Wales or lairds in Scotland. In Scotland the nobility were more demographically stable than their English counterparts, were still given to violence and the blood feud, and, in the face of a less assertive central authority, enjoyed considerable local political independence. Their influence against other social groups was demonstrated when the town of Aberdeen entered a bond of manrent with the early of Huntly in 1463, setting up an arrangement which lasted for 130 years. In Ireland, too, the native aristocracy were prone to raiding and feuding, and still demanded military service from those under them: indeed, at the end of the century many Irish nobles had licences from the crown permitting them to keep armed retainers. In Wales, conversely, over the century the gentry distanced themselves from the traditions of bardic poetry and vendetta, adopted English as their first language, and came to regard wealth as a more certain guide to social prestige than bloodlines. In England sixty or so peers (the number remained fairly constant over the century) enjoyed wealth, prestige, and power. Beneath them were the gentry, as we have hinted a broadly defined group, some of whose members were enjoying considerable economic success and upward social mobility. What all these groups had in common was that their existence depended upon their ability to extract a surplus from the bulk of the rural population over whom they ruled. Yet traditional ideologies, as well as practicalities, meant that even in economically advanced lowland England the relation between landlord and tenant was rarely a purely economic one: in many areas population density was low, certainly in 1500, tenants were not always easy to replace, they provided food for the lord in an economic system which was still heavily dependent on payment in kind, while the lord might sometimes need his tenantry for displays of power or support in warfare or feuding.

These tenants were a large and varied body. In Scotland, as we have noted, farming was usually a group activity, based on settlements called farmtouns or kirktouns in the Lowlands and bailes in the Highlands. These arrangements were modified over the century, most notably in the middle decades, by the practice of feuing. This involved the selling off of land, most frequently by the church and the crown, as a means of raising cash quickly, and has often been seen as a disruptive development working to the disadvantage of the peasantry. More recent research has modified this picture; it is now known that many feus were sold to sitting tenants, and that although the immediate costs of buying a feu were high, in the long term the arrangement worked to the advantage of the feuar. Tenurial arrangements were no less complex in England, although they are better documented and have been more deeply researched. Broadly, over half of English tenants held their land by copyhold, that is by customary tenures involving low rents. As inflation gained momentum in the sixteenth century, it became clear to landlords that their rents had to be increased, and on many manors this led to attempts by landlords to overturn copyhold tenures, and replace them by leaseholds which would allow the extraction of higher rents from tenants, and which could be adjusted as changing economic circumstances dictated. There has been considerable controversy over how far landlords could pursue such policies, and it is now accepted that English peasants proved surprisingly successful at resisting their landlords through both central and local courts. What is clear, however, is that the changes of the period saw the clear delineation in the English countryside of a stratum of rich yeoman farmers, doing well out of the economic circumstances of the times, and in many villages, especially those with an absentee landlord, more or less controlling village affairs. It is doubtful if the Gaelic-speaking areas of Ireland had a peasantry in the classic European sense, but even there it is possible to see gradations among the tenantry, with some tenants doing well, and others existing as poor sharecroppers.

The subordination of tenants to their landlords was an accepted part of social arrangements. So too, perhaps more certainly in theory than in practice, was the subordination of women to men. The history of women in sixteenth-century Britain is still a largely unwritten subject, while the sheer availability of source materials means that uncovering the history of the female half of the population of these Islands is a more viable project for England and Wales than for Ireland and Scotland. Learned opinion, as in the rest of Europe, held that women were morally, physically, and intellectually inferior to men, it was axiomatic that, at every point in the social hierarchy, wives should be governed by their husbands, while it is significant that women's wages were usually lower than men's for equivalent work. English common law, in particular, practically denied the legal existence of women other than mothers, and, indeed, the adoption of English law in Wales brought disadvantages for Welsh women, who had previously enjoyed a happier legal situation. But the history of sixteenth-century women should not simply be written as one of oppression. Fortunes varied according to social rank: but perhaps most importantly, the household, in both agriculture and manufacturing, was the basic unit of production, and the wives of yeoman farmers and craftsmen had an important role in household management, and one which was clearly valued by their menfolk. The image of women which comes through many of the legal and administrative records of the period demonstrates that many of them were strong and forceful social actors, and that male domination, insofar as it was an issue in real life, was something which was uncertain and constantly being renegotiated.

The agriculture in which the bulk of the population, male and female alike, was involved was a traditional one, backward by modern standards but already in many respects complex and sophisticated. There is, even in lowland England, little evidence of those agricultural improvements which were to appear in the next century, although it is perhaps noteworthy that the first book to appear in Welsh, published in 1546 by Sir John Price of Brecon, was a volume of hints for farmers. Yields on crops were low, and animals small, with an average sixteenth-century cow, for example, weighing about a quarter of its modern equivalent and producing one-sixth of the milk. The strains of oats and barley grown in the Scottish Highlands produced only a three- or fourfold return, while it has been estimated that wheat yields per acre in Britain rose by 30 per cent over the sixteenth century, to about 10 bushels (the figure for 1900 was 32 bushels). For the arable farmer, manure was the crucial problem, and one of the major advantages of the various mixed farming systems which existed was the provision of animal manure. At the beginning of the century, although harvest failures were not unknown, the agricultural base was generally capable of feeding the population: as we shall see, this situation was to grow less certain in the decades immediately before 1600.

Although agriculture was the fundamental economic activity in this period, what was often a slow and piecemeal urban development provides evidence of the existence of trade and industrial production. In England, as we have seen, London came to dwarf other urban centres, although there were a number of decent sized towns like Norwich, Bristol, and Newcastle, and a number of slightly smaller ones like Exeter, York, or Coventry. In Scotland there was a smaller urban sector, and, more particularly, an absence of those medium-sized market towns which were so important to the local economy in England and Wales and an almost total absence of urban centres in the Highlands. The most important towns in Scotland were the east coast centres which had long established traditions of trading, the four most important towns being Edinburgh, with around 10,000 inhabitants by 1600, Dundee with about half that total, and the slightly smaller Aberdeen and Perth. Over the century, Edinburgh was to establish itself as the major city in Scotland, seat of the royal court and administration, and took a large share of Scotland's trade. The other noteworthy urban development in Scotland was the first stirrings of what was going to be a major phenomenon in the seventeenth century, the expansion of Glasgow, whose population rose from some 4,500 in the 1550s to about 7,000 by 1600. In Ireland, the largest city was Dublin, with perhaps 10,000 inhabitants by 1600, other major centres being Limerick with 5,500, Galway with 4,000, and Waterford and Cork with about 2,400 apiece. All of these were, of course, coastal. Communication difficulties precluded the development of large inland urban centres in Ireland, although there were a number of locally important towns, among them Kilkenny, Navan, Ardee, and Kilmallock. Wales enjoyed a network of about fifty market towns, but no Welsh urban centre was impressive in its size. The largest, Carmarthen, Wrexham, and Cardiff, all had populations of less than 3,000. During the century, an increasingly large proportion of these populations, despite earlier prohibitions, became Welsh, and even small towns might be seen as cultural melting pots for their Welsh and English inhabitants: thus one Welsh commentator could, in a rather unlikely analogy, describe Brecon as the Constantinople of Wales.

The larger towns, as well as providing employment opportunities and apprenticeships, also offered various services: you might go to them for legal or medical advice, to buy luxury goods, or to obtain credit. They also enjoyed complex occupational structures. In Norwich, for example, 103 trades are listed for the period 1500–1558, and taxation records for the 1520s allow a more detailed analysis of occupational structures in English towns. Generally, about a half of the male workforce would be involved in the clothing, food and drink, and building trades, after which various locations might display specialities: leather making in Northampton, for example, or textile production in Coventry or Norwich. Specialization can also be traced in the Scottish towns of the period. Perth was a craft town, possessing a broad manufacturing and a relatively small textile sector, with the trade incorporations paying as much tax as the merchants. Glasgow was home to a wide variety of craftsmen, many of them in manufacturing trades. Dundee had a large textile sector, while Edinburgh was distinguished, certainly by the end of the century, by a number of craftsmen working on luxury goods, among them silversmiths and goldsmiths whose work was widely respected, and a large fishing industry. All of these major Scottish centres were dominated by merchant elites, those of Glasgow and Perth being mainly involved in internal or coastal commerce, those of Edinburgh and Dundee mainly in exports and long-distance trade.

Despite the presence, and importance, of urban craftsmen, most industrial activity in this period was rural. Almost all areas of the British Isles were home to local wool and textile industries, usually producing rough cloth for local consumption. The first half of the century was marked by the continuation of a fifteenth-century boom in wool exports from England, and especially eastern England, to Antwerp, although this trade was shattered by the disastrous slump in the early 1550s. Textile production was also well established in East Anglia, where increasing dependence was being placed on production by rural workers. Many of the processes in textile production could be performed by women or children, and hence many poor families became dependent on textile working to earn a few extra pence. The cheapness of the labour force allowed those in control of the trade to undercut skilled workers in urban guilds, while the low quality cloth produced in the countryside found a ready export market. There was also a widespread leather processing industry, some metallurgical production, and some extractive industry, with lead, iron, tin, and, most importantly, coal being mined. Coal production, especially on Tyneside, and in Scotland and South Wales, was to expand rapidly in the seventeenth century, notably in response to the ever-growing demands of the London market. But coal was already being mined extensively on Tyneside, in Yorkshire, in Flintshire, Ewloe, Buckley, Mostyn and Hope in Wales, and in Scotland. Indeed, one of the most advanced pits of the period was that run by a Scottish knight, Sir George Bruce of Carnock. He reopened an old Cistercian pit at Culross, and it soon had workings which demonstrated both the best mining technology of the age and a fair degree of capital investment.

Generally, however, it was trade rather than manufacturing or mining which attracted entrepreneurs in this period. Overall, the British Isles demonstrated their relative economic backwardness by exporting primary goods and importing finished or luxury ones. Scotland exported unprocessed raw materials, like wool, hides, salt, fish, live-stock, and coal, much the same was true of Ireland, while the boom in English wool exports in the first half of the century was essentially based on providing raw or unfinished materials for the sophisticated textile industry of the Southern Netherlands. Yet patterns of overseas trade were well established. The east coast Scottish ports had a long tradition of trading with France, the Low Countries, the Baltic, and Scandinavia, although in the sixteenth century England came to fig-ure more prominently, and France, a growing taste for French wine among the Scottish nobility notwithstanding, less so. Ireland simi-larly showed a distinctive pattern, Irish ships trading with Lübeck and Danzig in the Baltic, with a number of French ports, including Bordeaux and La Rochelle, and with ports on the northern and west-ern edges of the Iberian Peninsula. English trade, based on London, Newcastle, Hull, Southampton and Bristol, was similarly mainly to northern Europe, although the second half of the century did see the emergence of trading companies dedicated to longer distance trade. The Russia or Muscovy Company was founded in 1555, the Turkey Company (later to be amalgamated into the Levant Company) in 1581, and the Africa Company in 1588, while by the end of the century English entrepreneurs, adventurers, and politicians were already look-ing with interest towards the Americas. As yet the importance of this long-distance trade was small, but the first steps towards the com-mercial take-off of the next century, by the end of which the British Isles were to play a vital role in the Atlantic economy, had already been taken.

## The forces of change

The previous pages have provided an overview of the economic and social structures obtaining in the sixteenth-century British Isles. But even this brief description has been unable to avoid the fundamental fact that over the century new developments affected some at least of these structures. In many areas, of course, economic practices and social structures remained relatively static, and there may have been little in 1600 which would have surprised an observer from 1500. Other aspects of the social and economic life of the period, conversely, did experience change, sometimes of a fairly profound nature. We thus confront another difficulty: for if, when discussing the economic and social life of this period, balancing the local against the national is a complicated process, so too is balancing the continuities against what was new. Nevertheless, it is to the latter that we will turn, and to which the second half of this chapter will be devoted.

The key factor in socio-economic developments in the early modern period was changes in population movements. Writing the population history of the late medieval and early modern periods is, it will be appreciated, a very approximate science, but the main lines are now clear enough. Europe was moving towards a subsistence crisis around 1300, with the population on the verge of outstripping agriculture's ability to feed it, but in the middle of the fourteenth century the Black Death arrived, and at least one-third of Europe's population died. The plague did not go away, and recurring outbreaks kept the population static until the decades around 1500, when, possibly due to the gradual retreat of the plague, possibly because of a favourable economic situation which encouraged slightly earlier marriage, and thus extended the fertile period of wives, population began to increase. The introduction of parish registers in England in 1538 has eased the work of historical demographers, and we know a reasonable amount about population movements after that date. Registers also permit some broader insights into the demographic patterns. People in England and Wales (it was probably much the same in Lowland Scotland) tended to marry fairly late, women in their mid-twenties and men in their late twenties. The demographic regime was marked by high birth rates and death rates: the birth rate, taking Europe as a whole, was 30–40 per 1,000 of population, compared to 16.2 per 1,000 in 1970, with death rates at 30–35 per 1,000, as opposed to 12.3 per 1,000 for men and 11.2 for women in 1970. Average life expectancy was 30–35 years, less than half current expectations, although this average was badly skewed by high infant mortality: maybe a half of children could be expected to die before their first birthday. A man or woman who lived to 20 might expect to go on until old age, although the accidents of everyday life and the occasional epidemic precluded any certainty on that point.

Estimates of national populations in this period vary, and those quoted here should be regarded as rough guides only. England, for which we have the most reliable information, probably experienced a rise in population from perhaps 2,500,000 in 1520 to over 4,000,000 in 1600 to over 5,000,000 by 1630 (it should be noted that it is probable that this last total was lower than that for 1300). The population of Scotland rose from 690,000 in the mid-sixteenth century to 800,000 by its end. Wales had a population of 250,000, or perhaps a little more, in 1536, and 405,000 in 1630. Estimates of Ireland's population vary widely. There is some suggestion that the population stood at about 1,000,000 in 1600, and that warfare had rendered it static throughout the century, although others have argued for an increase from 1,000,000 in 1500 to 1,400,000 in 1600. The rate of increase was not uniform throughout the century. In England, where the records are fullest, there seems to have been a more rapid rise towards the end of the century, while in the late 1550s demographic growth temporarily ended, probably as a result of a newly arrived killer disease graphically described as the 'English sweat'. And, throughout, regional densities of population varied enormously. In England, more people were settled in the south and east. In Ireland, half the population lived in the Pale, although this only constituted one-third of the country's total land area. And in Scotland the modern concentration of population in the Lowlands had yet to occur, with roughly half of Scotland's people living north of the Tay. Population density in 1600 varied throughout the British Isles, with maybe twenty people to a square mile in Ireland, and nearly four times that number in England and Wales.

The increases in population may sound modest enough, but their implications were massive. One of the phenomena which has long been familiar to economic historians of the sixteenth century was the price rise, that prolonged bout of inflation which had serious repercussions throughout the European economy. There were doubtlessly a number of factors at work here, and earlier scholars have singled out the circulation of silver from the Americas and currency debasements as causes of the price rise. These may have contributed, but it is now accepted that it was the increase in population which was crucial. The agrarian base was having severe problems in feeding a growing population. The poor would eat bread before anything else, and grain prices rose faster than any others: in England they increased by a factor of six over the century, in Scotland they doubled between 1525 and 1550, and then underwent a sixfold increase between that date and 1600 (Ireland, with less of a money economy and lower population density seems to have largely avoided the price rise). When the harvest failed, the poorest third of the population sometimes faced actual starvation, or perhaps more frequently the risk of death through disease striking at their enfeebled bodies. And, while the price of bread increased, the earning power of the labouring poor declined. Only about a half of the population of England, and smaller proportions in other parts of the British Isles, were fully dependent on money wages by 1600: this was still an economy which to a large extent was characterized by subsistence farming and payments in kind. But most of the labouring poor owed at least part of their living to waged work, and the population increase, by flooding the labour market, created a situation where employers could afford to pay less. A series of calculations for England (there are strong indications that a similar situation obtained in Scotland) suggest that real wages declined steadily over the sixteenth century, reaching their nadir in the second and third decades of the seventeenth century, when the purchasing power brought in by a day's work was one-third of what it had been in 1500. Life at the bottom of society was always difficult in the late medieval and early modern periods: but around 1600 conditions for many of the poor were terrible.

Faced with rising agricultural prices, landlords set out to ensure that the value of their rent rolls would rise correspondingly. It was in the late sixteenth century that the tendency for English landlords to try to convert copyhold tenures to leaseholds, and thus raise rents, became marked. The period also saw an increased concern for effective estate management among these landlords: the sometimes beautiful estate maps which survive from Elizabethan England were not the product of some sudden taste for cartography, but rather of a desire for landlords to gain an accurate impression of their holdings. The need for more efficient farming may well have also created added inducements for enclosing land, although it is now generally accepted that, despite some well-known contemporary comments, enclosure was not so large a problem in this period as it has been portrayed by past historians. More seems to have taken place in the fifteenth century than the sixteenth, and the conversion of arable land to sheep pasture, which attracted considerable adverse comment from early Tudor moralists, would not have made economic sense after 1550. Many middling peasants, 'husbandmen' in southern English terminology, were squeezed out of their holdings, and forced to join the ranks of the labouring poor. In much of England, Lowland Scotland,

and many parts of Wales hundreds of thousands of people had no choice other than to accept deteriorating working conditions and worsening real wages in their efforts to feed themselves and their children. So far, working out how an English agricultural labourer's family survived economically in the years around 1600 has defied historians.

But, as our reference to landlords increasing their rentals suggests, hardship for some meant opportunities for others. Society was more fluid than has sometimes been imagined, and the net result of the sixteenth-century changes was to increase this situation. Even before the price rise, there had been opportunities for upward social mobility. Both the fluidity and the processes of mobility are demonstrated by Thomas Spring of Lavenham in Suffolk, described on a legal document of 1508 as 'clothworker alias yeoman alias gentleman alias merchant', who was to rise to the rank of esquire by the time of his death in 1523, and whose son was to be accepted among the local gentry and knighted. The late sixteenth century provided more opportunities for such people, while even established landed families did well from their rents. The value of the Herbert estates in Glamorgan rose from some £450 in 1570 to £1,169 by 1631. The rental of the Mansel family's estate at Margam in Wales rose from just over £109 in 1550 to just under £1,100 in 1632. It is no surprise that this was the era of the 'great rebuilding' in England and Wales, when gentry and noblemen alike built splendid new houses on their profits from rents. Yet this prosperity was also shared by yeoman farmers. Those among them who held land capable of producing a surplus even in a dearth year, and who were aided by business acumen and a little luck, were also able to do very well, some of them being able to attain gentle status. This meant, however, that social stratification, especially in southern and eastern England, was accentuated. In many villages there was a growing economic gulf between a handful of yeomen and the mass of the poor, a gulf which also became a cultural one as literacy, respectability, and godliness came to spread among the yeomanry and other village notables.

Literacy, indeed, was becoming desirable and more widespread. The Reformation meant that, in England, Wales, and lowland Scotland, the ability to read the Bible and the ever-increasing body of devotional works became important to the individual believer. The development of a more complex economy placed greater weight on written contracts and written records in general, so that literacy became a useful skill. Moreover, the practice, in England at least, of the printing of chapbooks and ballads meant that reading for leisure was also a possibility. Educational establishments flourished from the mid-sixteenth century. There was a wave of foundations of grammar schools, most of whose statutes included the implanting of right religion in young minds as a prime objective, while there is also scattered evidence of local schools, frequently run by clergymen, where children would be taught reading and writing for a few pence. Access to literacy was always determined by social rank and by sex. Literacy was almost universal among the English gentry and peerage by 1550, at which date maybe 40 per cent of yeoman farmers had achieved at least a basic literacy, while samples of tradesmen and husbandmen fluctuate between 10 and 20 per cent. Figures for Scotland are not available until the 1630s, when perhaps 25 per cent of men were literate. But throughout the early modern period, men from the labouring poor, and women of all ranks below the gentry, were illiterate. Access to education was clearly dictated by one's position in the social and gender hierarchies.

More generally, despite gentry and yeoman success stories, the economic conditions of the period seemed geared to produce casualties at the bottom of society. One of the outcomes of demographic growth and its economic consequences was an upsurge in vagrancy. From the mid-century onwards English observers, joined a little later by their Scottish counterparts, decried what they saw as the new problem of vagrant, 'masterless' men or women who did not work, who flouted the values of respectable society, who spoke an impenetrable argot, and who turned all too readily to crime. Recent research on such vagrants as were apprehended suggests that these contemporary fears were overdrawn: the dangerous poor existed, but they were neither as dangerous nor as numerous as some sixteenth-century observers thought. Although the rogue pamphlets of the period described an organized hierarchy of criminal vagrants who frequently operated in groups, official records reveal a less threatening situation. There is little evidence of organized crime or hierarchies among the vagrants, but rather of people down on their luck, many of them on the road looking for work, and willing to beg or resort to casual theft if no work was forthcoming. Rather than organized gangs, vagrants tended to travel alone (young adult males were numerically the most significant element), or in small groups, normally consisting of a married couple and their children. Despite the presence of a criminal element among them, and the tendency that many of them must have had to steal occasionally, the main significance of early modern vagrants is as reminders of the fragility of life for the poor.

While those in authority saw the vagrant as a danger, they were aware of their responsibility to provide for the deserving poor, not least because the Reformation and the subsequent dissolution of religious foundations had removed religious mechanisms for charity. It was England which produced the most effective system. Local experiments began early in the century, with the licensing and badging of beggars in many towns, among them York, where 'masters of beggars' were also appointed by the civic authorities in 1515. These local experiments continued over the century, and interacted with (and probably helped inform) a developing corpus of parliamentary legislation which resulted in the great Poor Law Act of 1598, reinforced by further legislation in 1601. This provided for the collection and disbursement of a poor rate in every parish, thus devolving responsibility to a local level, and, incidentally, helping to integrate the parish into secular government. In Scotland a Poor Law Act, closely modelled on an English Act of 1571, was passed in 1579, and this was extended in 1597 when the responsibility for supervising poor relief was passed on to local kirk sessions: attempts at compulsory rating on the English model proved impossible to implement in Scotland.

One of the elements which helped concentrate the mind of officialdom on the desirability of a poor law, and certainly something which fuelled concern over vagrancy, was fear of disorder. Aware of the instability of the world in which they lived, and with their sensitivity to humankind's sinfulness sharpened by Reformation theology, a broad spectrum of people, from monarchs down to yeoman farmers, were obsessed by the need to maintain harmony and order. England's rulers, at least, had their fears about such matters fuelled in 1549 by a rash of peasant risings, possibly engendered in part by popular misunderstandings of the plans for agrarian reform being discussed by Protector Somerset's regime. There were isolated risings from the south coast up to the north Midlands (memories of the repression of the Pilgrimage of Grace in 1536 probably helped dampen trouble further north), and there were two large revolts, apparently unconnected, one in the south-west and one in East Anglia. The rising in the south-west was prompted by the objections of a conservative local society to religious change. Trouble started, in both Cornwall and Devon, when priests tried to introduce the new Prayer Book on Whitsunday. The rebels marched on the regional capital, Exeter, which they proceeded to besiege. The East Anglian revolt was about economic grievances, and, despite recent research which has demonstrated the dimensions of the revolt in Suffolk, is normally associated, and indeed named after, the leader of the Norfolk rebels, Robert Kett. The eastern rebels besieged and in fact took their regional capital, Norwich. Both risings were put down later in the summer, the royal forces being augmented by foreign mercenaries gathered for war against the Scots. The repression involved considerable bloodshed, with perhaps 3,000 of Kett's rebels being killed outside Norwich. The rebellions of 1549 still await comprehensive research, but it is obvious that they represent a late example of the old style of peasant rebellion, with leadership being provided by those confident and assertive yeomen farmers who were used to leading their communities and bargaining with outside authority. Developments in the late sixteenth and seventeenth centuries were to convince such men that they had a sufficient stake in social stability to deter them from similar activities.

But if the old style mass peasant risings had finished, a new form of disorder had arrived: the grain riot. The participants here were normally agricultural labourers, poor craftsmen, and their womenfolk, this last group often playing a leading role. As might be imagined, such riots became more frequent as conditions hardened at the end of the century: eleven incidents of grain rioting are recorded, for example, in Kent in the period 1585–1603, with a cluster in the years 1595–6. Generally such riots, many of which took the form of what the modern world would call demonstrations, illustrate the limited aims of the participants. They normally involved only a small number of people, whose objective was usually to prevent export of grain out of their immediate area (Kent was firmly locked into the London food market) or to fix prices. Local authority normally treated these disturbances surprisingly leniently, with justices of the peace (themselves perhaps men with little enthusiasm for grain merchants) often negotiating with the rioters and showing a willingness to defuse

further trouble by bringing prices down. Conversely, authority sometimes acted very quickly and decisively when it was faced by rumours
of rebellion. Thomas Bird, a weaver from Sandwich, was arrested in
1586 after loose talk about a planned rising involving 800–900 men, in
the course of which he declared his intention 'to hang up the rich
farmers that had corn at their own doors'.

Scotland, probably as a result of the generally vertical nature of
social relations, saw little by way of peasant revolt, but the sixteenth
century did witness considerable unrest in Scottish towns. This most
often took the form of disturbances by members of the craft
incorporations against ruling merchant elites. An Act of 1469 had
allowed burgh councils to make themselves self-perpetuating, but
also required each craft to elect a member to represent its interests in
town government. The effect of this seems to have institutionalized
conflict between merchants and the trade incorporations, which were
in any case becoming stronger and better organized. The various
'risings' and 'commotions' came to a head with a full-scale riot at
Edinburgh in 1582 at the time of burgh elections. The incident was
followed by an official arbitration presided over by the young James
VI which led to a new constitution for the city in which craftsmen
were allowed a minority presence in the city council and in which the
deacons of all of Edinburgh's fourteen crafts should be consulted in
financial matters. Urban commotions, however, were to continue into
the seventeenth century. In 1612 the craftsmen of Stirling demonstrated publicly and raised their 'blue blanket' flag when the town
council tried to levy a duty on grain brought into the town.

Occasional acts of public disorder might have caused temporary
disquiet for those in authority, but by the 1590s something like modern patterns of crime were beginning to appear. Again, information is
easier to gather for England. There the bad harvests of 1596–8 were
followed by a rise in property offences, notably thefts and burglaries,
recorded in the archives of the criminal courts of counties as distant
as Essex and Cheshire. Evidence from the south-west supports the
view that these years saw both an increase in crime and a hardening
of the criminal law. In 1598 it seems that seventy-eight people were
sentenced to death by the courts of assize and quarter session in
Devon. Two years earlier, in September 1596, a Somerset justice of the
peace, Edward Hext, had written a letter to Lord Burghley in which
he foresaw looming social breakdown in the face of criminal

vagrants, thieves, and food rioters. To men like Hext, fear of disorder must have been a constant worry in the late 1590s.

The shifts in theological emphasis which had accompanied the Reformation also provided officialdom and villagers alike with a new source of disorder: the witch. England passed its first witchcraft statute in 1542, which, after its annulment, was followed by another in 1563, in which year, coincidentally, the Scottish Parliament passed its own witchcraft Act. Witch prosecutions in the two countries followed different paths (there seems to have been little by way of formal prosecutions in Ireland or Wales). In England it seems that witch accusations were normally isolated, and were frequently initiated by richer peasants who blamed misfortunes on poor, often elderly, women within their communities, many of them with an existing reputation for witchcraft. Most relevant trial records are missing, but they survive for south-eastern England. In Essex, at least, there appears to have been steady and quite heavy prosecution in the second half of Elizabeth's reign. In Scotland there were few prosecutions until 1590, when fears that witches were operating against the house of Stewart led to mass trials at North Berwick in 1590–1, followed by an indeterminate but probably substantial number of executions. James VI, as was appropriate for somebody who saw himself as the witches' intended victim, took an active interest in these trials, and in 1597 published a tract against witches, the *Daemonologie*. That year also saw another large-scale witch-hunt in Lowland Scotland, probably sparked off by a bad harvest: this craze was ended when the Edinburgh authorities, disturbed by the number of prosecutions, intervened to curb them. Despite the differences, there was, however, one similarity in English and Scottish witchcraft accusations: over 80 per cent of those accused of malefic witchcraft were women.

Riot, crimes against property, vagrancy, and witchcraft all involved the lower orders. Those in positions of authority at London, York, Dublin, Ludlow, and Edinburgh also found much to dismay them in the doings of the nobility. Traditionally, the nobility's main function in society was to fight on society's behalf, and habits of noble violence tended to stray off the battlefield and disrupt the smooth running of everyday social interactions. The problem was especially acute in Ireland and Scotland, where the nobility were still addicted to raiding and the blood feud. In Ireland, English control was too weak for anything effective to be done about the more boisterous practices of the Irish nobility, while the need to rule through at least sections of the nobility meant that they had to be allowed their retinues. Thus, in the mid-sixteenth century the earl of Kildare had 200 men to look after his horses, forty foot boys to run errands for him, and 160 kerns, all of whom were lodged on local inhabitants (their opinions on this aspect of the noble lifestyle have not come down to us). In Scotland feuding was still endemic, and it has been estimated that in the 1590s there were usually fifty feuds in progress at any one time. This was clearly unsatisfactory for that celebrated theorist of monarchy, James VI, and by 1600 he was attempting to discourage the practice, which was in any case to become less popular in the early seventeenth century. In Wales the gentry seem to have discarded the blood feud along with other elements of Celtic culture. The English nobility in the sixteenth century gradually turned away from violence as a method of problem solving, although the process had only been partially completed by 1600. Indeed, by that date the arrival from Italy of the duel provided the English nobility with a form of violence which helped set themselves apart from other people, and involved one of the things they were most concerned about, their honour.

The diminution of noble violence over much of the British Isles was a local symptom of much broader changes which were affecting noblemen all over Europe. Partly, the changes were cultural and educational. Renaissance concepts of gentlemanly behaviour were spreading from northern Italy, and it was beginning to be fashionable to be cultivated as well as being able to fight: it is no accident, if we may limit our remarks to England, that peers and gentry began to send their sons to Oxford and Cambridge in large numbers in the later sixteenth century. It was also to do with economics. The times made noblemen and gentry sensitive to the need for tight financial management, and, despite the historical myths about the financial ineptitude of the nobility in this period, there is ample evidence, at least from England, of noble involvement in a wide range of economic activities. George Talbot, 9th earl of Shrewsbury and a representative of a very old noble family, demonstrates this point. He exploited his demesne on a massive scale, he operated three iron works and a steel works, he owned three lead mines, coal mines, and a glass works, was active in supporting overseas trade and exploration, in fact owning a ship, the *Bark Talbot*. And there was also, to return to those values of Renaissance nobility, a widely culturally diffused model of the relationship between the nobleman and his ruler. Central government and the court did, of course, provide rich pickings for the lucky or successful noblemen, for example in the form of pensions, offices, gifts, or the contacts that might lead to fortunate marriage alliances. But the English landed elite gradually came to see it as an honourable and appropriate thing to serve their monarch not just on the field of battle, but in the council room and in county administration. Cultural changes coincided with a growing feeling among the privileged that they had a stake in the regime.

The peculiar political and economic trajectory of Ireland means that such changes were less marked there, although it is possible to discern something of the arrival of these new cultural patterns in that most troubled part of the British Isles. But they were certainly present in Scotland. As we have noted, the Scottish nobility had unusual powers, with many governmental functions devolved down to them. This situation was unlikely to change, not least because it is unclear how far the crown was capable or even desirous of making changes. But it is possible to trace something of the changing relationship between the crown and the monarch. Running a nation state was increasingly seen as something a nobleman might participate in directly rather than through kinship ties or tenant loyalty, and although the landed nobility still dominated Scotland that domination was increasingly being expressed through patronage rather than traditional methods of lordship. Moreover, if James VI did not quite create a *noblesse de robe*, the burgeoning central administration in Edinburgh did offer opportunities of advancement for nobles or their sons. The cultural shifts were also there. Scottish nobles became more educated and more cultured, more aware of Renaissance values, and, as they rebuilt their houses, tended to adopt a distinctive architectural style which leant heavily on Dutch and French models. It is instructive that one explanation for the Scottish nobility's retreat from the blood feud is that after 1603 they were extremely anxious to avoid practices that their English counterparts might regard as backward.

Urban elites were similarly becoming integrated into the royal regime. As we have noted, one of the features of urban life in the larger English and Scottish towns was the entrenchment of oligarchy. The merchants who controlled town councils were anxious to retain power, and, generally speaking, even allowing for such incidents as the remodelling of Edinburgh's constitution, they did so. The trend was even more marked in Ireland, notably in Cork, Youghal, and Galway. In Galway a group of fifteen merchant families provided all but one of the town's annually elected mayors between the granting of the first charter in 1484 and the Cromwellian remodelling of 1654. The position of many Irish towns as Anglo-Irish enclaves in a Gaelic hinterland precluded that social interplay between town and country which was so common in England. What urban elites throughout the British Isles did with their power is instructive. In most towns the urban council had the right to administer justice, implement poor law policies, and generally control the populations which Providence had placed under them, most of whom had no representation and little say in civic affairs. Governmental concerns for a well-ordered society ran parallel to those of urban patriciates. The accretion of wealth enjoyed by so many merchants in British and Irish towns over the sixteenth century was accompanied by a consolidation of their place at the top of urban social structures.

# Conclusion

In writing this overview I have been forced to be very selective in choosing which themes to bring forward: my objective has been that of providing a coherent framework which will permit some sort of comparative context within which the various national and regional experiences I have touched upon might be understood. As I come to its end, I am acutely aware of what, perforce, has been denied detailed treatment. Perhaps the most important of these is domestic life, the history of the family and the household, the world where women enjoyed the greatest influence in their respective societies. Obviously, there is much to be written on this area, not least because the household was the basic unit of social organization, of socialization, and in many cases of economic production, and because family life was, for most people, an experience of fundamental importance in this period. Similarly, I am aware that I have written little on the experience of work. For most people work in this period, whether agricultural or manufacturing, was unpleasant: working conditions were bad, hours were long, wages in most cases low (almost invariably more so for women than for men), and injury or disease connected with employment frequent. Assessing the quality of life of our sixteenth-century forebears is difficult. There was much to dismay them: the worsening conditions of life at the bottom of society, the near-helplessness of all social groups in the face of disease, the disaster that a cattle-raid or the arrival of an army might bring, and, in an age that was innocent of insurance, the ruin that might follow a more prosaic misfortune like a house fire. Life was uncertain, hard, and short. Yet human beings have a great capacity for survival, and when the documentation allows us access to these people's thoughts, they come to us with surprising frequency as well-rounded human beings making their way through life as best they could.

Trying to summarize the experiences of the various parts of the British Isles in the sixteenth century is difficult. It is possible to see a steady congruence of the experiences of England, Lowland Scotland, and Wales, but it would be facile and misleading to lump them together, not least, let us remind ourselves, because all of these geographical units held within them a wide range of social and economic microsystems. What we can discern is a diversity of experiences which demonstrate that the processes of economic and cultural integration which we would consider the hallmark of a modern state were as yet far from complete. That the next century was to see great steps in this direction was something which would have been unclear to many observers in 1600, and would, in fact, have not been considered as very desirable by many of them. Similarly, historians trying to analyse the social and economic life of the British Isles in the sixteenth century should try not to be too conscious of what was to follow that century, and endeavour not to be too avid in their search for the roots of future developments.

**Figure 4** Abraham Ortelius's 1570 map of the British Isles, 'Angliae, Scotiae et Hiberniae Sive Britannicar. Insularum Descriptio', deriving from Mercator's pioneering map of 1564, based on a map drawn by the Scottish Highlander John Elder. Note the extraordinary amount of detail included; but also that 'the British Isles' was a normal geographical description of the archipelago before the events of 1603.

# 2

# The limits of power: the English crown and the British Isles

Steven G. Ellis

The chief legacy of the Tudors in terms of state formation was per-haps to create the circumstances in which a multiple monarchy coterminous with the British Isles emerged in 1603. This development was the product of two separate processes. In the first place, the reduction of all Ireland to peace and civility—which, in effect, meant the conquest of the hitherto-independent Gaelic parts—had long been an English ambition. It represented the final phase of a process of monarchical expansion and centralization in the Tudor state which also saw the imposition of standard English structures of local gov-ernment in other outlying parts, notably Wales and the English far north. Essentially, this involved the welding into a composite mon-archy of those territories ruled by medieval kings as 'parcels' or dominions of the English crown. Second, there was the Union of the Crowns with Scotland, which brought together under one king two very different, and traditionally hostile, kingdoms. This was the half-intended result of the dynastic marriage in 1503 between Henry Tudor's daughter, Margaret, and King James IV of Scots, and it was foreshadowed too in the projected but abortive marriage involving the future Edward VI and Mary, queen of Scots. Ironically, it was Scotland which supplied England with a king: English kings had long had designs on this smaller and weaker kingdom to the north, even though the Tudors no longer aimed forcibly to incorporate it into the

English state. In another sense, however, the new multiple monarchy also reflected traditional English claims to overlordship throughout the archipelago.

Yet the unification of the British Isles was never a priority of the Tudor monarchs. None of them showed much real interest in, nor travelled widely throughout these remote borderlands to which they laid claim. Unlike the Yorkist kings who knew Wales and the north well (and may even have visited their father in Ireland), only Henry Tudor knew Wales (from his childhood there); later Tudors might occasionally venture to York on the southern fringes of the British upland zone; but no Tudor monarch ever visited Ireland or Scotland. For the most part, they confined themselves to their royal palaces and houses concentrated in south-east England. Indeed, the early Tudors in particular showed far more interest in recovering the territories in France which Henry VI had lost at the end of the Hundred Years War (1337–1453).

## Geography and society

Herein lay an important paradox. Most of the British Isles lies in the upland zone. And in the sixteenth century this region had markedly different patterns of settlement and land usage from lowland England. Moreover, despite talk by historians of an English nation state, the Tudor monarchy was in practice multi-national, with French, Irish, Welsh, even Scots among the king's subjects. It has been plausibly suggested that already by 1500 two-thirds of the archipelago's inhabitants could speak one of the various English/Scots dialects (albeit dialects which were not necessarily mutually intelligible); but in reality this high proportion is largely explained by England's far higher population density (monoglot Celtic speakers in England being confined to small pockets in west Cornwall and the Welsh Borders). In terms of geographical area, about half the British Isles remained predominantly Celtic in speech and culture, notably Wales and the extensive Gaelic parts of Ireland, Scotland, and Man. Thus, the Tudors' relative unfamiliarity with conditions outside lowland England left them very poorly equipped to govern these other territories, given the fundamental differences in terms of geography, culture, patterns of settlement, and land usage within the British Isles. They found it hard to visualize a well-ordered, civil society greatly different from the familiar, well-populated landscape of the south-east.

Nonetheless, until the 1530s, the British Isles as seen from London could roughly be divided into three main areas. There was, first, the extended lowland region of southern and central England which had constituted the original area of the Anglo-Saxon kingdom and which remained the heartland of English royal power. This was a heavily populated region of numerous towns and nucleated villages, with dispersed patterns of landholding, small parishes and manors, and political power shared between the nobles, rich merchants, and a prosperous gentry. Within this region, medieval kings had built up a centralized and uniform system of government, with the country divided into shires, each of which was ruled by the same combination of local officials, headed by sheriffs, escheators, and coroners, and the ubiquitous JPs holding their quarter sessions—all done in accordance with a uniform code of law, English common law, and supervised by royal commissioners and the king's judges on their biennial circuits.

From this base, medieval kings had traditionally dominated the upland districts to the north and west. The far north of England, and the Principality and Marches of Wales were part of a second, geographically distinct, region of the Tudor state, which also included the lordship of Ireland and was less firmly controlled from London. This was a predominantly marcher region of conquest lordships which had been added piecemeal to the realm of England in the period c.1090–1290. It had a very different landscape, with great stretches of pastoral upland and boggy lowland, and fewer towns or prosperous gentry. Ties of lineage were much stronger here among its more scattered, often Celtic-speaking population, and society was frequently dominated by great magnates with compact holdings and a warlike tenantry. Links with the centre were attenuated. English common law and the standard structures of English local government operated in some parts, alongside great feudal franchises and march law, but in practice this was a more militarized region with a predominantly military system of administration.

Finally, there was Scotland and Gaelic Ireland which were also part of the upland zone and where, in some respects, conditions resembled those of the Tudor borderlands, particularly in terms of their more militarized, clan-based societies and native Gaelic culture. Yet, despite traditional English claims over them, these were areas which, in practice, were independent of the Tudor monarchy. Scotland indeed was a separate monarchy under its own Stewart kings who faced very similar problems in the government of the disparate lands they ruled, notably in terms of cultural divisions between Scots, Gaelic, and Norse, and the highland–lowland divide. Yet, with far fewer resources than their Tudor counterparts and a much smaller (and more vulnerable) lowland base from which to dominate the Highlands, the Stewarts were more reliant on their nobles to rule the provinces and less tempted to centralize their authority. Indeed, Scottish kings did not feel threatened by Gaelic culture, or the late medieval Gaelic Revival, and in the 1490s James IV troubled to learn the language.

# Metropolitan perspectives and 'the Celtic fringe'

The English administrative capital, London, was ideally situated for the rule of the Anglo-French empire which the English monarchy had just lost, with easy access by sea to Normandy, Calais, even Gascony. Its location in the south-eastern periphery of the British Isles, however, made it far less suitable as a capital for an emerging British state. Even in modern times, London's location has provoked tensions between the constituent parts of the British state, but in Tudor times problems of communication were far more severe. For instance, orders and supplies for Tudor armies campaigning in Ulster during the Nine Years War (1594–1603) commonly travelled by land to Chester, then by sea to Dublin, and onward by sea or land to the military outposts at Dundalk and Carrickfergus. There is a temptation to view King James's 'crown of the three kingdoms' (England, Scotland, and Ireland) as a kind of 'manifest destiny', the inevitable result of far-sighted planning by Tudor monarchs. But at least until mid-century, Tudor ambitions remained focused on reviving traditional English claims to the crown of France. Their lack of sustained interest in the British upland zone constituted a major limitation on royal power.

Moreover, even when events attracted their attention, English kings and their officials had long held a low opinion of their inhabitants. In the twelfth century, Giraldus Cambrensis had dismissed the Welsh as an untamed and undisciplined people, living like animals. Though now partially anglicized, they remained light-headed and liable to rebel. The Irish were 'a barbarous people' with 'primitive habits'[1] and were likewise relegated to the nether links of the great chain of being: Polydore Vergil saw them as 'wild men of the woods', 'savage, rude and uncouth'. Many of them had also migrated to Scotland, another savage land. Even Scottish officials castigated Gaelic ('the Irish language') as 'one of the chief and principal causes of the continuance of barbarity and incivility amongst the inhabitants of the isles and highlands'.[2] The people of the Scottish Lowlands were perhaps more civil, but those Scots who infiltrated into northern England were beggarly rogues, thieves, and reivers (cattle rustlers), who undermined border defence. Of course, the king had some loyal English lieges in the upland zone, but their relations with the natives raised suspicions in London of degeneracy and corruption by the natives' evil ways and beastly habits.

These English perceptions of the peoples of 'the Celtic fringe' as intrinsically evil and savage can be traced back to William of Malmesbury in the twelfth century. During the fourteenth century, moreover, the English—so historians have described it—also discovered that God was an Englishman (which explained recent English successes in the Anglo-French wars). And both ideas continued in Tudor times to exercise a powerful influence on English policy towards the benighted natives of the British Isles. Since God was an Englishman, 'civility' (as the manifestation of English culture) was self-evidently closest to godliness; and to the extent that other peoples fell short of English norms, they were less civil. Thus, the classification of the archipelago's inhabitants in terms of civility and savagery supplied the Tudors with a deceptively simple model for the extension of royal authority. Not only was this task a Christian duty, representing the triumph of civilization over savagery; but it was thought that simply by imposing the cultural and administrative norms of lowland

---

[1] Andrew Hadfield and John McVeagh (eds.), *Strangers to That Land: British Perceptions of Ireland from the Reformation to the Famine* (Gerrards Cross, Bucks., 1994), 27.

[2] Gordon Donaldson (ed.), *Scottish Historical Documents* (Edinburgh, 1974), 178.

England on these remote and savage parts would turn them into little Englands, reducing them to peace and civility. Even so, while the Tudors were conscious of their divine mission to civilize, they were in no great hurry to discharge these duties, since they also had other, more urgent responsibilities. Accordingly, for almost the first fifty years of Tudor rule, until the developing crisis over Henry VIII's divorce and the Reformation prompted the monarchy to tighten royal control there, Tudor intervention in the upland zone was generally sporadic and piecemeal.

# Henry VII and the Tudor borderlands

In reality, the problems of Tudor government in the borderlands were far more intractable than contemporary Tudor analysis implied, but the Tudors only gradually became aware of these difficulties from the 1530s, when the suggested remedies failed to achieve the expected results. Henry VII was more concerned to secure the new dynasty against internal and external enemies. His policies in the borderlands were essentially conservative, although his Welsh birth and descent were an advantage in his dealings with Wales. Indeed, while Wales seemed to present a similar range of problems to Ireland and the far north of England, the basic problem there was the fragmentation of power and authority. There was no single territorial entity called Wales, but rather about 130 marcher lordships in the east, and the six counties of the Principality in the west. This fragmentation was the product of an earlier military frontier between the original areas of English settlement in Wales and those parts still controlled by native Welsh princes before the Edwardian conquest. The lordships, moreover, were divided between enclaves of Englishries ruled by march law, and Welshries where native customs prevailed; and the population was similarly divided between English and Welsh.

These divisions were replicated elsewhere, notably in parts of Ireland. In part, the reasons for this had to do with concepts of nationality, the determinants of which were not just place of birth, but chiefly law, language, and culture. The English nation *c.*1500 comprised all those of free birth, English blood and condition, born in territories under the allegiance of the English king: thus, English nationality was in the first instance a legal status, and included the English of Calais, Ireland, and Wales, not just those born in England. Traditionally, only freeborn Englishmen had access to the king's courts: the mere Irish living in the Englishry and the mere Welsh were treated like serfs and were legally disabled from holding many royal offices. The Scots and the Irish living in Gaelic parts were aliens, and frequently enemies to the crown. Henry VII's belated sale of charters (1504–8), granting whole communities in north Wales the status of freeborn Englishmen, anticipated the more general emancipation of the Welsh in 1536. Yet charters had long been sold to individuals: Scots or 'wild Irish' living among the English could also purchase their freedom. Henry VII also continued Edward IV's device of establishing regional councils to supervise local government, but the decisive factor in the rule of the early Tudor borderlands was the king's handling of the great territorial magnates there.

In Wales, starting in 1490, the king exacted from marcher lords an 'indenture for the marches', requiring each lord to take surety from his men for good behaviour, due appearance in court, and to surrender suspects on request for trial elsewhere. Given that king's personal application to the minutiae of government, this no doubt had some impact in curbing the country's lawlessness, but Henry VIII had little interest in this work. Thus, more important in the longer term was the fact that many of the larger lordships came into crown hands by inheritance or forfeiture. Twenty-two comprised the earldom of March and passed to the crown in 1461; the attainder of Sir William Stanley in 1495 brought in four more; and the attainder in 1521 of the 3rd duke of Buckingham, lord of Brecon, Caurs, and Newport, removed the last of the great marcher lords capable of challenging royal power. With landed influence now increasingly concentrated in crown hands, the council of Arthur, prince of Wales, at Ludlow, was given greater powers to enforce law and order in the Welsh Marches and English border shires. After Prince Arthur's death, this Council in the Marches continued to operate (1502–4) under a president, Bishop Smyth of Lincoln, as likewise after 1509, albeit ineffectually, when it became the king's council.

By contrast, the Tudors had no natural ties with Ireland and the English north where good rule and good lordship were seen to depend far more heavily on effective arrangements for defence. In the far north, for instance, large tracts of marchland lay waste in 1485, following the recent Scottish war. Yet Henry VII's main priority was to stifle any challenge to his position from disaffected nobles in regions which were solidly Yorkist. The king deliberately excluded the Nevilles and the Percies, the ruling magnates, from offices which were traditionally theirs, notably the wardenships; diffusing power instead among lesser landowners; and also reducing the crown's usual financial and military subventions for the defence of the Borders. For instance, separate royal constables were appointed for the chief royal castles of Berwick-on-Tweed and Carlisle, with their garrisons.

Initially, however, Henry had little choice but to reappoint as king's lieutenant and warden-general Henry Percy, earl of Northumberland, whose failure to support Richard III at Bosworth had been crucial to the Tudor victory. In Ireland, likewise, there was no obvious alternative as deputy-lieutenant to the ruling magnate, Gerald Fitzgerald, earl of Kildare. Thomas Butler, earl of Ormond, clearly preferred life at court to service in Ireland; and despite an ominous delay, Kildare eventually recognized Henry, following the example of the nominal lieutenant, John de la Pole, earl of Lincoln. In spring 1486, Northumberland apparently foiled a plot by Francis Viscount Lovell to seize the king at York. The following year, however, both Lincoln and Lovell with 2,000 German mercenaries joined Kildare in Ireland, where a Yorkist pretender, Lambert Simnel, was crowned Edward VI in Dublin. Recruiting large numbers of Gaelic kern, they then invaded England, landing at Furness in Lancashire, and immediately made for Richard III's old power base in north Yorkshire. Although the two Lords Scrope joined them, Northumberland's speedy response again steadied York and the north-east, so prompting the Yorkists to strike south and risk an early engagement with the larger royal army, in which they were routed.

In 1489, further disturbances occurred in Yorkshire following new tax demands, despite an earlier exemption negotiated by Richard in 1474 in return for service against the Scots. The collector, Northumberland, was murdered, a full-scale rebellion began, and York was again besieged. Exploiting regional tensions, the king issued a proclamation that the Yorkshiremen intended 'to rob, despoil and destroy all the south parts of this ... Realm',[3] but he was forced to raise

[3] S. G. Ellis, 'Crown, Community and Government in the English Territories, 1450–1575', *History*, 71 (1986), 190.

another army to crush the revolt. In the aftermath, he replaced Northumberland with a rank outsider, Thomas Howard, earl of Surrey. And whereas Northumberland had contracted to defend the Marches in wartime in return for £3,000 a year, Surrey's salary as lieutenant was only £1,000, with his troops in wages. This change was an extension of Yorkist policy, both in Ireland and in the West Marches, where a minor peer, Thomas Lord Dacre, was appointed lieutenant. It reduced both costs and the political influence of the ruling magnates: Northumberland, for instance, had on his death been retaining 84 lords, knights, and squires costing over £1,700.

In Ireland, relations with Kildare remained strained, despite a royal pardon concerning Simnel, but when the earl reacted equivocally to another Yorkist pretender, Perkin Warbeck, he was finally dismissed from office (1492). Disorders ensued, as the king attempted to balance Kildare influence by building up the Butlers, in the form of Lord Ormond's illegitimate elder brother, Sir James Ormond, appointed joint-governor with the archbishop of Dublin. Yet unlike the north, where the 5th earl of Northumberland was under age, Kildare was well able to protect his local standing, and the ensuing feud with the Butlers threatened to attract Warbeck back. The king was eventually forced to despatch another expedition to Ireland, led by Sir Edward Poynings who, as deputy-lieutenant of Calais, had been counteracting Warbeck's intrigues in the Netherlands. In summer 1495, after port-towns and nobles in Munster had declared for him, Warbeck did indeed return, blockading Waterford (July–August); but Poynings broke the blockade with his artillery, after which Warbeck fled to Scotland. The following year, he led a brief Yorkist-Scottish invasion of the far north which failed to attract support and degenerated into a border skirmish. And after a third descent on Cork in 1497, he was finally captured in Cornwall.

In large measure, the equivocal response to the new Tudor dynasty in Ireland and the north reflected local perceptions of serious short-comings by the Tudors in the discharge of their basic duties of providing good rule and defence for their subjects. Good rule still depended far more on the region's resident ruling magnates, chosen instruments of the popular Yorkist kings, than on an unknown absentee king. By contrast, the most striking manifestations of Tudor authority were the intrusion of rank outsiders like Poynings and Surrey. It was perhaps only when opposition to the Tudors became increasingly identified with support for England's traditional enemies that the Yorkist loyalties of these regions finally evaporated.

Within a few years, however, improved relations with Scotland also supplied Henry VII with a convenient solution to his northern problem. In 1497, following James IV's abandonment of Warbeck, a seven-year Anglo-Scottish truce was signed, and this time the truce was consolidated into a formal peace treaty—the first with Scotland since 1333—concluded in 1502, with provision for a marriage between King James and Henry's daughter, Margaret. In practice, this 'treaty of perpetual peace' barely lasted ten years—a decent interval, nonetheless, by contemporary standards—but peace with Scotland allowed Henry to scale down arrangements for the defence of his northern frontier. Surrey returned south, being replaced initially by Archbishop Savage of York, appointed president of a restored northern council in 1501. The council's authority was restricted to Yorkshire, however, and it lapsed again on Henry's death in 1509.

Further north, the existence of extensive liberty jurisdictions, akin to the Welsh marcher lordships, hindered the work of government. Border rule was now entrusted to local gentry and minor peers, notably Thomas Lord Dacre who had by 1511 amassed authority over all three Marches. Yet, in the absence of the traditional ruling magnates to supervise border rule and defence, the region's precarious peace dissolved into feuds and reiving. In particular, the semi-autonomous kinship groups living close to the frontier and known as the border surnames became virtually uncontrollable: Bishop Fox was reduced to excommunicating them in a bid to maintain a semblance of order and secure restitution for robberies. Yet, once peace with Scotland had extinguished the main threat to Tudor rule, Henry VII was prepared to tolerate such disorders as preferable both to renewed dependence on 'overmighty subjects' like the Percies and the high costs of a more effective system of border rule. The peace commissions of the three most northerly shires were both smaller and renewed less frequently under Henry VII than they had been under the Yorkists. Moreover, the combined salaries of the three wardens or lieutenants was now less than £400 per annum, and much of this was recouped by reviving the ancient practice of farming the shrievalties. For instance, from 1506 Nicholas Ridley of Willimoteswick, a lawless borderer, paid 100 marks a year for the privilege of serving as sheriff of Northumberland. Yet no sheriff or escheator of Northumberland accounted at the exchequer between 1461 and 1515, and by 1526 quarter sessions had not been kept there for a long time.

Affairs were marginally better in the West Marches, even though financial compositions sometimes replaced trials for murder. Power was gradually concentrated in the hands of Lord Dacre, who controlled the wardenship, the captaincy of Carlisle, and the shrievalty of Cumberland, as well as holding the strategically vital baronies of Burgh and Gilsland against the Scottish border. Dacre's ancestral possessions were extremely modest, but his wife was heiress to the wealthier Lord Greystoke. Henry VII exploited this, gradually allowing Dacre to acquire the Greystoke lands in return for loyal service. The Greystoke inheritance included estates throughout the north, so that by the time Dacre became warden-general in 1511, his standing had been transformed from that of a poor border baron to a major northern magnate. He continued to rule all three Marches until a few months before his death in 1525.

# Foreign war and the borderlands under Henry VIII

In the changed circumstances following the old king's death, however, Dacre needed all his increased landed endowment and *manræd* (the military service available from his tenants and connection), since the young Henry VIII's belligerent foreign policy soon breathed new life into the Auld Alliance between France and Scotland, with James IV 'aboutward to have stolen the town of Berwick'.[4] In the West Marches, following a programme of castle-building and military reorganization on his estates, Dacre could raise 5,000 men from his battle-hardened tenantry to invade Scotland. Yet he was hard put to control the strategically more important East and Middle Marches from his modest territorial base around Morpeth. For major campaigns the king sent north a lieutenant with command of an army royal, but otherwise Dacre was expected to defend the Marches with minimal assistance. He intrigued against the French party in Scotland

---

[4] S. G. Ellis, 'A Border Baron and the Tudor State: The Rise and Fall of Lord Dacre of the North', *Historical Journal*, 35 (1992), 256.

and tried to make the Scottish Marches ungovernable. Yet, if the king had exploited effectively the opportunity provided by the English victory in the ensuing Anglo-Scottish war, all this should have been unnecessary.

James IV's invasion of England in 1513 in support of his French allies ended in shattering defeat at Flodden, with twelve earls, five prelates, and the king himself all killed. In the short term, the northern levies under the earl of Surrey's command could easily have occupied the Scottish Lowlands, but Queen Catherine as regent ordered the army disbanded to save money for Henry's invasion of France. Much more shortsighted was Henry's squandering of the promising diplomatic opportunities created by the accession to the Scottish throne of his young nephew, James V, with his mother, Margaret Tudor, heading the regency council. Henry remained far more interested in recovering England's erstwhile continental possessions than in consolidating Tudor influence at the Stewart court and thereby securing the northern Marches.

Essentially, therefore, the limits of royal power and the limitations of Tudor policy were graphically exposed by conditions in the far north where the Borders remained lawless and disturbed. After Dacre's dismissal in 1525, allegedly for maladministration, bands of up to 400 thieves roamed the Marches, eventually necessitating a military campaign to subdue them. Attempts to curb noble power and the magnates' bastard feudal connections had simply stoked disorders, leading to a virtual collapse of local government; and continued Tudor reliance on the Dacres as a more trustworthy alternative to the unreliable Percies had eventually created a new 'overmighty subject'.

Early Tudor rule in Ireland was equally reliant on noble power. Following Kildare's reappointment as deputy-lieutenant in 1496— this time with full royal backing following the earl's marriage to Henry's kinswoman and guarantees for his conduct—Earl Gerald consolidated English influence in the Pale Marches and even extended it further afield. As in the north, Henry VIII was long content to maintain the administrative arrangements devised for Ireland by his father; and in 1513 when the old earl finally died (shot while watering his horse in the river Barrow), the king soon appointed as deputy, Gerald Fitzgerald, the young 9th earl of Kildare. The Kildares exploited the governorship to reconquer ancestral estates from the

Gaelic Irish, constructing or enlarging castles and towers to protect their tenantry and strengthen the English Marches, much as Dacre was doing in the north; and they expanded into Gaelic Leinster, the midlands, and east Ulster. Yet in Ireland, the Marches were more fluid because there was no agreed border line, and because individual Gaelic chiefs were far weaker and more divided than the Scottish crown and community. Accordingly, Kildare wielded much more influence there, building up a Gaelic clientage network and cross-border alliances to protect the English Marches in a way which was far less feasible for Dacre in the Scottish Borders. Moreover, although the two magnates both had unusually compact lordships and very comparable landed incomes (over 2,000 marks a year), in terms of wealth and landed influence Kildare stood head and shoulders above any other magnate in Ireland. From a Tudor perspective, however, Ireland was even less strategically important than the English north; and to divert scarce resources to rule and defend this remote outpost from a bunch of savages was—as Henry VIII described it, when surveying the dismal achievements of Surrey's expedition there in 1520–22—'consumption of treasure in vain'.[5] Yet, with decisive interventions and other convincing demonstrations of royal power an even rarer occurrence in Ireland than the north, Tudor rule also remained more dependant on noble power. In both regions, long tenure of office helped to transform a local noble into a great regional magnate; but the personal system of defences and alliances built up by the two ruling magnates to offset the shortcomings of royal government made their replacement extremely difficult when circumstances dictated a change of Tudor policy in the later 1520s.

## Internal reconstruction

The Anglo-French treaty of 1525, followed by peace with Scotland, brought to an end the first phase of Henry VIII's reign during which foreign affairs, and particularly foreign war, had dominated the political agenda. For the next fifteen years, until the fall of the king's

[5] S. G. Ellis, 'Tudor Policy and the Kildare Ascendancy in the Lordship of Ireland, 1496–1534', *Irish Historical Studies*, 20 (1976–7), 239.

pre-eminent councillor, Thomas Cromwell, the developing crisis over the royal divorce and the Reformation meant a growing preoccupation with internal security. This prompted in turn a renewed drive to strengthen royal control and promote good rule in the Tudor borderlands. The most striking manifestation of this new initiative was the revival—at the expense of ruling magnates—of the regional councils, now associated with a junior member of the royal family as figurehead, to supervise local government. Yet these quasi-bureaucratic initiatives were weakly supported; and in all three borderlands the chief result was to antagonize established local interests. In Wales, following the death in 1525 of Sir Rhys ap Thomas, effectively a Tudor viceroy there, a reconstructed council was set up under Princess Mary at Ludlow, with Bishop Vesey of Exeter appointed president and Walter Devereux, Lord Ferrers, receiving ap Thomas's old offices as justice and chamberlain of south Wales. The result was a feud between Ferrers and ap Thomas's disappointed grandson, Rhys ap Gruffydd.

For the north, the king's natural son, Henry Fitzroy, was created duke of Richmond and despatched to Sheriff Hutton to head a new council. Initially, the council's authority was extended to the Marches, where the earls of Westmorland and Cumberland served as Richmond's deputy-wardens. Yet, without financial and military assistance, neither proved able to rule effectively in opposition to the traditional ruling families, the Percies and Dacres. In 1527 the ensuing disorders forced the king to back down. The council's authority was again confined to Yorkshire, and William Lord Dacre secured his father's office of warden of the West Marches and, after renewed feuding with Cumberland, also the captaincy of Carlisle in 1529. Across the Pennines, the young earl of Northumberland as warden was allowed £1,000 with 69 gentry retainers and other officials costing £486 a year to help him restore order. In effect, therefore, Henry had restored the *ancien régime*. Yet these changes strengthened the Marches at a time when deteriorating relations with Scotland were again threatening war. Hostilities eventually began in 1532 over an 'ungracious doghole' in the West Marches, called the Debateable Land, and continued half-heartedly for eighteen months with the French offering to mediate. Yet as soon as peace was signed, Dacre was arrested for treasonable communications with Scots in wartime and replaced by his old adversary, the earl of Cumberland. Moreover,

French mediation also stretched to eventually successful negotiations with James V for a French bride to consolidate the Auld Alliance, so further undermining Tudor influence in Scotland.

Even less successful were Henry VIII's interventions in Ireland. They began in 1520 when the earl of Surrey made a reconnaissance in force to discover 'by which means and ways your grace might reduce this land to obedience and good order'.[6] Surrey's report—that it could only be done by compulsion, with an army of 6,000 and colonists from England—proved remarkably prescient, but it was not what Henry wanted to hear. Rather than lose face by reappointing Kildare, the king turned to his rival, the earl of Ormond, so stoking the feud between the two families. In fact, Kildare soon had to be allowed home to control his own kinsmen and defend his estates from the border Irish; and Ormond proved no more able to defend the English Pale from Kilkenny castle than could Cumberland control the West Marches from Skipton castle. Kildare was then reappointed deputy, but the Kildare–Ormond feud continued virtually unabated, amidst mounting violence and disorder, as both sides encouraged their Gaelic allies to raid their rival's lands. 1528 marked a nadir when, following the summons of the two earls to court in another bid to end the feud, Kildare's nominal deputy, Lord Delvin, was kidnapped by O'Connor. The ensuing 'O'Connor's Wars' prompted further royal initiatives, first, the duke of Richmond's appointment as absentee head of an executive 'secret council' in a weak imitation of the northern conciliar experiment (1529–30), and then the despatch of troops with an experienced commander, Sir William Skeffington, to stabilize the military situation. Kildare's obstructive attitude to these changes earned him lengthy periods of detention in England (1519–23, 1526–30), interspersed with short spells as deputy (1524–6, 1532–4). Yet, despite all these experiments, the king could find no real alternative to continued reliance on an 'overmighty subject' like Kildare as deputy, or the heavy cost of maintaining an outsider, such as Poynings or Surrey.

Overall, therefore, the early Tudor achievement in the borderlands was insubstantial. Apart from ending residual support for Yorkist pretenders, the Tudors failed to promote good rule there, or even to defend them properly, so that the Marches remained disturbed and

---

[6] Ibid.

faction-ridden at a time when lowland England was becoming more peaceful and prosperous. Henry VIII's handling of the ruling magnates was particularly inept: deprived of the king's confidence and support, they lacked the status and resources to maintain firm control, but understandably they resented the crown's intrusion of other nobles, weakly supported, to offices they saw as rightfully theirs. In practice, the Reformation crisis rapidly led to a breakdown in all three regions, forcing the king into administrative reform and a more interventionist policy.

# Rebellion, centralization, and uniformity

Prompted by Cromwell, the king began in 1534 a major overhaul of provincial government which lasted throughout the 1530s. Those charged with ruling the more remote provinces were replaced by more trusted crown servants, and the king later reorganized the councils and other institutions of regional government. In Ireland, Skeffington was reappointed deputy in place of Kildare; in the north, Cumberland again displaced Dacre as warden of the West Marches; and in Wales Bishop Rowland Lee replaced Bishop Vesey as president—all in the same month. The overall thrust of the changes— probably Cromwell's suggestion—was to centralize control and bring marcher administration more into line with arrangements for lowland England. In each case, the changes strengthened central authority and reduced aristocratic influence, but they also cost more, exacerbated political tensions, and did not necessarily lead to stronger government.

In Ireland and the English north, the charges of treason levelled simultaneously (May 1534) against Kildare and Dacre, allegedly because of their contacts with Irish and Scottish enemies, look like a pre-emptive strike by Henry against potentially the most dangerous of the nobles suspected of plotting against him. Dacre was disgraced and dismissed following his arrest, fined £10,000 on a lesser charge, and forbidden to reside in the Marches; but his unexpected acquittal on the main charge of making private treaties with Scots enemies in wartime left the king still dependent on his cooperation to govern the West Marches but unable to use him as warden. By contrast, Kildare's resistance to his dismissal sparked a major rebellion lasting fourteen months and costing £40,000 to suppress. The attainder of the earl and his supporters also precipitated the collapse of the system of defences and alliances by which English rule had been consolidated during the Kildare ascendancy, and the dissolution of the monasteries further undermined traditional power structures. Yet appointing an English-born deputy and other key officials to a remodelled council did nothing to address the resultant crisis of lordship, which Gaelic chiefs exploited to encroach on the English Marches, and the king was forced to maintain a permanent garrison, usually 500 men before 1547. Moreover, since the increased costs of the new governor and garrison far outstripped the profits of the wasted marchlands confiscated from Kildare and the Church, the lordship became an increasing drain on English finances. The crown remained generally unwilling to accept this deficit as the price of increased control: hence the general neglect of Ireland, punctuated by the periodic volte-face and frenetic bouts of activity which characterized Tudor rule after 1534.

Northern developments broadly followed the same path, but with significant differences. In particular, the government's efforts to strengthen royal control in response to the Reformation crisis were further advanced when the Pilgrimage of Grace broke out. By 1536, the royal divorce and supremacy had been followed by new demands for taxation in peacetime, the suppression of feudal franchises and lesser monasteries in the region, and the crown's imminent acquisition of the Percy inheritance. Accordingly, the Pilgrimage attracted stronger popular support than Kildare, and rebel demands were more specific, even though they reflected a similar combination of noble, regional, and religious grievances. The Pilgrims demanded a parliament at York or Nottingham to redress grievances and repeal unpopular legislation. In the north-west, moreover, socio-economic grievances were prominent among the peasantry; and in Cumberland the rebel captains pointedly urged the Commons to organize resistance 'when the thieves or Scots would rob or invade us', 'because the rulers of this country do not come among us and defend us'.[7] Everywhere in fact, the great noble houses stood aside, and without active

---

[7] Michael Bush, *The Pilgrimage of Grace: A Study of the Rebel Armies of October 1536* (Manchester, 1996), 335.

magnate support the northern council proved powerless to contain rebellion. This pattern of noble-inspired revolt in defence of regional autonomy was to be a recurring feature of the border response to Tudor centralization, presenting a most serious challenge to the regime. Yet the government was not even able to make an example of all the leading rebels because, to do so, would have left the Marches undefended and ungovernable. Altogether, about 75 executions followed the Kildare rebellion, compared with 178 executions after the Pilgrimage, although the latter figure was swollen by the execution by martial law of 74 Cumberland peasants.

In the aftermath, the northern council was remodelled, and proved fairly successful in containing simmering discontent in Yorkshire. In the Marches, Henry nominated himself warden-general, in a grandiose but meaningless gesture, appointing gentlemen deputy-wardens to replace the ineffectual Cumberland and the recently deceased Northumberland. The king's acquisition of the Percy and monastic estates, and then Hexhamshire and Redesdale by 'exchange', established the crown for the first time as a major landowner there, while concurrently the 1536 statute strengthened royal control over the region's extensive feudal franchises. Militarily, however, the changes weakened the Marches by undermining established structures of lordship, even though the king fee'd 66 local gentry in a bid to strengthen the *manræd* at the wardens' disposal. The new arrangements cost the king over £2,600 a year in fees, but this was far less than the crown's additional landed income there. In other words, this apparent extension of royal power was really only a redistribution in the crown's favour of the region's existing financial and military resources, public and private.

Initially, the deputy-wardens had only to contend with the activities of the border surnames, since the 1534 peace with Scotland still held and James V too was keen to maintain good rule on the Borders. Yet once war recommenced in 1542, they were soon in difficulties, lacking tenants to defend the Borders. The great landowners, since they were no longer entrusted with the wardenship, had less need of border service from their tenants, and so raised rents and entry-fines in response to inflation. For instance, where the 4th earl of Northumberland had raised 1,000 spearmen from his tenants in Northumberland, the 6th Earl could only raise a hundred. By 1543 there were only 300 horsemen throughout the shire, and the great Percy castles there, now in crown hands, were in decay for want of reparations. Northumberland was no longer able to defend itself in wartime, so the king was forced to station a garrison of 2,500 men there, now commanded by a southern noble, and conciliar supervision of the wardenries was abandoned. Overall, therefore, the impact of the northern reforms was very uneven: Tudor rule was more firmly established in sheltered parts like Yorkshire, but the Marches remained weak and the border surnames uncontrollable. After Henry's death, the Somerset regime soon moved to strengthen the Borders by rehabilitating the Percies and reappointing Dacre as warden.

The basic reason for this failure was continued poor relations with Scotland. By 1540, relations were again coming under strain over redress for border offences, religious differences and, especially, James's refusal to be drawn into an English alliance which Henry desired as a prelude to another invasion of France. In September 1541 war became almost inevitable when James, afraid of kidnapping, refused to come, as expected, to an interview at York where Henry awaited his nephew. Eventually, as Henry's army launched a border raid, the king's printer issued a *Declaration* in late 1542 which formally reasserted traditional English claims to overlordship over Scotland as part of the king's 'imperial' status throughout the British Isles. Henry even contemplated advancing the border to the Forth, with cooperative Scottish lords swearing allegiance to him as 'supreme lord of Scotland', as the earl of Angus had done in 1532. Yet what followed owed little to Tudor policy. A Scottish army attempting a surprise raid on the English West Marches was itself surprised and routed, with around 500 landowners taken prisoner, and three weeks later James V died suddenly, leaving a week-old daughter, Mary, on the throne.

This time, unlike Flodden, Henry did at least appreciate the extent of his opportunity. Yet because his main priority remained France, he tried to exploit it indirectly. If the king had simply unleashed his army to occupy Scotland, he would probably have succeeded in his aim of controlling Scotland by marrying his son, Prince Edward, to Queen Mary and so procuring a dynastic union, despite the poor state of Anglo-Scottish relations. Yet far less realistic was his ostensibly statesmanlike attempt to procure it by consent (so avoiding the cost of conquest). The Solway Moss prisoners were entertained at court, sworn to the project and meanwhile to Mary's upbringing in

England, and sent home to work as an English party in Scotland. Henry did succeed in negotiating the Treaty of Greenwich (1543) with the earl of Arran, the Scottish governor, including provision for the marriage, but not for Mary's English upbringing; and having, as he thought, secured control of Scotland and his northern frontier, the king then declared war on France, whereupon Arran defected to the French party and the treaty was annulled. Henry's subsequent attempts to coerce the Scots into accepting the treaty simply proved counterproductive. Far from strengthening the English party, the sack of Edinburgh and Leith in 1544 during what became known as the Rough Wooing merely drove the Scots into the arms of the French, who in 1545 sent 3,500 troops to support their allies. Thus, when hostilities petered out following the conclusion of the Anglo-French peace of 1546, Anglo-Scottish relations remained as bad as ever.

The one substantial achievement of Henry's reign was the union with Wales, where there was no frontier to defend. The feud between Ferrers and ap Gruffydd finally erupted in riots between their respective retainers at the Carmarthen sessions in 1529. Ap Gruffydd was eventually tried and executed on a trumped-up charge of treason in 1531, but under the slack President Vesey disorders simply continued elsewhere. Finally, the energetic Bishop Lee took charge, armed with five statutes to strengthen his authority and instructions to restore order. Boasting that he would 'make one thief hang another',[8] Lee scoured the Marches for thieves and robbers, hanging even gentlemen. More important in pacifying Wales, however, was the so-called Act of Union—the statutes enacted and gradually promulgated, 1536–43. Effectively, they abolished the distinction between Marches and Principality by shiring the marcher lordships, imposing English law and administrative structures throughout Wales, and creating a new kingdom of England and Wales. Sheriffs, JPs, and other English local officials were introduced, Welsh shires and ancient boroughs received representation in Parliament (one member each, not the normal two, so as to reduce costs), Welsh law and custom were abolished, and the English language was made compulsory for administrative and legal business. Administratively, therefore, Wales

---

[8] Peter Roberts, 'The English Crown, the Principality of Wales and the Council in the Marches, 1534–1641', in Brendan Bradshaw and John Morrill (eds.), *The British Problem, c.1534–1707: State Formation in the Atlantic Archipelago* (Basingstoke, 1996), 122.

was now assimilated to England, and 'the mere Welsh' received the same rights and privileges as Englishmen.

Lee opposed the changes, arguing that the natives were not ready for English-style self-government. 'There are very few Welsh in Wales above Brecknock who have £10 in land', he declared sternly, 'and their discretion is less than their land.' In the event, Wales was excluded from the requirement that JPs have an annual landed income of £20; but others were equally mistrustful of the Welsh gentry as 'bearers of thieves and misruled persons'.[9] Yet in Wales, where native Welsh gentry had long served as deputies of the mainly absentee, English marcher lords, the gentry were less dependent on the marcher lords because there was no frontier to defend and found their privileges increasingly irksome. Moreover, whole communities had long petitioned for grants of English law and land tenure. Thus, the Union attracted considerable support in Wales, particularly since it ended the threat that the Lancastrian penal code (which, *inter alia*, excluded Welshmen from office) might yet be enforced against the native Welsh gentry. In other respects, however, the Union was far from being the unqualified blessing which Elizabethan apologists implied. Lee's presidency was long remembered for its draconian rule— reputedly 5,000 executions in six years—and initially too, the Union's language clause created tensions. The English bishop of St Davids, for instance, urged the establishment of grammar schools whereby 'Welsh rudeness would soon be framed to English civility'.[10] In the longer term, however, the Union did lead to a strengthening of law and order. It also promoted the idea of a single territorial entity called Wales, in place of the region's late medieval fragmentation, so helping to foster a more territorial sense of Welsh identity. Moreover, although the status of the Welsh language, hitherto the most potent symbol of Welsh identity, had been downgraded, this change was partly offset by efforts sponsored by the Welsh gentry, who still patronized bardic culture, to promote religious services in Welsh.

In the wider context too, the successful implementation of Tudor reform in Wales came to be seen as offering a blueprint for the reduction of other borderlands to peace and civility, despite the

---

[9] Glanmor Williams, *Wales and the Act of Union* (Bangor, 1992), 20.

[10] Peter Roberts, 'Tudor Wales, National Identity and the British Inheritance', in Brendan Bradshaw and Peter Roberts (eds.), *British Consciousness and Identity: The Making of Britain, 1533–1707* (Cambridge, 1998), 14.

fundamental differences between these marchlands. Success in Wales strengthened official convictions that the mere extension of standard English administrative structures to other outlying parts would automatically promote good rule. Thus later on, when reform initiatives in Ireland ran into trouble, leading officials with experience in both countries, notably Sir Henry Sidney and William Gerard, urged the application to Ireland of 'the Welsh policy'. In the short term too, experience in Wales was seen as offering lessons for Ireland. After the Kildare rebellion, the lordship's continuing military weakness had eventually led, in the circumstances of mounting mistrust by the Gaelic chiefs about the government's real intentions, to an unprecedented joint invasion of the Pale by O'Neill and O'Donnell in 1539. Although the chiefs were routed at Bellahoe, the so-called Geraldine League did not then collapse, as experienced observers predicted; and Henry was forced to despatch reinforcements and to mount a new initiative. What followed, the strategy devised by the incoming deputy, Sir Anthony St Leger, which is now known as 'surrender and regrant', bore some striking similarities to, as well as profound differences from, 'the Welsh policy'. As with Wales, Tudor reform addressed Ireland's political fragmentation by attempting to incorporate the Gaelic chieftaincies with the English lordship into a single political entity, with the Gaelic peoples accorded the same status as freeborn Englishmen. Yet, rather than union with England, the means whereby the island's medieval partition between Englishry and Irishry would be abolished and English government extended throughout would be the erection of Ireland into a separate Tudor kingdom. This involved Gaelic chiefs recognizing English sovereignty in return for feudal charters confirming the lands they occupied. Thus, the Gaelic lordships would be shired as English counties, and 'the mere Irish' would become English subjects rather than Irish enemies, with protection at common law for their lands and goods.

This was an extremely ambitious undertaking: Ireland was four times the size of Wales, which had taken seven years to assimilate administratively into England. Moreover, the strategy also entailed the break-up of the old Gaelic world extending into Scotland, the assimilation of the Gaelic peoples into separate 'foreign' kingdoms of Ireland and Scotland, and a parallel acceptance by those *Gaedhil* living in Ireland of the Tudors with whom, unlike the Welsh, they had no natural ties. Yet, of all the Tudor initiatives for Ireland, 'surrender and regrant' most nearly matched ultimate aims with available resources, providing for a gradual extension of English rule with Gaelic cooperation. Initially, moreover, a promising start was made, with the creation of O'Neill and O'Brien as earls of Tyrone and Thomond respectively, the rehabilitation of the earl of Desmond, and other peerages for MacGillapatrick (Lord Fitzpatrick of Upper Ossory) and for one of the 'degenerate English', Burke of Clanrickard (earl of Clanrickard). For the local English, the initiative promised lucrative leases of ex-monastic land, as prospects for peace improved, and provincial office in an extended administration. By 1544–5, moreover, the consequent reduction in racial tensions even permitted an unprecedented deployment of Irish troops in France and Scotland.

Conversely, some destabilizing pressures were slower to manifest themselves. Tudor reform held fewer attractions for the local elite than in Wales because the Pale gentry were already English subjects, not 'mere Irish'. Yet initially, Ireland's new status as a separate kingdom had seemed to represent a reassuring statement against further Tudor centralization, so allaying tensions which had emerged in the Dublin administration between local English and newcomers from England. Moreover, while he lived, the old king's refusal to countenance any increase in the administration's annual shortfall of c.£4,000 made good from England ensured continued reliance on the Englishry as the mainstay of Tudor rule.

In practice, however, Ireland's new status had little impact on Anglo-Irish constitutional relations. Although now styled a kingdom, Ireland remained an English dependency, not a sovereign kingdom. Policy for Ireland, and much other legal and governmental business was still determined by king and council in England; Irish lawsuits were tried on appeal by the English king's bench; Irish officials were appointed under the great seal of England, and without a licence so warranted, the Irish Parliament could not meet nor enact legislation. The English Parliament, moreover, still legislated occasionally for Ireland, for instance the Edwardian reform legislation, even though Ireland was not accorded representation there. Thus in practice, this alleged 'constitutional revolution' simply supplied a mechanism for incorporating Gaelic Ireland into the Tudor state, broadly along Welsh lines. As power was concentrated in the hands of king and privy council, the local Englishry found itself increasingly excluded from the making of policy, with disastrous results in the longer term.

# The mid-Tudor crisis and the advance of Protestantism

After 1547, the Edwardian regime was prepared to pay for results and experimented with plantation in a bid to force the pace. The English garrison was quadrupled; and when a rising in Leix and Offaly by the O'Mores and O'Connors allowed the confiscation of their lordships, the Pale could be extended by colonization. Forts Governor and Protector were established to defend the settlers and, with other strongpoints at Nenagh and Athlone, secured military control of the midlands. Later, the earl of Sussex had Leix and Offaly shired as Queen's and King's Counties, and tried to turn the garrisons into self-sufficient colonies, while herding 'deserving natives' into Gaelic reservations along the Shannon. Yet the emphasis on coercion and colonization soon proved counterproductive. Anglo-Gaelic relations again broke down, so spoiling hopes that plantation rents would cover defence costs and make conquest self-financing. And as the annual deficit snowballed from £4,700 to £35,000 a year, Queen Mary reappointed St Leger with orders to pacify the natives, cut the garrison, and reduce costs.

The Leix–Offaly plantation was apparently inspired by Protector Somerset's Scottish policy, which aimed to coerce the Scots into implementing the Treaty of Greenwich. Another English invasion led to a further heavy Scottish defeat at Pinkie (1547), but this time English garrisons were established throughout the Scottish Lowlands. The eventual aim was a puppet kingdom controlled from London, but meanwhile an English Pale would protect the 'assured Scots' and, as in Ireland, strengthen defences by advancing the frontier into enemy territory. Military costs, exceeding £140,000 a year, proved enormous, however, and the arrival of a French army of 10,000 in 1548 soon turned the garrisons and their 7,000 troops into a liability: they were eventually withdrawn in 1550. By contrast in Ireland, where there was no agreed frontier, it proved more difficult to extricate the army on which, in deteriorating political conditions, the administration became increasingly reliant. 1,500 troops were now seen as an effective minimum to maintain royal authority.

Of fundamental importance in the shaping of early modern power structures and national identities in the British Isles was the advance of Protestantism. Viewed from the peripheries, the Tudor Reformation was a religious manifestation of the same policies of centralization and cultural imperialism which had characterized Tudor rule, particularly since the 1530s. Most obviously, this development was reflected in the injunctions of the royal supremacy and the parallel upsurge of ecclesiastical legislation by a parliament in which the borderlands remained seriously underrepresented. Moreover, since the Reformation involved a shift from a visual presentation of Christianity to a bibliocentric one, its enforcement created major problems in the 'dark corners of the land' where parishes were larger and poorer, and levels of literacy much lower. For Celtic-speaking parts of Wales, Ireland, and Cornwall, however, the introduction of English Prayer Books and Bibles was not just an intensification of existing pressures for uniformity: it amounted to a policy of cultural imperialism against the indigenous cultures of these regions. In the event, the New Testament and the Prayer Book were soon translated into Welsh (by 1567), but Gaelic translations did not come until much later (1603 and 1608 respectively), and Cornish translations not at all. Moreover, the need to operate through two languages further dissipated reforming energies. Thus, religious divisions exacerbated the government's difficulties in consolidating Tudor rule in the borderlands. In Wales, where the local gentry profited substantially from leases of confiscated monastic possessions, the effects were not too serious; and in the longer term, a native Protestant tradition, rooted in the concept of a primitive national church which was theologically reformed and culturally British, became a central aspect of Welsh identity. In Ireland, however, where in the longer term soldiers and settlers from England were the chief beneficiaries of the monastic dissolutions, and in the far north, where the local elite was even more solidly recusant, the government soon ran into major difficulties over the need to enforce religious uniformity. Moreover, the very nature of the Elizabethan settlement—with a reformed theology grafted onto an essentially Catholic liturgy and polity—was also to prove an obstacle to future religious union with Scotland. In line with the peculiar concept of the royal supremacy, the Tudor Reformation reflected state power as much as continental Protestantism; whereas the Scottish Reformation was not only a much later phenomenon, and more typically Calvinist in its polity or structure, it also developed more in opposition to the state.

# The Reformation and the emergence of a British state system

Initially, however, the spread of Protestantism eased the government's difficulties in defending its northern frontier. The Anglo-Scottish war of 1557–9 represented not only a final sputter of the competing Anglo-Burgundian and Franco-Scottish alliances which had divided the British Isles for centuries but also marked something of a nadir of British influence in Europe. Dynastic marriages had reduced the Tudor and Stewart monarchies to quasi-satellite states within the rival Habsburg and Valois multiple kingdoms; and both monarchies went to war at the behest of their respective senior partners. In November 1558, Henry II achieved by diplomacy what Henry VIII had failed to do by bullying, when the Scottish Parliament confirmed the 'crown matrimonial'. Yet concurrently, the Habsburg–Tudor union was dissolved by Mary Tudor's unexpected death and the accession of her Protestant half-sister, Elizabeth. This transformed Anglo-Scottish relations, holding out the possibility of English assistance for Scottish Protestants and nationalists opposed to Scotland's projected status as a French province. There followed the Scottish revolution of 1559–60, another English invasion, and the Treaty of Edinburgh (1560) which in practice established a second Protestant regime in Britain. The diplomatic volte-face of 1558–60 not only spelled the end of the Auld Alliance, with the advent of cordial Anglo-Scottish relations based on a common commitment to Protestantism, it also marked the emergence of what was in effect an increasingly self-contained, British state system. Subsequently, Elizabeth's Scottish policy was minimalist, confined to occasional interventions to maintain a pro-English Protestant regime in Scotland, despite initial proposals for a union and the crisis following Queen Mary's deposition. In 1586, after the outbreak of the Anglo-Spanish war, she did agree to a Scottish subsidy of £4,000 a year, with an undertaking to uphold any right James VI might have to the English crown; but the real reason James remained well-disposed was not Elizabethan diplomacy but that, privately, he remained confident of the English succession, and meanwhile he would do nothing to upset Elizabeth unduly.

Improved relations with Scotland also reduced the government's dependence on the great territorial magnates for border defence. Whereas the previous decade had seen something of an aristocratic reaction, with the Fitzgeralds and Percies restored, and Dacre and Northumberland again appointed wardens, Elizabeth's accession saw Northumberland replaced by a southerner, Lord Grey de Wilton. Following Dacre's death in 1563, Elizabeth alternated the wardenships between lesser nobles like Lords Scrope and Eure or southerners like the earl of Bedford or Lord Hunsdon. The major crisis came in 1569, following Queen Mary's deposition and flight into England, which sparked off a court conspiracy centring on the duke of Norfolk, with whom the earls of Northumberland and Westmorland were allied. The northern earls sensed their opportunity to rescue Mary, restore Catholicism and, with it, their traditional influence in northern government. Yet their rising (November 1569) after Norfolk's arrest was poorly coordinated and quickly collapsed. There followed a clash between the queen's forces and Leonard Dacre whose battle-hardened tenantry, more than the earls', did at least remain willing to fight for their lord. Ironically, however, Leonard Dacre had been alienated by Norfolk's claims to the Dacre inheritance. Following the attainder of Dacre and the earls, northern patronage was reorganized to build up a court party.

For Elizabethan Protestants, however, the main threat to stability was now the solidly Catholic sympathies of the region's traditional ruling elite, not Scottish invasion. Elizabeth's officers there were frequently chosen more for their reliability than their landed influence, even though they might lack the status to command ready obedience. In consequence, local government suffered. The far north remained very disturbed, as the gentry squabbled among themselves, and also costly to rule. After more than twenty years' experience there, Sir Ralph Sadler wrote despairingly in 1559 that the Borders were 'in such disorder' through theft and robberies, and so weak in the recent Anglo-Scottish war, that English borderers 'paid the Scots certain rent and tribute' to save them 'from burning and spoil', 'which I never heard of before'.[11] Yet even though the incidence of blackmail increased under Elizabeth, and was eventually prohibited by statute in 1601, the English Marches were gradually destroyed by Scottish reivers, as border service was undermined.

Throughout the border region, and also in Ireland, the more disturbed conditions meant that the typical gentry residence remained the defended towerhouse, which was almost unknown in lowland England. Indeed, in the worst affected Middle Marches, the region's growing poverty even led to the replacement of towerhouses by poorer quality pelehouses. By the early 1580s, 'the decay of the Borders' and the decline of border service were occasioning serious disquiet in official circles. Musters of horsemen in Redesdale, for instance, had dwindled from 300 in 1558 to little more than twenty by 1586. It remains unclear how far leading officials recognized the monarch's central responsibility for this fundamental Tudor failure to maintain good rule and defence: but since 'the king can do no wrong', scapegoats had to be found. Already in 1537, Archbishop Cranmer had attributed the Pilgrimage of Grace not just to 'unlearned priests and monks', but to the 'barbarous and savage' nature of the people there, who were ignorant of 'farming and the good arts of peace', religion, 'culture and more gentle civilisation', while in the 'furthest regions on the Scottish border', clans lived 'in perpetual battle and brigandage', surviving solely on 'pillage and plunder'.[12] Archbishop Parker likewise warned Secretary Cecil in 1560 that if bishops were not soon appointed to northern sees, the region would become 'too much Irish and savage'.[13] Yet, whereas 'the malice of the wild Irish' supplied an easy excuse in Ireland for the obstinate refusal of the natives to embrace the benefits of English civility, in point of fact the northerners were more English than the Tudors, and Tudor officials were hard put to explain their 'degeneracy'. In the far north, at least, they were driven to suggest that the borderers were not really civil Englishmen at all. William Camden dismissed them as nomads, while more optimistically, reports of visits by the famous preacher, Bernard Gilpin, to the inhabitants of Tynedale and

[11] S. G. Ellis, 'Civilizing Northumberland: Representations of Englishness in the Tudor State', *Journal of Historical Sociology*, 12 (1999), 120.

[12] Diarmaid MacCulloch, *Thomas Cranmer, a Life* (New Haven, 1996), 178.

[13] J. Bruce and T. T. Perowne (eds.), *Correspondence of Matthew Parker, D.D. Archbishop of Canterbury* (Parker Society; Cambridge, 1853), 123.

Redesdale suggested that 'their barbarous wildness and fierceness [is] so much qualified that there is hope left of their reduction unto civility'.[14]

# National identity and the collapse of the Gaelic world

By Elizabeth's reign, the Reformation was also interacting with Tudor expansion to transform the Gaelic world, albeit in unanticipated ways. When John of Islay, last lord of the Isles, died a pensioner at the Scottish court in 1503, he was eulogized by a bard from Ireland in conventional terms which belied his inability to control the powerful Clan Donald and its territories stretching from Lewis to Antrim. John of Islay had dreamed of a royal progress to Tara for inauguration as high king of Ireland, and the elegy extolled traditional MacDonald claims to sovereignty over the *Gaedhil* [ = Irish] of Ireland (*Éire*) and Scotland (*Alba*). Yet the Scottish crown's initially ineffective forfeiture of the lordship in 1493 exerted increasing pressure on this the most powerful, extensive, and aggressive of the Gaelic lordships and was finally enforced in 1545, after Donald Dubh's untimely death at Carrickfergus while treating with Henry VIII against his sovereign. Later medieval senses of Irishness were predominantly cultural rather than geographical, as MacDonald claims show, focusing chiefly on a distinct Gaelic nation and culture, with its separate language and legal system, although traditional senses of identity had identified the *Gaedhil* with the land of Ireland and the defunct high kingship.

Henry VIII's erection of Ireland into a kingdom thus served to revive more territorial concepts of Irishness, excluding the 'Irish' of Scotland but now extending to *all* Ireland's inhabitants. This included *Gaill* ( = foreigners, English, Scots) who traditionally refused to see themselves as 'Irish', as well as *Gaedhil*, as common subjects of the king of Ireland. Concurrently, the spread of Protestantism also eroded traditional pan-Gaelic ties between Ireland and Scotland. Much to Elizabeth's embarrassment, the first printed book in Gaelic, published in Edinburgh in 1567, aimed to exploit these traditional

[14] Ellis, 'Civilizing Northumberland', 121.

ties, harnessing the bardic tradition to the cause of reform: Bishop John Carswell's translation of Knox's *Book of Common Order*, 'especially for the men of Scotland and Ireland', reflected the advance of the Reformation in Gaelic Scotland and noted the inconveniences 'to us, the *Gaedhil* of Scotland and Ireland . . . that our Gaelic language has never been put into print'.[15] Yet even though in Ireland the Gaelic chiefs initially made no difficulty about accepting Henry VIII as Supreme Head of the Church of Ireland, opposition to the Reformation quickly built up there, particularly among the friars, as Carswell observed. Thus, the eventual impact of religious reform interacting with monarchical expansion was to create novel Scottish and Irish senses of identity: in both countries the rival *Gaedhil* and *Gaill* now became common *Albanaigh* or *Éireannaigh*, respectively, in the new Gaelic terminology. The difference was that in Ireland this development occurred primarily in opposition to the state: a new sense of Irishness based on faith and fatherland united the Catholic Irish against the Protestant New English, but traditional pan-Gaelic ties with Scotland were undermined by the development there of a Protestant Gaelic tradition.

Thus, following the advent of better Anglo-Scottish relations and the emergence of religious divisions between Scottish and Irish Gaeldom, the Gaelic world looked increasingly weak and vulnerable to renewed expansion from London and Edinburgh. As dynastic union looked likely to resolve the problems of England's northern frontier, the Tudor assimilation of Irish Gaeldom seemed the one outstanding question in regard to the unification of the British Isles.

# The Tudor conquest of Ireland

For most of Elizabeth's reign, Ireland remained a festering sore in the Tudor body politic. In the far north, Elizabeth had gradually reduced noble power, excluded the great magnates from office, and inserted outsiders instead without bringing about a wholesale alienation of the local elite; but in Ireland similar friction between the local Englishry and outsiders eventually proved a serious complication, with

[15] R. L. Thomson (ed.), *Foirm na n-Urrnuidheadh: John Carswell's Gaelic Translation of the Book of Common Order* (Edinburgh, 1970), 10–11.

Old English and New English officials increasingly divided over the best way to reduce Gaelic Ireland and Elizabeth concerned above all to reduce her expenses. In this context, the basic difference between the two borderlands was that in the north the frontier was of declining military importance, whereas in Ireland deteriorating Anglo-Gaelic relations heightened its importance and, with it, the military role of the great magnates. In the short term, moreover, the expansion of Tudor rule in Ireland actually compounded the government's difficulties: the erection of new shires like King's County simply shifted the problem of defence away from the standing fortifications of the Pale; and the transformation of Gaelic chiefs into English-style nobles by surrender and regrant, for instance Donald MacCarthy More who became earl of Clancare in 1565, was far from creating a new Tudor service nobility in Ireland. It merely added to the numbers of old-style territorial marcher lords there whom Tudor officials increasingly distrusted as overmighty subjects.

At different times, Tudor policies for Ireland drew on the whole range of medieval English political ideas and governmental devices developed for the conquest and assimilation of outlying territories. Gaelic chiefs were made responsible for the conduct of their clansmen and dependents through the system of booking and pledges, as with the northern surnames. 'Surrender and regrant' transformed Gaelic lordships into shires and tribal holdings into feudal tenures, although under Elizabeth the chiefs resisted new attempts to establish the leading clansmen as tenants-in-chief rather than mesne tenants, as previously, since this threatened to reduce their political influence. English settlers were introduced to control strategically important districts: briefly in Kerrycurrihy manor near Cork (1568–9), and in east Ulster against the Scots (1570–3); more ambitiously and generally in large parts of Munster (1585–90) after the Desmond rebellion. Regional councils were established in Connaught (1569) and Munster (1570) to oversee the rule of outlying parts; but reflecting the increased militarization of society there, the Irish councils rapidly acquired a more coercive character, fuelling resistance through their heavy reliance on military retinues and martial law, in contrast to the operation of the established regional councils in the borderlands elsewhere. Successive compositions in the Pale and Connaught turned the obligation to military service, the right of purveyance, and their Gaelic equivalents into an alternative system of military taxation which funded the queen's troops but further undermined the role of the Irish Parliament. After 1543, parliaments in Tudor Ireland met only briefly in 1557 and 1560, and then again in 1569–71 and 1585–6; but mounting resistance to the government's bills reflected the growing alienation of the local community. Even so, by 1590 Tudor rule had been gradually extended until only Ulster lay outside the system of shire government.

These measures were as much a response to the successive crises which punctuated the politics of Elizabethan Ireland as the result of far-sighted planning. Ambitious but weakly supported initiatives were, by turn, authorized by ambitious governors like Sussex and Sidney and countermanded by the queen either because they cost too much or in response to opposition by disaffected Palesmen, influential magnates like Ormond, or powerful chiefs like Shane O'Neill. Moreover, the tendency was for originally distinct Gaelic and Old English forms of dissent to coalesce because Tudor policy aimed also to strengthen royal control over outlying English districts. The result was mounting unrest and a wave of rebellions: the Butler rising and the earl of Thomond's rebellion were Irish echoes of the intrigues surrounding Norfolk, but there were more extended phases of rebellion in the south and west (1568–73), in Leinster and Munster (1579–83), and the Nine Years War in Ulster (1594–1603) which, in 1598, spread into Connaught and Munster. Initially, insurrections in English Ireland generally followed the mainland pattern of political demonstrations within a context of overall obedience—by contrast with the localized Gaelic 'wars of independence'—but movements of political opposition increasingly coalesced with an originally distinct tradition of resistance to Protestantism, so that resistance became increasingly general, ideological, and entrenched. Politics thus degenerated into an increasingly ruthless kind of military struggle, with mounting atrocities on both sides.

Yet only by attracting substantial military assistance from Spain could the victims of Tudor expansion hope to succeed. Even the most formidable of these resistance movements, the Ulster confederacy led by Hugh O'Neill, earl of Tyrone, had little hope otherwise of matching the superior resources of the Tudor state; and Philip II showed scant interest in Irish affairs until the 1580s, and then only as a means of countering Elizabeth's interference in the Spanish Netherlands. The confederates won occasional victories, and the English military machine became increasingly stretched in the 1590s to find money and men for Ireland in addition to commitments in France and the Netherlands and in the face of hardship and famine at home. Altogether, 42,500 troops were levied for service in Ireland during the War, representing perhaps 19 per cent of available manpower in England and Wales. Indeed, from 1596 onwards warfare in Ireland was the largest single expense in the wider war against Spain: payments from England averaged £104,000 a year, besides the cost to individual counties (Kent paid £3,324 altogether, Lancashire £5,500) of equipping and transporting the sixteen separate levies of troops for Ireland. In this context, the 3,500 Spanish troops who eventually landed at Kinsale in 1601 proved insufficient to tip the scales, and Lord Mountjoy's ruthless but professional campaign gradually crushed the rebellion. The War cost Elizabeth over £1 million, but with Tyrone's surrender at Mellifont, the political unification of the British Isles was finally completed.

# The Crown of the Three Kingdoms: an unstable inheritance

By 1603, therefore, the Tudors had finally achieved a long-term goal of English monarchs with the consolidation of monarchical power to the west and north of lowland England. Essentially, the aim had been to break down local autonomy and extend royal authority and English civility by a strategy of political centralization, administrative uniformity, and cultural imperialism. Together, the completion of the Tudor conquest of Ireland and the Union of the Crowns with Scotland spelled the end of the traditional military frontiers whose policing and defence had created such problems for the Tudors. Even before this, however, the great provincial magnates and their warlike tenantry had been tamed, and within a few years the Borders would be reduced to middle shires and English local government likewise extended throughout Ireland. In that sense, therefore, the events of 1603 were a vindication of Tudor policy—at least when viewed from London.

It is doubtful, however, whether, when weighed against the serious shortcomings of Tudor government in terms of the maintenance of peace, good rule, and defence, this achievement would have appeared so impressive to the long-suffering inhabitants of the Tudor borderlands. Essentially, they had been required to conform to the political and social norms of lowland England while still living in a turbulent march; and the numerous feudal franchises of the upland zone had been replaced by shires, despite the inevitable shortage of substantial gentry families to operate this type of local government. As so often, the *reductio ad absurdum* of Tudor policy occurred in Ireland, where Gaelic chiefs were expected to promote tillage and build stone houses as 'marks of English civility', regardless of local conditions, and where eventually in 1608 the most disruptive of the border surnames, the Grahams, were transplanted to Co. Roscommon on the assumption that this 'naughty and factious people' would reduce the wild Irish to tillage and civility simply because they were English.[16]

In the longer term, too, the manner of Tudor expansion and centralization was to exert deep-seated pressures on the political stability of the new British state created, in effect, by the events of 1603. This was most clearly the case in Ireland where the manner of the conquest alienated the local Englishry and left a bitter legacy of sectarian and racial animosity, with an administration controlled by a colonial elite of New English adventurers dependent on a standing army to maintain authority. Yet Tudor centralization also marginalized Wales and the English far north in an extended English nation-state and was reflected, for instance, by the fact that in the 1601 Parliament they had only 29 and 16 MPs, respectively, in a lower house of 462. The basic problem, however, was that lowland England was untypical of the British Isles as a whole, and London was not very accessible from Carlisle and Carrickfergus. Thus, any attempt to centralize power and replicate elsewhere conditions in the south-east was bound to create tensions, given the differences of geography and of communication in a pre-industrial society. Initially, King James's experience of Scotland's more fragmented power structures, decentralized administration, and cultural pluralism helped to mitigate the rigours of the Tudor system. Yet, following Tudor practice, the attempt to rule both Scotland and all of Ireland as dependent kingdoms from London soon ran into trouble.

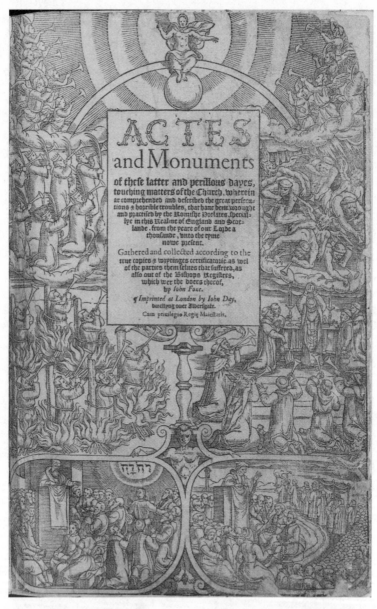

**Figure 5** Title page, 'Foxe's Book of Martyrs'. This design was evidently derived from the title page of a Lutheran Gospel Commentary published in Nuremberg in 1526, and was first used in 1563. It exploits the binary possibilities of illustration flanking the text by depicting an eternal opposition between the forces of (Protestant) good and (Popish) evil, presided over by God, who will ensure ultimate victory for the good. It symbolizes the Protestant culture of England which Foxe helped to create.

# 3

# The change of religion

## Diarmaid MacCulloch

Christianity's twenty-first-century profile in the four nations of the British Isles is a result of seventeenth-century upheavals: in particular the civil wars between 1640 and 1660. The picture has been blurred by the arrival and naturalisation of many other world faiths, by modern Christian ecumenism, and by general decline in institutional religion, but the fourfold character can still be recognized. English religious life is divided between a majority church priding itself on having evolved a distinctive 'Anglican' synthesis of historic Catholicism with Protestant reform, and a Protestant Nonconformity which has developed in reaction to this synthesis: still on the outside is Roman Catholicism, despite its numerical strength. Ireland presents majority Celtic Roman Catholicism and minority Anglo/Scottish Protestantism: Wales equally sharply confronts Celtic Protestant Nonconformity with English-oriented Anglicanism, while Scotland is dominated by an established church with a self-consciously Presbyterian and Calvinist tradition.

This modern picture looks little like Britain's religious profile in 1600. The Reformation transformed religious life throughout the islands, but the modern evolution was not inevitable. Up to the 1640–2 explosion in all four nations, the religious situation was not nearly so clear-cut, and radically different outcomes were possible. In that sense, an account of the sixteenth-century Reformation which stands on its own, inevitably ends the story too soon. As we examine what happened, one theme remains inevitable, and an essential part of mid-seventeenth-century breakdown: a convergence resulting from the increasing power of England, the most prosperous and populous of the four nations. For most of the period, England set the pace, and increasingly dominated the other polities. But there is a still greater fact to notice: as a movement which convulsed all Europe, the Reformation was the one sixteenth-century event which deeply and immediately affected all parts of the British Isles.

## Reform and inertia 1500–1520

In 1500 the four quarters of the archipelago were at their most distinctive in religious practice. England was an unusually well-run part of the Western Church: its large and well-endowed dioceses were administered by senior clergy who displayed the unimaginative conscientiousness required by a church which felt no threat to its future. The generally admirable intellectual and administrative calibre of England's bishops may have been connected to the fact that most unusually in Europe, the higher nobility rarely became clergy (a puzzling absence, given that English bishops were said to be equalled in wealth throughout Europe only by their Hungarian counterparts): most leading clerics were drawn from Oxbridge-educated sons of yeomen and lesser gentry. The atmosphere of regulation was symbolized by the relative success of a three-century campaign to impose clerical celibacy on secular or non-monastic clergy as well as regular clergy (monastic, living under a rule): this had been achieved to a much greater extent than in most other parts of western Europe, and certainly more than in other parts of the British Isles. The hostile commentator William Tyndale, writing in 1530, made the distinction between England and other countries where concubinage (irregular clerical partnerships with women) was official, including neighbouring Wales. He said (perhaps with some justification) that higher English standards had been maintained because Lollard criticism had forced more secret lust on the English clergy than in countries where there had been no dissenting challenge. [1]

The English Church had a vigorous devotional life, structured

---

[1] *An Answer to Sir Thomas More's Dialogue, the Supper of the Lord . . . and William Tracy's Testament expounded. By William Tyndale . . .*, ed. H. Walter (Parker Society; 1850), 40–1.

reasonably efficiently by diocese and parish, with lay piety strongly expressed in parish gilds. These had a variety of functions in popular worship, but everywhere they provided a means for ordinary people to benefit from the Church's prayers, so important to steer their souls after death through the painful years of purgatory towards the heavenly bliss of God's presence. Gilds were connected with the impulse to found chantries to send up soul-prayers in the mass, the highest form of approach to God. The founding of chantries still showed especial strength in the north of England. Besides this, eucharistic life was a kaleidoscope of devotions to holy places and tombs of saints both officially and purely locally recognized. There was nothing static about this activity: some cults and shrines lost their popularity, but new ones took their place, like the devotion to the Name of Jesus (vigorously promoted by Henry VII's mother Lady Margaret Beaufort), pilgrimage to King Henry VI's tomb at Windsor, or the cult of St George (first fostered by the monarchy, but taking widespread popular roots when the Reformation interrupted it). Popular devotional practice and church life often needed no official encouragement; they interacted with fun and enjoyment on holy days (holidays), and had a life of their own. For instance, the 'hocking ceremony', an Eastertide custom involving days of mock kidnaps of men by women and vice versa, became widespread as a method of parish fund-raising in the provinces in the late fifteenth century, but it never reached London.

Among regular clergy, the orders of friars retained a slightly double-edged esteem among the laity as skilled confessors and dramatic preachers. Bequests to them for prayers are exceedingly common in late medieval English wills, but the constant pastoral contact of such charismatic and high-profile figures with the laity (particularly with women) provoked some lay anxiety and a tradition of scandalous stories. Alongside them, the various monastic orders were mostly conscientious enough in maintaining their communities: for instance, numbers of English Benedictine monks studying at university, particularly at Oxford, seem to have been rising in the early sixteenth century, proof of the continuing intellectual liveliness of their houses. Like the laity as a whole, the nobility and gentry had transferred most active patronage of new foundations away from monasteries to chantries; only the Crown remained a major patron of new ventures in the regular life, in particular with late fifteenth-century foundations of Observant Franciscan friaries near the royal palaces at Greenwich and Richmond. The royal foundations generally remained some of the most impressively devout and respected of monastic houses, particularly Henry V's Bridgettine monastery at Syon (Middlesex) for nuns and attendant clergy: this even established its own printing press to produce the devotional literature for which there was an increasing lay demand.

Otherwise, English monks' problems were not so much that the laity despised them, but that the exuberant piety of the parish could now get on very well without them, at least in southern England. There the parochial system was concentrated and efficient, and parish churches could provide altars at which clergy could offer up soul-prayers. In northern counties, parochial boundaries were frozen in thirteenth-century patterns which even then had offered sparse coverage for pastoral care. Monasteries therefore continued to play a more central social and religious role. When the Pilgrimage of Grace exploded in the north in 1536, all houses already suppressed in north-west England were reopened by the Cumbrian and Lancashire rebels, and almost all houses can be shown to have supported the rising. It is noticeable that in the far north, the monasteries at Carlisle and Shap were among the last that the government closed in 1540, as if Henry VIII anticipated further trouble and postponed action against them as long as he could.

Lollardy, the protest movement inspired in the late fourteenth century by John Wyclif, had been decisively expelled from the universities during the early fifteenth century, but it was holding its own as a minority dissenting group with long-established bases, mostly in the south-east and the river systems of central lowland England. Often it showed a paradoxical symbiosis with official Catholic parish structures, as the substantial folk who were Lollard leaders also took their place in everyday administration of their community. Lollards showed much interest when the first rumours reached England after 1517 that there was a new outbreak of rebellion against the Church in Germany, led by a dissident monk, Martin Luther. They used their clandestine network developed over more than a century to spread Lutheran books. Not all Luther's ideas struck chords with these dissidents, and their sturdily sceptical piety, suspicious of outward show and preoccupied with living an ordered, godly life, was to shape English Protestantism's future just as much as Luther's idiosyncratic and paradoxical message of justification by faith alone. Nevertheless, they recognized Luther as an ally against the old system, and promoted a renewed dissidence. By the late 1520s this was producing a variety of movements of reform, to which from 1529, far away in Germany, the nickname 'Protestant' was applied. In a British context, the word was not used until at least 1553, and the earliest stages of these movements are perhaps better labelled evangelical.

The Church in Wales (formally part of the English metropolitan province of Canterbury) showed most of the drawbacks and virtually no signs of the new departures apparent in England. It was politically fragmented, divided especially between Welsh-speaking regions and 'Old English' (mainly in urban enclaves), and it served a region only gradually recovering from the dire effects of unsuccessful early fifteenth-century rebellions against English rule. Most Welsh religious houses had in any case always been poorly endowed. Distinctive was popular piety, oriented more than England's towards shrines which owed little to the Roman Church's imposition of the parochial system; pilgrimage was on the increase in fifteenth-century Wales. However, there was little native religious leadership: virtually all bishops were Englishmen looking for wealthier dioceses back home. The Welsh were not isolated from wider national life, despite English racial condescension. Some escaped Welsh poverty by going to university, particularly Oxford—notably to All Souls College, which did much to train ecclesiastical lawyers active in national church administration. Others took a different route, into royal military service which maintained a number of permanent garrisons on the kingdom's frontiers. One of the most significant of these was Calais, which proved a conduit of ideas to Wales in the Reformation, as garrison soldiers returned home to tell of the new religious experiences on offer on the other side of the English Channel.

Ireland exhibited a three-way split between Dublin's Pale, more dispersed and independent enclaves of medieval 'Old English' settlement, and Gaelic lordships (the largest area of Ireland); these produced a Church of contrasting characters. Religion in the Pale was closest to the English experience: Dublin boasted not one but two well-endowed cathedrals (one with a sizeable Augustinian monastery attached, like Carlisle in England), and the Pale's clerical leadership was self-confident, proud of its Anglo-Norman heritage and determined to keep the alien and expanding world of Gaelic culture at bay.

Ireland was not a poor country, and its clergy both English and Gaelic, were drawn from the ranks of the gentry, who were also intimately involved in the finance and organization of the Church. Church wealth in the Gaelic lordships was dominated by the system of coarbs and erenaghs, hereditary holders of rights in church lands, who might be in minor orders, but might equally be laypeople. These were concentrated in the north and west, but many other parishes exhibited a tendency to draw clergy from the same family over successive generations. Whatever the benefits or drawbacks of this close involvement of gentry in parish finance, organization, and staffing, during the fifteenth century the Gaelic lordships witnessed a remarkable and distinctive flowering of reformed Catholicism centring on the Observant Franciscans. This spread eastwards to affect the whole island and has left a haunting legacy of late medieval conventual ruins. Irish monasticism, in contrast to the friars, failed to reform itself, despite some efforts particularly among the Cistercians.

Scotland promised institutional reform by establishing two archbishoprics independent of England (St Andrews, 1472; Glasgow, 1492), but the promise was not fulfilled: the episcopal structure remained distorted by early medieval concentration of cathedrals in fertile low-lying plains, even in the Highlands, and by an extraordinary confusion of boundaries among eastern dioceses. Overall, the Church's wealth was channelled aside to benefit the landowning elite. Scottish noblemen had always been inclined to impose themselves on ecclesiastical high office, but the tendency accelerated after James IV's death (1513), to the detriment of an effective Scottish episcopate. The parochial system in the Lowlands, in theory comparatively well-endowed, was subverted by diversion of funds to de luxe collegiate chantry foundations designed to save the souls of the nobility; significantly, the remnants of these churches form some of the most lavish examples of late medieval Scots building. Monasteries, like cathedrals, were concentrated in the Lowlands, with the exception (on both counts) of the ancient island abbey of Iona, erected into a cathedral at the beginning of the sixteenth century for the diocese of the Isles (Sodor). Like the rest of the Scottish Church, monasteries were more affected by secularization than their relatively untainted English counterparts; by the sixteenth century, nearly all were presided over by commendators, non-monastic sons of the gentry and nobility. By contrast, the orders of friars showed signs of reform and reconstruction: the last friary (the Carmelites of Edinburgh) was founded as late as 1526, a quarter-century later than anything in England. There were also marginal traces of Lollardy in south-west Scotland, but its connection with the English movement (presumably through coastal trade routes in the Irish Sea) remains to be explained.

Among these four nations, English predominance was as yet weak. Scotland in particular was theoretically at war with England for two centuries down to James IV's and Henry VII's treaty of 1502; it was more oriented in politics and religion to the Baltic and to its traditional ally France. In the far north, indeed, Shetland remained a world apart until the 1570s, more intimate with Norway and Hanseatic towns than with Edinburgh. The secular legal system of Orkney and Shetland remained separate until 1611, although the islands had been fairly loosely united to the Archbishopric of St Andrews in 1472. The sense of Scottish separateness from England was growing rather than diminishing. A glance at late medieval Scots architecture reveals this: an almost complete absence of English Perpendicular forms and all-pervasive analogies with French Flamboyant. In 1507 James IV ordered use of the newly published Aberdeen Breviary in Scots churches, and forbade importation and sale of the English Sarum Use for the liturgy in Scotland: no doubt a commercial decision, but also a cultural one.

# The London colonial enterprise 1520–1558

The characteristic of this period was assertion of dominance not merely by England, but by the English capital and its hinterland. To be more precise, it was the assertion of Henry VIII's ego. Henry was well aware of his ancestors' claim to lordship over the whole archipelago; furthermore, after clashing with Pope Clement VII over the annulment of his marriage to Catherine of Aragon, he suddenly became alerted to the supposedly ancient truth that he was Supreme Head of the Church within his dominions. However, earlier in Henry's reign, his own self-assertion had marched uneasily with that of his long-term chief minister, Thomas Wolsey, for whom the king obtained a cardinal's hat from Pope Leo X in 1515. Wolsey (in whose career it is always difficult to disentangle self-aggrandizement from an eager concern to do his master's bidding) additionally became papal legate *a latere* in 1518. This made him the pope's prime representative in the realm of England, outclassing the Archbishop of Canterbury's normal legatine powers, and giving him a degree of control over both provinces of the English Church (Canterbury and York) which had no recent precedent. Such power echoed his political supremacy, expressed in his life grant of the office of Lord Chancellor in 1515. The Irish Church, however, quietly ignored his efforts to extend his legatine power to Ireland.

Wolsey might have used his exceptional position to tackle aspects of church life and administration which needed reforming; he was, after all, a former Oxford don with a good claim to be a humanist scholar, and he was keenly interested in education (to the extent of lending his name to a Latin grammar prepared for his cherished school in his native Ipswich). However, although his legatine office busily creamed off profitable routine business from other church courts, he made few innovations. Very unusually among English bishops, he spent little time in his successive dioceses; even Henry VII's minister Cardinal-Archbishop John Morton had done his best to visit Canterbury and regularly ordain clergy there. Wolsey was regarded by senior churchmen as soft on heresy, although he was fairly energetic against Lutheranism when it appeared on the English scene in the 1520s—we might also consider that his policy of persuading religious reformers to recant was more effective than creating martyrs. He did little to promote English monastic reform, and was indeed almost unique in the kingdom as a non-monk heading a monastery (the wealthy St Albans Abbey). Ironically, he was instrumental in attacking the independence of the Observant Friars, one of the few English religious orders which needed no reform at all. Otherwise, his one major programme of real change in the Church was to close a clutch of small monasteries in the south-east, to finance his Ipswich and Oxford colleges. This might be considered a sensible redeployment of resources, but it was too closely associated with his own image of grand self-indulgence, and aroused local fury, even riots when some monasteries were closed. Wolsey succeeded in alienating virtually the entire monastic world. He also employed in his dissolutions one of his servants who put the experience to use in the next decade: Thomas Cromwell.

Wolsey was broken by his failure to get the Aragon marriage

annulled: the king had convinced himself that God urgently demanded the annulment, and the pope was obstructing it. From the moment when this obstruction became open, at the end of a hearing of Henry's case at Blackfriars, London, in summer 1529, Henry began looking around for an alternative strategy to secure what he and God wanted. He put his team of theological experts to the task of showing that he and his predecessors had always had the right to decide the most momentous religious questions: that England was, in contemporary political jargon, an empire, without any superior on earth. They duly found what he wanted in (among other places) the stories of King Arthur, which appeared to them to be perfectly respectable history.

Among these researchers was a diplomat and Cambridge don, Thomas Cranmer, on whom the discovery of the royal supremacy had a traumatic effect: it propelled him out of his previous conventional piety and distaste for Martin Luther into a hatred of the papacy and a new preoccupation with the Reformation's message. This crystallized during one of his diplomatic missions, when he expressed his newfound convictions by marrying the niece of a Lutheran theologian in Nuremberg—an act of rebellion against the celibacy rule of the old Western Church. Great was his alarm when he found that Henry VIII, valuing an efficient and trustworthy royal servant, had chosen him to succeed the late William Warham as Archbishop of Canterbury. However, Cranmer kept quiet about his wife, returned to England, and went through all the necessary bureaucracy to secure papal cooperation with his consecration, while secretly repudiating papal obedience—all because of his genuine reverence for Henry, coupled with a new passion for reforming the Church. He presided over the annulment of one royal marriage and the open acknowledgement of a new marriage to Anne Boleyn, his patroness, herself a vigorous promoter of the evangelical cause. He was now able to work closely with his old acquaintance, the king's new chief minister Thomas Cromwell, by now also a discreet but highly motivated evangelical, who was given the equivalent of Wolsey's former legatine powers in the name of the king, with a new title as Vice-Gerent in Spirituals. Surviving Cromwell's fall in 1540, Cranmer was able to protect the evangelical cause and many leading like-minded clergy from the worst of the ageing King Henry's occasional lurches towards traditional religion. By the end of the reign, much of the old world had been dismantled (including the dissolution of monasteries and the destruction of shrines and some religious imagery), while Henry, still in control of contending religious factions in high politics, had quite consciously allowed his son to be tutored by committed evangelicals and to be guided into a new reign by a set of evangelical politicians.

The clearest expressions of London's hegemonic strategy over the rest of Britain flowed from Henry VIII's break with Rome. Legislation between 1533 and 1536 passed in the English Parliament affected not only England but Wales (at that stage without parliamentary representation). Parallel enactments in the puppet Dublin Parliament were enforced in the areas of English rule in Ireland; in 1537 the proctors of the Irish clergy, the one group which was vigorously to oppose the royal supremacy, were permanently excluded from the Irish Parliament, easing the path for further legislation there. The dissolution of all monasteries over which the Tudor monarchy had control, administered by Cromwell with remarkable speed and efficiency between 1532 and 1540, suppressed all monastic life throughout England and Wales and in about half of Ireland. All English and Welsh friaries were dissolved in a single campaign in 1538, accompanied by much negative government propaganda to neutralize public worries: the friars included some of the most effective preachers of traditional faith and thus posed real danger to Cromwell's plans. In Ireland, they could only be suppressed in English-controlled areas, and it is noticeable that in 1536, the Dominican order constituted a new independent province for Ireland: one means of stemming the destruction of the friars' work.

Throughout the 1540s and 1550s, Lord Deputy Sir Anthony St Leger attempted to anglicize the Irish nobility, in the wake of the defeat of 1530s rebellions, to end Ireland's separateness. However, such efforts were not consistently backed from London and produced meagre results; this was particularly true of evangelical religious policies which Cromwell had exported from England to Ireland on the back of the break with Rome. George Browne, a former English friar made archbishop of Dublin to enforce Cromwellian religious changes, found that his clergy adamantly refused to take part in the preaching campaign which he ordered. Browne found little support from the Dublin secular administration, and after 1540, he lapsed into intimidated passivity. The Palesmen showed little sign of resentment against monastic dissolutions, and accepted the royal supremacy without demur, but they were much more resistant to any attempt to undermine traditional sacramental life.

In England, Edward VI's accession (1547) brought a regime based on a close association of politicians headed by Edward Seymour, duke of Somerset, and with Archbishop Cranmer as a prominent member. It immediately began accelerating religious changes. There were constraints: the Holy Roman Emperor Charles V's suspicion combined with hostility to change from most bishops and noblemen. Yet even in the first year, a royal visitation promoted renewed destruction of religious imagery, an official collection of homilies (sermons) set forth evangelical theology, the old heresy laws were abolished, and the final dissolution of chantries was enacted. Cranmer welcomed to England many prominent overseas reformers displaced by Catholic victories in central Europe; his vision of the Church was resolutely international, and the refugees whom he found most congenial were non-Lutherans (the 'Reformed') like Martin Bucer and Peter Martyr Vermigli. Over the next few years, he masterminded two successive versions of the Prayer Book in English, the second (1552) far more radical than the stopgap version of 1549; he also formulated a statement of doctrine (the Forty-Two Articles) and drafted a complete revision of canon law. Cranmer was cautious in orchestrating the pace of change, to the annoyance of many less politically-minded evangelical clergy, and his caution was justified when a major uprising in western England in summer 1549 specifically targeted religious innovation, notably his Prayer Book. Yet simultaneous popular commotions in south and east England, far from showing unhappiness with the government's religious agenda, displayed positive enthusiasm for it, and indeed their demonstrations seemed fuelled by an excitement about the reformation in church and commonwealth which Somerset's official pronouncements ostentatiously proclaimed.

The result of this sudden eruption of trouble was Somerset's summary removal in October 1549 by his colleagues, to be replaced by the reassuringly less colourful John Dudley, earl of Warwick (later duke of Northumberland). Yet the Reformation continued and accelerated its pace, encouraged by Cranmer and the young king's evangelical enthusiasm: evangelical bishops supplanted several conservatives, which in turn made it easier to impose the religious revolution. The work was suddenly halted by Edward's fatal illness in 1553; he and Northumberland tried to divert the succession from Henry VIII's traditionalist daughter Mary to a Protestant member of the royal family, Jane Grey, but the scheme met an unexpectedly fierce national rejection and popular resistance. Mary rode to London in triumph; the Protestant cause was thrown into disarray, and it looked as if England's Reformation was over.

Edwardian efforts at introducing the Reformation to Ireland met with characteristically cautious backing from Lord Deputy St Leger and other senior administrators. Caution was necessary, when not merely Robert Wauchope the papally appointed archbishop of Armagh and Irish primate, but also the royal appointee to Armagh, George Dowdall, offered opposition to change—Dowdall eventually fled in defiance in 1551. Yet official compromise avoided too much confrontation with suspicious traditionalists and kept most from breaking with the established Church. Remarkably, there was no official dissolution of Irish chantries on the English model. The 1549 English Prayer Book was introduced to Ireland; a Dublin edition was published in 1551, a year after any English edition, and there was even a Latin version, which could meet the problem for the Gaelic lordships that government plans for a Gaelic translation were not implemented. Moreover, the more radical 1552 English liturgy was not imported, to the horror of the evangelical enthusiast John Bale when he arrived from England to be Bishop of Ossory; he could not see that to have secured widespread Irish use of even Cranmer's first Prayer Book was itself a considerable achievement.

Mary's 1553 restoration of traditional religion to Ireland (welcomed with much enthusiasm by the Irish clerical elite) was modified in one crucial respect: the Pope was persuaded to modify his twelfth-century predecessor's grant by recognizing Henry VIII's fait accompli in proclaiming an Irish kingdom. Mary was not going to lose that title, and her determination was coupled with the beginnings of a new policy towards her second kingdom: the implementation of plans to plant settlers in Leix and Offaly mooted in her brother's reign. As the flagship of English policy in Ireland into the seventeenth century, plantation proved to be fatal to 'Old English' loyalty to England, and an obstacle to any similar loyalty taking root among Gaelic lords. It was thus a Catholic monarch who began the colonization which created the resentment out of which Irish Catholic nationalism was eventually borne.

That was one of many ironies to afflict this most loyal daughter of Rome. She won the crown with every advantage in July 1553: defeating and humiliating Jane Grey's Protestants in a virtually bloodless coup, she had the chance to exploit conservative frustration and fury at Edwardian changes. Anxious to restore England to papal obedience, she enlisted the help of her cousin, the long-exiled Cardinal Reginald Pole, a distinguished humanist and advocate of major reform in the Western Church, who was made papal legate *a latere* to England and became her close adviser. Although the English political elite spun out negotiations in order to ensure that they could retain recently acquired church estates and wealth, Pole eventually arrived in November 1554 and England was reconciled with Rome. Mary could rely on widespread national satisfaction at the restoration of the Latin liturgy and traditional devotion, and she successfully outfaced opposition to her marriage to one of Europe's most powerful Catholic monarchs, Philip II of Spain.

Nevertheless Mary ended her reign as the enemy of a new pope, Paul IV: passionately anti-Spanish because of Spanish rule in his beloved homeland Naples, he entered war with Mary's husband Philip. He also revoked Pole's legateship for England; there had been a long vendetta between the two men, and now Paul sought to summon his old enemy back to Rome and put him on trial as a heretic. Pole had to rely on Mary's defiance of the pope to continue in his conscientious efforts at restructuring the English Church, reforms which in some respects (such as his plans for clerical seminaries attached to cathedrals) anticipated the later work of the Council of Trent. Yet all this work, which was much more creative than a mere restoration of the pre-1533 situation, was left unfinished at Mary's death in 1558. Pole had nurtured his talents in Italian exile for more than two decades, but had little time to display them in England. His efforts at sorting out the chaos of clerical finance became an unintended gift for Queen Elizabeth's new Protestant settlement.

In Scotland, English policy after the Scots defeat at Flodden (1513) was repeated military and dynastic interference, culminating in the duke of Somerset's disastrous garrisoning policy from 1547 to 1549, after which the English gave up interventionism for a decade. From the 1530s, this attempt to impose an English protectorate in Scotland was linked with the English Crown's break with Rome and England's increasingly radical religious policies. James V's anti-English strategy included not only his two marriages to French princesses (the second being Mary of Guise in 1538) but also his demonstrative hostility to Scots evangelicals. This did not stop him from simultaneously taking advantage of papal worries that he might defect from Rome, in order to extract a virtual exclusion of real papal power in Scotland, and to impose heavy clerical taxation without papal protest. Moreover, in one of his last decisions before he died in 1542, he came down against sending a delegate to the imminent Council of Trent which was called to reform the Roman Catholic Church: so no government representatives from Britain ever appeared at Trent's various sessions. A pro-English government in Scotland under James Hamilton, earl of Arran, went on in 1543 to make some moves to imitate what Henry VIII had done in England, but it was quickly overthrown; thereafter, English-style Reformation in Scotland was handicapped for a generation by resentment against the patent English quest for hegemony. Cardinal David Beaton, who up to his murder by Scots evangelicals in 1546, dominated a pro-French and militantly traditionalist regime, exploited this fury in the interests of Catholicism.

Yet there was a significant double strategy in the enterprise which Somerset relaunched in 1547: he invaded and devastated Scotland in order to secure the marriage of the boy Edward and the even younger Mary, queen of Scots, but he also sought to charm the people of Scotland into a union, using a newly coined rhetoric of British identity in printed and preached propaganda. It was in 1548 that the term 'Great Britain' first came into general use, prominently in the work of a unionist Scots writer, James Henrisoun, and the context was Protestant.[2] There was genuine popular enthusiasm in south-west Scotland for the evangelical message which English preachers brought, and it is remarkable that pro-English feeling in the western Highlands seems to have survived throughout the 1540s (but then the English were devastating the Lowlands!). By 1603, a union of crowns seemed a natural outgrowth of religious links set up in the Edwardian era,

[2] 'Great Britain' is discussed, particularly in relation to James Henrisoun, in M. Merriman, 'James Henrisoun and "Great Britain": British Union and the Scottish Commonweal', in R. Mason (ed.), *Scotland and England 1286–1815* (Edinburgh, 1987), 85–112, esp. 85, 95.

instead of the bizarre mismatch of ancient enemies which it would have been a century before.

In the meantime, Mary, queen of Scots, was married not to King Edward but to a French prince, and her mother Mary of Guise took over from the earl of Arran to lead a devoutly Catholic regime with reformist intentions. International tensions meant that she had little contact with Mary of England's work in restoring and redeveloping Catholicism. The links of her leading reforming Catholic clergy were rather with Germany and Paris, and they are perceptible in the work of John Hamilton, archbishop of St Andrews, who soon after his arrival in office in 1549 instituted two successive councils to consider reform. His Scots catechism of 1552 (admittedly drafted, it seems, by an English Catholic exile) shows a concern to be conciliatory to evangelical critics of the Church, in a manner characteristic of various major efforts at reform in the archdiocese of Cologne in the 1530s and 1540s. The Regent Mary, desperate to maintain disintegrating national unity, forced another church council to meet in 1559. It achieved little, and its failure represented one of the last European attempts at ecumenical reconciliation (closely followed in France by the abortive 1561 Colloquy of Poissy). In despair, several leading Scots humanist Catholic clergy went straight over to the Protestant cause.

## Responses to religious revolution 1520–1558

The English government's expansionist aims and the jurisdictional revolution caused by the break with Rome ran in parallel with the continent-wide upheaval which stemmed from Luther's attack originally narrowly focused on the indulgence system. Before Thomas Cromwell steered Henry VIII towards fitful and cautious involvement with the Reformation, evangelical ideas had already found a response in some parts of Britain. In both Scotland and England, academics and merchants with continental links were prominent in bringing ideas over; penetration was small-scale in England through the early 1520s, until a sudden burst of activity was inspired by the arrival of the first English printed New Testaments, translated by the refugee Oxford scholar from the Forest of Dean, William Tyndale, and published abroad in 1525/6. One cannot underestimate the impact of this new vernacular translation on those who read it. It remained at the heart of Reformation in the English-speaking British Isles; surreptitiously read and discussed, it worked on the imaginations of those who had no access to public preaching because of official repression or lack of provision. It may be significant that there is a perceptible nationwide decline in ordinations in England during the 1520s: perhaps the traditional church was losing its grip on those thinking of a clerical career.

Cromwell and Cranmer began the slow work of supplementing bible-reading by recruiting and financing preachers. In 1537 Cromwell also persuaded Henry VIII to order general provision of English Bibles for parish churches, and further promoted an official translation in 1539. Even after Cromwell's fall, the parishes were in 1541 given an effective extra spur to provide Bibles by the threat of fines if they did not. The resulting popular enthusiasm for the Bible was sufficiently noticeable for Henry VIII to take fright. In 1543 he pushed Parliament into ordering that only upper status groups in society, presumably deemed less excitable, should be allowed to read it at all—an Act which is curiously like the many statutory attempts to legislate people into wearing clothes appropriate to their degree (sumptuary legislation). Interestingly, in the same year the Scots Parliament dominated by Arran passed an Act which for the first time allowed lieges, that is landowners, to possess the Bible, thus giving the Scots approximate parity of access to the Bible to its newly restricted access in England.

In both England and Scotland, therefore, between the 1520s and 1550s enthusiastic evangelical communities emerged in ports all along the east coast, while in south-east England, evangelical activists merged inland into pre-existing Lollard groups. Probably ordinary people were more affected than clergy and the landed elite, who had more emotional and financial investment in the old system. Radical reformers and Continental Anabaptists cultivated the same territory, and radicalism showed signs of substantial growth in Edward VI's reign while official English Protestantism established its new identity—resulting in two radicals being burned at the stake by a panicky regime, which had only just abolished the late medieval heresy laws directed against Lollardy. These deaths were not forgotten by either radicals or Catholics when Mary I turned likewise to a policy of burning heretics, this time the Protestant activists of Edward VI's church. More than three hundred were burned, among them prominent church leaders including Cranmer; Mary did not relax persecution when it became clear that the campaign was not destroying Protestant morale. Protestants who fled the country began developing a cult of the martyrs, which when embodied in a major narrative by John Foxe (published in English in 1563), became one of the defining features of future English Protestantism. If anything characterized the majority English approach to religion over three centuries from the reign of Elizabeth I, it was hatred of Roman Catholicism. This has been described as the most consistent English political stance of the early modern period.

For Scots Evangelicals, traditional trading links with the Baltic and north Germany were initially as important as those with England; they therefore had a direct relationship with the rapidly institutionalizing Lutheran churches which was not so easy for the English, faced with Henry VIII's studied hostility to Martin Luther. However, Scots reformers of the 1540s did not gain even the limited foothold in government which Archbishop Cranmer and his allies enjoyed in Henry VIII's last years: Scotland failed to follow the example of similar northern states like Denmark and Sweden and embrace an official Lutheran Reformation. Many Scots evangelicals fled to England, particularly when the Protestant noblemen governing in the name of Edward VI pushed the English Reformation into a more radical path than Luther's. One reformer in particular, John Knox, was deeply impressed by what was going on in Edwardian England, though he also bitterly criticized the English government's stage-by-stage introduction of change. Henceforward, English reforming patterns played a leading role in the Scottish Reformation.

Wales and Ireland experienced no similar popular movement. In Wales, ordinary people were outraged when shrines and sacred images were destroyed, and there was little native base for sympathy with change: Lollardy was a foreign phenomenon, which had been identified by one patriotic poet with the alien English. The governments of Henry VIII and Edward VI made no effort to present new ideas in the Welsh language; the few pioneer writings in Welsh were the private initiative of individual Welsh evangelical enthusiasts. Such activity had virtually no parallel in Ireland. Yet in neither country during the 1530s and 1540s was there any strong sign of continued loyalty to the pope. The Welsh in particular had a pride in the Welsh origins of the Tudor dynasty which Henry VII had been careful to cultivate; Welsh bards contrasted fifteenth-century miseries with the prosperity and improvements in Welsh status brought by the new dynasty. As a result, this markedly traditionalist nation gave no support either to the religiously conservative rebellions in northern England in 1536/7 (the Pilgrimage of Grace) or in south-western England against the English Prayer Book in 1549. Welsh passivity in this second wave of unrest is particularly striking.

## Official Protestant crusades 1558–1603

Once more in 1559 a Protestant regime under Elizabeth put in place reforming legislation for England and Wales, duly echoed by the Dublin Parliament. The pattern chosen by the queen was to resurrect matters as they had been in late 1552, towards the end of her brother's reign, including Cranmer's second Prayer Book barely modified, and his doctrinal statement (shortened to Thirty-Nine Articles when finalized in 1563). This settlement, with little change in its official structures, still governs the Church of England. There followed a decade of precarious political balance in English local and central government between reformers and Catholic sympathizers. This collapsed in 1568–9, and prominent Catholics started to become recusant, that is, they refused any longer to attend services of the established Church. However Catholic activists badly mismanaged a rebellion led by northern noblemen in 1569–70, and there was no further serious internal challenge to the Protestant ascendancy. This left the government free to enforce its will: using the old church's diocesan and parish structure for Protestant purposes, and isolating those who remained loyal to Rome by legislation and official pressure which turned them into a harassed minority among the gentry and nobility. Catholics went abroad to train for the priesthood, and returned to a dangerous underground missionary ministry in which the reward was often imprisonment, torture, and death; yet their heroism could do no more than sustain a minority community led by a network of devoted gentry and largely dependent on gentry households.

Elizabeth's policy was designed to establish a broad Protestantism which would not encourage controversy through following the latest

European attempts to make doctrine more precise. Although it was Francis Bacon rather than Elizabeth herself who described her as loath to make windows into men's souls, she expressed a similar agenda to her French Catholic suitor Henry, duke of Anjou, during marriage negotiations in 1571: 'Neither doth the usage of the divine service of England properly compell any man to alter his opinion in the great matters now in controversie in the Church'.[3] Her legislated Church was in place to secure outward conformity, and she firmly resisted any changes which might threaten this aim. She discouraged attempts by her bishops, mostly veterans of Edwardian forward policies, to legislate for further reform in the 1563 Convocation of Canterbury, and equally she frustrated them when they switched their efforts to Parliament. By the end of the decade the bishops began to realize that they were prisoners of the queen's immobilism, committed to enforcing her settlement rather than improving it.

In Wales, official policy showed a remarkable advance on earlier incompetence: Welsh identity and cultural distinctiveness were treated as allies rather than as obstacles. In a new departure, most bishops appointed to Wales after 1559 were native Welshmen, and several of them gave patronage to the bards who played an important part in Welsh society. The authorities also worked creatively alongside the handful of Welsh Protestant enthusiasts to encourage the publication of Welsh translations of the English Prayer Book and Bible. The Bible completed in 1588 was decisive not only in winning the Welsh to Protestantism, but in preserving Welsh as a viable language into modern times. A significant factor in integrating the Welsh cultural and social elite into the agenda of a Protestant government was the foundation in 1571 of a new college in Oxford University, Jesus College, which immediately developed the already significant Welsh presence in the university. The contrast with Elizabethan policies towards Ireland is sadly instructive. England's strategy of new colonial settlement inevitably made the Irish see the English as enemies, while the English saw Gaelic culture as an

[3] Elizabeth I's remarks about religion to Henri, duke of Anjou, were to be conveyed through her envoy Sir Francis Walsingham, and are contained in a letter from Elizabeth to Walsingham on 11 May 1571: Sir Dudley Digges (ed.), *The Compleat Ambassador, or two treatises of the intended marriage of Qu. Elizabeth of Glorious Memory* . . . (London, 1655; Wing D.1453), 99: I am indebted to Dr Susan Doran for alerting me to this quotation, particularly through her further use of the letter in S. Doran, 'Elizabeth I's Religion: The Evidence of her Letters', *Journal of Ecclesiastical History*, 51 (2000), 705.

obstacle to their schemes. The Gaelic aristocracy now allied with agents of the Counter-Reformation and with England's Catholic enemies on the Continent, principally Spain, which made repeated if unsuccessful efforts to aid Irish Catholics with expeditionary forces. As the older Irish clergy died off, their replacements had to make the choice between allegiance to Elizabeth or allegiance to the pope.

Like England, Scotland began a new political Reformation in 1559, when frustration with French influence discredited Mary of Guise's Catholic policies and led to a Protestant insurrection encouraged by fiery preaching from activists like John Knox. The rising was led by prominent members of the nobility (strengthened by adherence from the earl of Arran, heir presumptive to the throne), but it also relied on popular violence which included the comprehensive sacking of certain (mostly urban) monasteries and friaries—a Protestant aggression without parallel in any other stage of the Reformations in the British Isles, and an anticipation of what Calvinists would do in France and the Netherlands over the next decade. During 1560 a new Protestant Church (the 'Kirk') was legislated into existence. Knox had been inspired by his Marian exile in John Calvin's Geneva, and his plans for the Kirk were now modelled on Geneva and other Reformed Churches rather than on England. Some of the bishops of the old church joined the new to take up leading roles in administration. The revolution was aided by the English government, in a vigorous military intervention which avoided the mistakes of the Edwardian adventures in Scotland; yet the success of this English investment in Scots Protestantism was balanced by the uncomfortable fact that the Scottish Reformation was based on a rebellion against God's anointed monarch. The contrast with the shape of the English Reformation, directed at every turn by the Crown, was significant, and it constantly recurred up to the end of the seventeenth century.

The Scottish situation was complicated by the arrival from France in 1560 of Queen Mary, a young woman who moved from inexperience through attempts at inclusiveness and conciliation to exceptional political incompetence, alienating Protestant politicians who had done their best to remain loyal to her. The ensuing civil war resulted in a series of Protestant and mostly pro-English regimes ruling from 1567 in the name of her infant son James VI, after Mary had fled to the reluctant and embarrassed hospitality of Elizabeth of England. Amid complex political manoeuvres, a remarkable ecclesiastical compromise was evolved for the Scottish Kirk. A reformed church polity was founded to cover the whole country, but it was to coexist with the ghost of the old Catholic church system preserved for the lives of its old office-holders; they continued to draw two-thirds of their revenues even if they did not play an active part in the new church.

This was a shrewd and realistic expedient. The many absentee and pluralist clergy in the pre-Reformation parish system must have made the compromise about parish revenues easier: after all, hardly any of those resources had benefited medieval parishes anyway, and providing a third of them to the active parish minister would normally represent an improvement in the real finance available to working clergy. Half the old clergy in any case chose to work actively in the new Kirk. Scottish monasteries were not suppressed (although the potentially more dangerous mendicant orders were), and they were allowed to fade gradually away: a significant measure of their irrelevance to Catholic survival. Several were legally remodelled into secular lordships: a logical step, since they had generally been headed by a layman in any case. In what amounted to an optional Reformation, there was little opportunity for the formation of a distinctive and self-conscious Catholic recusant grouping, in contrast to England and Ireland, and it took early seventeenth-century Franciscan missionary work to win a few of the Western Isles back to Catholicism. Some noblemen remained Catholic, and given King James's wish to be as inclusive as possible to magnates willing to be loyal, it was possible for them to gain high positions in royal favour: so the Jesuit-educated crypto-Catholic Alexander Seton, earl of Dunfermline, took a leading place in Scottish government for nearly three decades from the 1590s.

Activist Scots Protestants were capable of being more hardline than the Reformations of Switzerland and Geneva which they so admired. For instance, from 1561 the Kirk officially disapproved of the non-scriptural feast of Christmas; when it adopted the Helvetic Confession of Faith in 1566, it explicitly excluded the observation of Christmas which the Swiss had allowed. However, after the death of the anglicized and comparatively moderate Calvinist John Knox (1572) two tendencies emerged. One was a broadly-based Protestantism accepting the institution of bishop/superintendents and a strong role for the secular government in church affairs, rather on the

English model; the other, led by Andrew Melville after his return from Geneva in 1574, was a more doctrinaire Presbyterianism, determined to assert the Church's independence of Crown interference. Threeway political struggles between these two groups and Catholic noblemen in the 1580s resulted in further compromise: as James VI reached political maturity, he struggled with considerable success to increase the power of the bishop/superintendents and of the Crown within the system, but he also allowed the growth of a nationwide structure of presbyteries.

# Godly people 1558–1603

When Elizabeth came to the throne, convinced Protestants were certainly in a minority in England, let alone Wales, and to create a godly Protestant realm was an enormous task which the authorities had to undertake in partnership with unofficial enthusiasts. The partnership was not always comfortable: Protestants were accustomed to being an innovative, destructive, and often persecuted force, and they took time to adjust to being pillars of the establishment. Many longstanding outlets of popular Protestantism such as propaganda plays and ballads were gradually sanitized and silenced by the authorities, as the regime felt itself more secure against popish superstition: the alehouse became an enemy of true religion, when in earlier days it had often been the only refuge for the godly against the established Catholic Church.

It was not surprising that the official settlement did not satisfy all enthusiasts, for its doctrine and organization made official in 1559 were fossilized from the earlier stage of the Reformation under Edward VI. Many of the most energetic Protestants had gone into exile under Queen Mary and had seen the functioning of more perfectly reformed churches, particularly in Geneva. Elizabeth excluded former exiles obviously associated with Geneva from high office in the new church, because she was furious with John Knox for challenging the right of women to rule (his disastrously timed *First Blast of the Trumpet against the Monstrous Regiment of Women*, 1558, had been aimed from Geneva against the previous English queen, Mary). Nevertheless (and although English contacts with the reformers of

Zurich remained important, particularly among older Church leaders), Calvinism's impact on English Protestantism was substantial.
Reformed ideas on predestination, as expounded by Calvin and his
successor Theodore Beza, became the usual framework for English
Protestants to discuss the problem of salvation. Reformed theologians assumed leadership in the two universities and hence in the
church, while at the same time Calvinist theological discussion provided a rallying-point for activist clergy and laity who felt that the
church settlement was unsatisfactory.

Disputes in the 1560s began over fairly marginal if symbolic matters like clerical dress and gave rise to the name 'Puritan' to describe
those wanting greater or lesser degrees of change. Soon, however,
areas of dispute widened to criticism of the bishops (now, in the face
of their own inclinations, defending the immobility of Elizabeth's
settlement) and in the end, the very notion of episcopal government
came under attack from those who believed that Presbyterian church
organization represented the will of God expressed in Scripture—by
divine law (*jure divino*). In response, the Church leadership encouraged increasingly self-confident and distinctive defences of the English establishment, culminating in Richard Hooker's writings in the
1590s. Some even played the Presbyterians at their own game by
maintaining that government by bishops was God's *jure divino* plan
for his Church. Clashes between conformists and Puritans resulted in
the suppression of the organized Presbyterian wing of Puritanism by
1591, but the impact of Puritans on the Church at a local level
remained enormous. At this stage, few left the official Church to form
or join separate, more radical Protestant groups; earlier signs of
growing numbers among radicals did not bear much fruit after 1558.

A different and subtler form of dissent from the English Protestant
settlement likewise had only small beginnings before 1600, but it was
to have great significance for the problematic future identity of the
Church of England and its worldwide offshoots. A number of clergy,
many of them Oxford and Cambridge scholars, consciously turned
away from the Church's Reformed consensus to emphasize continuity with the pre-Reformation past and to recover a Catholic identity
from ambiguities within the Edwardian and Elizabethan settlements;
they gave a new positive value to tradition, beauty, and ceremony in
worship. The group may have been inspired by the anomalous survival of cathedrals in the English church system: cathedrals retained

their traditional function of ordered worship led by professional musicians, and they thus exposed an unexpected aspect of Thomas Cranmer's Prayer Book otherwise not experienced in the average post-1558 parish church. One prime setting for this ethos was Westminster Abbey, the royal mausoleum church which behaved more like a cathedral than most cathedrals, and from the 1580s one London-born cleric with Westminster links, Lancelot Andrewes, took the lead in quietly encouraging like-minded clergy from his base in Cambridge University. However, this sacramental-minded clerical clique did not enjoy power in the Church until the later years of James I. It was then that the bewildered and increasingly angry Protestant majority in the Church gave this new movement the derogatory nickname 'Arminians', symbolizing what they saw as a rebellion against Reformed orthodoxy by borrowing the name of a rather different contemporary rebel against the Dutch Reformed Church, Jacobus Arminius.

In Wales, administrative instability continued in former marcher border areas with England even after the Acts of Union. It is noticeable that Catholic recusancy was generally stronger in eastern than western Wales; it may have been easier to maintain conservative dissent in the less effectively structured marcher region. Monmouthshire was indeed the strongest recusant area in the kingdom, apart from Lancashire. Yet government-encouraged efforts to root Protestantism in Welsh culture were paying off by the end of the century. Under Mary, the traditionalist north Welsh poet Siôn Brwynog had been able to stigmatize Protestantism as alien to Wales by contemptuously labelling it, like earlier Lollardy, as the 'ffydd Sayson' (English religion).[4] Fifty years later, such an identification was much less convincing, and by the early seventeenth century, the contraction of self-conscious Welsh Catholicism was signalled by decline in recruitment to the Catholic priesthood.

In Scotland, Reformation steadily gathered ground, establishing firm structures first in the east and south-west; it also made considerable headway in the Gaelic west because of vigorous backing offered by Archibald Campbell, 5th earl of Argyll, who threw the weight of his clan leadership behind Protestant evangelism. By the 1590s the old church was withering away as former office-holders died, while the

---

[4] Siôn Brwynog quoted in G. Williams, *Welsh Reformation Essays* (Cardiff 1967), 18.

presbyteries were taking a more consistent place in church administration. Altogether, the Reformation was much less directed from the
top than in England, and local government by Protestant activists was
fostered by the growth of presbyteries. Protestant radicalism outside
the Kirk was even more insignificant than in England; radical debate
centred on argument about the future organization of the Kirk itself.
The foundations were laid for a precocious system of parish-based
poor relief, and for an education system which would eventually
ensure widespread informed Protestantism; this included the foundation of a fourth university (Edinburgh, 1582), while England con-
tented itself with expanding its two existing universities. By the 1620s
the Scots clergy had been transformed into a virtually all-graduate
body.

A notable feature was the anglicization which this triumph of the
established Kirk involved, not simply on the part of anglophile King
James. From the first enactments of the 1560s, the language of the
Kirk's Bible and outline liturgy was English—they had, indeed, been
created for English congregations exiled under Mary. Moreover, the
English language used was that of Home Counties England, reflecting
the religious links of lowland Scots Protestants with London. John
Knox's wife was, after all, English, and the contemporary Catholic
controversialist Ninian Winzet sneered at Knox that he had forgotten
'our auld plane Scottis quhilk your mother lerit you'. A slightly later
Catholic controversialist ranted in a similar patriotic vein against the
authors of the Kirk's so-called 'Negative Confession' of Faith, drawn
up in 1581: 'you . . . not onlie knappis suddrone [chatter in the English
of England] in your Negative Confession, bot also hes causit it be
imprentit at London in contempt of our native langage'.[5] The lowland Scots language began to fade from secular as well as religious
literature. Scots literary Gaelic was for long equally neglected by the
Kirk, after a precocious start when John Carswell (superintendent of
Argyll and the earl of Argyll's protégé) translated the *Book of Common Order* (1567), the first printed book in either Irish or Scots

---

[5] Ninian Winzet's sneer at John Knox occurs in *Certain Tractates*, ed. J. K. Hewison
(2 vols.; Scottish Text Society, Edinburgh; 1888–90), i. 138, and the condemnation of the
Negative Confession is from the second part of John Hamilton, *Ane Catholik and Facile
Traictise*, (Paris, 1581; *RSTC* 12729), entitled *Certane orthodox and Catholik conclusions
vith thair probations, quilkis Johne Hamilton proponis in name of the Catholikis, to the
Calvinolatre ministeris*, sig. V viii[b] (I am indebted to Dr Jenny Wormald for drawing
these references to my attention).

Gaelic; nevertheless, highlands Protestantism was very ready to use the spoken Gaelic language in worship and psalm-singing.

In Ireland, notable religious energy was all on the Catholic side: the Counter-Reformation which was forming a political alliance with the Irish nobility also began to remould traditionalist religion in its own image, helped by growing national prosperity only partially disrupted by colonial wars. By the 1580s older conformist clergy were either dying off, or losing heart and quitting the established Church for the Roman obedience. Clergy were trained on the continent for the Roman mission, and built on the existing popularity of the friars, whose communal life continued in many parts of the west, often in their pre-Reformation buildings. This was not simply Gaelic religion; it included Old English regions as well, although some clerical missionaries were beginning the equation between Catholicism and Gaelic culture which would become one of the later myths of Irish history. It was an equation which the Catholic Old English deeply resented.

On the Protestant side, only a handful of major towns established anything like the life of a well-regulated English Protestant parish, although the foundation of Trinity College, Dublin in 1594 belatedly provided potential for educating a new Protestant elite which came into its own with the destruction of the Catholic nobility in later years. In contrast with the established Church in Wales, attempts to promote Protestantism in Gaelic were late and half-hearted. John Kearney, a Cambridge-educated clergyman, treasurer of St Patrick's Cathedral, Dublin, did publish a Protestant catechism and alphabet in Gaelic in 1571. This was the first Gaelic book printed in Ireland, and its specialist typeface has remained a standard for Irish Gaelic printing, while in Scotland (following the model of Carswell's pioneering text) Gaelic printing adopted Roman font. However, when a considerable amount of Protestant literature was put into Irish Gaelic after 1600, the opportunity for its widespread effectiveness had already been lost.

The outer wash of the European witch-craze hardly touched the Celtic nations of the British Isles, and persecuting activity was concentrated in the most advanced Protestant areas of England and Scotland. In England, it remained distinctively regional, and was particularly associated with areas of Puritan activism and social predominance like Essex. A late start in Scotland produced the most virulent persecution in the British Isles, encouraged for a time in the 1590s by James VI himself; his enthusiasm was later to embarrass him, but he was unable to halt the tide of frequently brutal investigations and executions which were encouraged by the Kirk, as part of its campaign to bring godliness to every aspect of Scottish daily life.

# A future British Church?

From 1603 the British Isles shared a single monarch; despite the ruling dynasty coming from Scotland, this proved London's final triumph as the Stewarts jettisoned their Scots identity. Although James VI and I was frustrated in plans to unite England and Scotland in a single kingdom of 'Great Britain' by the prejudices particularly of his English subjects, he was able to make a start on closer ecclesiastical union by further moves to remodel the Scottish Kirk, using the pattern of the Church of England as his ecclesiastical model. He made a number of cross-border ecclesiastical appointments as part of this strategy for a united British Church, and by a shrewd mixture of tact and bullying, managed to keep Scots resentment of his changes within bounds.

James had good reason to feel complacent about the English Church which he inherited. Through all the wrangles of Elizabeth's reign, the Church's leadership had battled (not always with much sympathy or support from her) to create a preaching ministry and a well-disciplined parish structure, regulated by effective church courts. By James's accession, these efforts were being met with overall success. The clergy were steadily more adequately educated, and renewed provision for schools (after mid-century disruption caused by the dissolution of chantries) was producing an increasingly high proportion of general literacy, important for informed Protestantism. By the early seventeenth century, Wales and the highland zone of England could be said to be predominantly Protestant as the lowland south and west had been since the 1580s, even though little had been done to remedy the defects of parochial organization in these areas. Puritans could take as much credit as the episcopate for the effort. James gave additional help to the English Church by ending the long-established Tudor raids on its wealth by Crown and nobility; in any case, overall funding of the parish ministry through tithes and local endowments of glebeland had not diminished in the Reformation upheavals, and if anything, had improved. The general recovery of the English Church from mid-century disarray can be traced in the evidence from the 1590s onwards of widespread restoration of church buildings and refurnishing for the Protestant liturgy.

In Ireland, the colonial enterprise continued apace, as Ulster, the most recalcitrant part of the Gaelic lordships, was turned over to English and Scots colonists after the flight of the Northern Earls (1607); other plantations took place in the south. At last there was a basis for a strong Protestant Church outside the Dublin Pale, even though the Scots component of the new settlements sheltered some alarmingly radical opinions. The turning-point for the established Church was probably the wars of the 1590s; after that, the parish churches lost what adherence they had maintained among the wider population. Protestantism became concentrated among the settlers, reinforcing its self-image by a strongly Calvinist theology which encouraged the idea of a godly elect minority battling against the Devil and the Pope. By contrast, pastoral and missionary work from Catholic clergy continued with combined backing from Gaelic and Old English nobility, with the government's resources too thinly stretched to do much about it; indeed officialdom tended to try to divide and rule by discreetly favouring secular Catholic clergy against the regulars. Nevertheless, all the signs were that given time, the Protestant Church based on a broad consensus backed by the Crown would take over most of the British Isles, as it was doing in Scandinavia. That this did not happen can be attributed to the political crisis provoked throughout the islands during the reign of James's son Charles: a story which lies beyond the scope of this survey.

Modern Britain constructs its Christian identities with reference to the various reformations of sixteenth-century Britain, but in doing so, often creates myths about what happened in those reformations. In England and Wales there is an Anglican myth, reluctant to perceive the reality of the established Church which James I inherited: a self-confident and emphatically Protestant body, resulting from an aggressive and destructive religious upheaval in the mid-sixteenth-century. For this Church, the label 'Anglican' seems anachronistic and misleading. Indeed, 'Anglican' as a word in English did not exist before the seventeenth century, and may indeed first have been used as a term of abuse in Scotland by James VI: in 1598, he genially assured a suspicious Kirk that his proposed strengthening of episcopacy would not take Scotland on the road to 'papistical or Anglican' bishops.[6] After that, the word was hardly used at all until the nineteenth century, when it was found to be convenient to describe the new situation of a church now spreading throughout the world, and the complicated theological identity which had evolved within this church.

In the Scotland of 1600, the established Kirk which commanded increasing consent was a mixed episcopal and presbyterian structure, in which bishops were not the alien figures of later Presbyterian legend. In Ireland, the religious struggle's outcome was still open, and as yet, Catholicism was not decisively identified with Gaelic identity alone: it commanded the allegiance of most of the country's Old English nobility and gentry who still considered themselves heirs of a proud tradition of loyalty to the English Crown. All various later national myths, however, were reactions to the continued encroachment of London on the autonomy of the regions most remote from it: an encroachment which in many different ways, the British Reformations did much to promote.

---

[6] James I's apparent invention of the word 'Anglican' is to be found in D. Calderwood, *History of the Church of Scotland by Mr. D. Calderwood*, ed. T. Thomson (Wodrow Society; 1842–9), v. 694.

**Figure 6** Elizabeth I enthroned as the Emperor Constantine in the initial letter of the dedication of the 1563 edition of John Foxe's *Actes and Monuments*. Iconographical evidence suggests that the three figures standing bare-headed on the right of the throne were intended for William Cecil (foreground), the publisher, John Day (in the middle), and Foxe himself. In the 1570 edition of Foxe, 'C' became the initial letter of 'Christ', rather than Constantine.

# 4

# Monarchy and counsel: models of the state

John Guy

It cannot be said that distinctively *British* theories of monarchy and politics evolved in the sixteenth century. Renaissance culture was pan-European: ideas (like printed books and manuscripts) crossed the Channel freely in both directions. This was equally true after the Reformation as before. Libraries were acquired in Paris, Basle, or Venice rather than in London, Dublin, or Edinburgh. Translations of classical and later writings were in vogue. Young aristocrats often travelled on the Continent after they had studied at university or the Inns of Court. Still, it was in the sixteenth century that classic 'British' models of sacral monarchy (mainly England) and popular sover- eignty (mainly Scotland) emerged. These were the ideas that underlay the British Civil Wars of the seventeenth century and shaped the Atlantic and colonialist traditions, notably in North America. They survived until the French Revolution unleashed more stridently 'nationalist' theories of popular sovereignty, and until the rise of nationalism in post-Enlightenment Germany created the stimulus for ideals of autonomy and self-determination that were more closely indexed to ethnic and racial concerns.

The rise of coherent (and rival) models of sacral monarchy and popular sovereignty was a key stage in the evolution of early modern British political consciousness. When James VI and I acceded to the English throne in 1603, his speeches and writings were tantamount to a refractive and reactive mirror to these debates. In a speech at Whitehall to members of both Houses of the English Parliament in 1610, he put his theory of monarchy into capsule form:

The State of Monarchy is the supremest thing upon earth: for Kings are not only God's Lieutenants upon earth, and sit upon God's throne, but even by God himself they are called Gods. There be three principal similitudes that illustrate the state of Monarchy: one taken out of the word of God; and the two other out of the grounds of Policy and Philosophy. In the Scriptures Kings are called Gods, and so their power after a certain relation compared to the Divine power. Kings are also compared to Fathers of families: for a King is truly *Parens patriae*, the politic father of his people. And lastly, Kings are compared to the head of this Microcosm of the body of man.

Kings were Gods, above ordinary men. Political science was divine. For James, the *arcana imperii* (the Tacitean phrase for the 'secrets' or 'mysteries of state' in imperial Rome) were too high for rational discussion. In winging such ideas, he experimented with language: his argument still had to be moulded into orthodoxy. Such exalted claims, first propagated by Henry VIII in the more intoxicated moments of his struggle with the papacy, had all along been challenged by 'conciliarist' or 'quasi-republican' voices. The model was circumscribed. It had been undermined by 'populist' Protestant theory in the 1550s, and by those critics of Henry VIII and (later) Mary Stewart, who had invoked idioms of limited or 'constitutional' monarchy against the theory of sacral monarchy. Yet something significant had occurred by 1610. The language of James's speech is not how Henry VII (in England) or James IV (in Scotland) would have conceptualized monarchy in 1500. A clearly audible change was the shift in the political culture from idioms of *dominium* and feudal lordship to those of 'divine right' monarchy linked to examples in humanist-classical literature.

# Kingship and lordship in 1500

Early modern theory of monarchy was blended from a mixture of feudal, scholastic, and classical ideas. In 1500 the concept most frequently invoked was *dominium* ('lordship'), which was used by the practitioners of Roman civil law and local or customary law to signify ownership of land. Late medieval lawyers dealt with forms of tenure in which an original holder of land did not relinquish his 'lordship' over it. The right to privileges known as feudal 'incidents' or 'pre-eminences' remained with the superior lord, of whom the king was chief. Idioms of feudal law also applied to royal jurisdiction and government, which is why St Thomas Aquinas, the leading scholastic thinker of the High Middle Ages, debated the powers of monarchy in this vein.

The fifteenth century saw the 'refoundation' of monarchies. Edward IV and Henry VII restored their authority by attainders and forfeitures coupled to the rigorous exploitation of the king's feudal rights. It could be said that the king's prerogative was the sum of these rights. James III's acquisition of Orkney and Shetland by marriage in 1468, the forfeiture of the Earldom of Ross in 1476, and the suppression of the Lordship of the Isles in 1493, worked to the same effect. In Scotland the role of the feudal lord was superimposed upon the more ancient status of chief of a clan or kindred. Tribal loyalty, with its obligations to protect and serve, placed noblemen at the heads of political networks that shaped the structures of power at every level. Kinship and lineage were crucial in England as well, since the king's coercive powers were limited. He relied on the nobility and leading gentry, whether in their own right or as Crown officials, to muster troops for his army, and these magnates were also his local agents. 'Public' or 'official' expressions of royal power were overlaid by 'private' or 'informal' networks of authority. To preserve his 'state', the king had to exploit his 'lordship' as a feudal suzerain. For his part, the king claimed that his feudal rights constituted a right of 'empire', symbolized by the closed or 'imperial' crown that he displayed at his coronation and wore with his purple robes when enthroned in majesty on days of 'estate'. (These ideas were drawn from the models of the Carolingian and Hohenstaufen dynasties of the Middle Ages; they pervaded the feudal monarchies of Europe and not merely those of the British Isles.)

In terms of political theory, kingship came from antiquity. God had vested sacral power in Moses and the kings of the Old Testament: the regal prototypes of David and Solomon dominated the literature. Classical authors had analyzed the forms of government, notably Aristotle, who defined the attributes of monarchy in Book III of the *Politics*, and less specifically Cicero in *De officiis* ('On Duties'), where the civic values of the Roman republic were defended and the tyranny of Julius Caesar excoriated. Of the medieval scholastics, Aquinas was less interested in who ruled than in the uses to which the ruling interest was put. He said that legitimate authority might be vested either in the community as a whole or in a single public person. In the end, he held that government by one man was the best, because unity of purpose could only proceed from unity of 'will', which was best achieved when the power of decision rested in one person. This did not give the king a licence to act irresponsibly, since his power was circumscribed by law and 'counsel'. It was not the king alone but the 'king counselled' who was supreme. An 'uncounselled king' was a tyrant, who ruled his realm for his own profit and not for the good of the community. Since kings were instituted for the public good, justice in its widest sense was their function. They were to keep the peace and defend the realm from attack, administer the law equitably and impartially, and uphold true religion and the Church.

Monarchy was fissured by a paradox. At one level the king was bound by law, at another he was free from it, an ambiguity latent in Roman law itself. The formulas that the prince is 'above the laws' and that 'what has pleased the prince has the force of law' were contradicted by a third principle: 'it is a word worthy of majesty of the ruler that the prince professes himself bound to the law'. When the preeminent English jurist Henry of Bracton (d.1268) glossed these passages, he argued that the king should be under no man 'but under God and the law'. The subordination of the king to the law was, however, voluntary. It sprang from an act of grace. Bracton imagined a divinely appointed ruler deputed as 'vicar of God', who was subject to no earthly restraints beyond his own wisdom. As Henry VIII's councillors knew, this was not a model of parliamentary sovereignty, but one of a self-limiting ruler who, by way of concession, or by way of enhancing his majesty and reputation, chooses to place the law above himself.

A 'populist' alternative was advanced by the lawyer and politician Sir John Fortescue, whose *Praises of the Laws of England* was written or revised to accompany the readeption of Henry VI in 1470 or 1471. His starting point was the formula of Roman law that held that the origin of public power lay in the people. Monarchy was justified because a 'body politic' could not be acephalous: it required a 'head'. If, however, the king was the legislator, he was not a *lex loquens* ('speaking law'). He did not 'give' the law except through the mouths of his judges, since he was educated to believe that it was better to rule according to law and to submit his prerogative and powers of equity to the direction of appropriate Crown officers than to risk becoming a tyrant. It was a set-piece argument by a theorist keen to enhance the efficiency of government and minimize the disruptive role of the nobles during the Wars of the Roses, but who was concerned to limit the discretionary powers of the king. Fortescue encapsulated his ideal in the formula *dominium politicum et regale* ('political and regal lordship'). Unlike the king of France, whose rule was *tantum regale* ('excessively regal'), the king of England ruled *politice* ('politically'). He did not change the laws or enact new ones, nor did he tax his subjects or impose other fiscal or military burdens, without their assent expressed in Parliament. Fortescue conceded that the king might need to rule *regaliter* for 'urgent causes', a view he had expressed more strongly in an earlier work, *On the Nature of the Law of Nature*. He evaded the dissonance by pointing up the contrast with France, where the administrative powers of the king had been increased by Louis XI; but his analysis of the French monarchy is unsubtle, and seems to be little more than an appeal to francophobia in a particular set of circumstances. The dichotomy between his constitutionalism and the model of 'imperial' kingship is more apparent than real.

# The theory of 'imperial' monarchy

When Henry VIII broke with Rome, he annexed the language of sacral monarchy to justify his royal supremacy over the English Church. The classic summary is the preamble to the Act in Restraint of Appeals (1533). The model relates to the *imperium* ('power' or 'magistracy') and the *majestas* ('majesty') enjoyed by the Roman emperors. In its classical and Renaissance forms, it is a proxy for the later concept of sovereignty. As invoked by Henry VIII, its origins lay in the propaganda invoked by the civil lawyers on behalf of the French king against the pope in the fourteenth and fifteenth centuries. In response to the pope's claim to exercise the 'plenitude of power' even in temporal matters, the civil lawyers answered that the king was 'emperor' in his realm (*rex in regno suo est imperator*); the pope had no authority to legislate for the kingdom, because the pre-requisite for legislation was *dominium*, and the pope had no *dominium* over the king's subjects. Both Henry VIII and Francis I claimed to be 'emperors' in their kingdoms, even if it was only Henry who broke with Rome.

'Imperial' theory still lacked some of the resonances that it later acquired. The idea that 'emperors' ruled, or claimed to rule, sub-ordinate territories was implicit in Edward Foxe's *On the True Differ-ence between Royal and Ecclesiastical Power* (1534), but the link was loose. There was not yet a definite association with the subjugation of provinces or colonies, although Henry VIII, like Edward I, initiated a policy of territorial centralization within the British Isles. He sub-sumed Wales administratively within the realm of England and asserted feudal suzerainty over Scotland. In Ireland, he altered his title from 'Lord' to 'King of Ireland' in 1541. The new style was justified on the grounds that it afforded the king the 'honours, preeminences, prerogatives . . . and other things whatsoever they be, to the estate and majesty of a king imperial appertaining or belonging'. As preda-tory in foreign policy as he was at home, Henry asserted 'tous et quelzconques droitz et souveraineté' over his remaining possessions in France. The crux was that the powers of 'emperors' were 'whole' and 'entire'. Kings who were 'emperors' recognized no superior. All rights, jurisdictions, pre-eminences, and privileges were derived from the 'imperial' Crown.

Henry VIII stretched the theory of 'empire' to its limits. His break with Rome was predicated on the model of the king as God's 'vicar' on earth whose *imperium* embraced both Church and State. Henry's redefinition of 'empire' was Caesaropapalist, subsuming 'temporal' and 'spiritual' affairs equally. The catalyst was his first divorce campaign. His advisers had compiled the *Collectanea satis copiosa*, which Henry first saw in the autumn of 1530. The agenda was, first, to define the king's regal power; and then to rediscover the 'original' constitution of the Church of England in order that the 'true difference' between royal and ecclesiastical power might become known. The *Collectanea* argued that since AD 187 the king of England had enjoyed secular *imperium* and spiritual supremacy within his realm, powers modelled on the kings of Israel and later Roman emperors. Furthermore, the pre-Conquest Church of

England had been an autonomous province of the universal Catholic Church under the king's authority as head. It was later that the pope had usurped royal power. If this were so, it followed that the break with Rome was not schismatic, but merely a return to the norm that had prevailed before the papacy annexed the 'plenitude of power'.

Although the royal supremacy was declared in Parliament, it was not equivalent to a doctrine of parliamentary sovereignty before the Revolution of 1688. It was modelled on the prototypes of ancient Israel and the Roman empire after Constantine's conversion to Christianity. Henry VIII's favourite kings were David and Solomon; his favourite emperors Constantine and Justinian. He could quote *verbatim* from the Old Testament and from Justinian's *Institutes*. The annotations in his personal psalter suggest that, by the 1540s, he perceived himself as David, and that he read the Psalms as a commentary on his own divine mission and regality. By exercising his *imperium*, the king could redefine the duties of 'his' clergy, summon church councils within his dominions, revise canon law, dissolve the religious houses, and even expound the articles of faith, which in Henry VIII's reign is what he did.

It is often claimed that, whereas the royal supremacy was 'imperial' under Henry VIII, the model was diluted after his death. His son was a minor, and it is argued that Parliament alone could reinstate Elizabeth I as supreme governor of the Church in 1559 by reversing the Marian reunion with Rome. Although an excellent debating point, this argument is flawed. Since Edward VI was only 9 years old at his accession, a regal prototype was found to match the circumstances. King Josiah was appropriated: one of the three kings of Judah whom the Protestants revered for his campaign against idolatry, who had succeeded to the throne at the age of 8. Josiah had purged Judah and Jerusalem of the 'carved images, and the molten images. And they brake down the altars of Baal in his presence' (2 Kgs. 22–3). It was in his reign that 'the book of the law' had been rediscovered by the high priest of the temple at Jerusalem, which provided a model for the Edwardian Prayer Books and policy of 'official' Reformation. In Edward's reign, the royal supremacy became a trojan horse for Protestantism: the model of Josiah made it imaginatively feasible for the councillors of a 'godly king' to undertake a programme of fast reformation on their own initiative, whilst protecting Edward's regality and preserving his right to assert his 'imperial' status when he reached the age of majority.

As to the Elizabethan Religious Settlement, it is not so far removed from the 'mingle-mangle' predicted by one of Sir William Cecil's advisers in late 1558. It has an ambiguity about it which may stem either from careful planning or from a mismatch between the queen's intentions and those of Cecil, her leading privy councillor and parliamentary agent, who as principal secretary to the duke of Northumberland in Edward's reign had been a prime mover of the Prayer Book of 1552. In practice, Elizabeth reinstated the model of strict separation between the administrations of Church and State that had set the norm in her father's reign. Whereas Edward VI's privy councillors debated the stripping of images from the churches and the reformation of doctrine, the Elizabethan Privy Council enforced the *status quo*. Ceremonial and confessional debates were once more reserved to the bishops in Convocation (the Church's own representative assembly). When Elizabeth expressed her personal views, she held her ecclesiastical power to be magisterial. When Archbishop Grindal clashed with her in 1577 over his support for the puritan 'prophesying' movement, she suspended him for daring to suggest that he owed allegiance to a higher power. Her case was that the *locus* of sovereignty and the *form* of administration in Church and State are different things. She might (most likely for gender reasons) delegate the exercise of her ecclesiastical authority to Convocation or to statutory commissioners empowered by her own letters patent, and she invariably did; but *imperium* was vested in her alone.

As much for an unmarried female ruler as for Henry VIII, therefore, the royal supremacy was sacral monarchy by another name. Since the Reformation legislation had been abrogated in Mary Tudor's reign, it followed that in 1559 Parliament was required to declare the royal supremacy to be in force again, to exact oaths of allegiance from office-holders and clergy, and to approve the new Act of Uniformity; but the role of statute was auxiliary. The regal power was undiminished at least in the eyes of the Crown. Integral to this line of reasoning was a model that imagined Parliament to be the queen's instrument of government for securing legislation and taxation, and not a political or representative council for the debate of Crown policy, as some of the more 'forward' or confessionally-minded Protestants in the House of Commons believed.

A modulation of the 'imperial' claim was the image of the 'godly prince' who would champion true religion against Antichrist. It is this depiction, inspired by the view of monarchy that was the norm among the English and Scottish exile communities in the leading Protestant cities of Europe in the 1550s, that emerges from John Foxe's *Actes and Monuments* (first English edition in 1563) and from the dedicatory Epistle to Elizabeth in the Geneva Bible (issued in multiple editions after 1560, although none was printed in England until 1576). In the second edition of the Geneva Bible (1561), marginal annotations to the Epistle posed a cluster of questions. What wisdom is requisite for the establishment of religion? What policy must be used for the 'planting' of religion? What is requisite for them that must give counsel by God's Word? The discussion pivots around the regal prototypes of Jehoshaphat, Hezekiah, and Josiah: the kings of Judah noted for their refusal to condone idolatry. The Epistle explains that when Jehoshaphat 'took this order in the church', he appointed Amariah 'to be the chief concerning the Word of God, because he was most expert in the law of the Lord and could give counsel and govern according to the same' (2 Chr. 19: 11). The Epistle skates on thin ice where Elizabeth is concerned, since the model of a 'chief priest' with 'authority and privilege' to determine 'all matters' of religion and 'God's Word', was not one that she proposed to emulate. Furthermore, the prototype of Josiah, which recurs in the Epistle and did not fade from the minds of those seeking the 'further reformation' of the Elizabethan Church, was subversive, since it imagined the queen not enthroned in 'majesty' like Constantine, but surrounded by her 'godly councillors' as in the reign of Edward VI, implementing with their assistance 'the book of the law'. The innuendo was that female rule, if insufficiently 'godly', was not sacral monarchy, but was tantamount to minority or acephalous (headless) rule.

A layered ambivalence enveloped the monarchy in Elizabeth's reign. In the end, the sacral model prevailed. Cawdrey's case (1591) was the trigger and the cause célèbre: the case, heard in the Court of Queen's Bench, was the appeal of a puritan minister deprived of his benefice that was designed to test Elizabeth's right to delegate the exercise of her disciplinary powers in ecclesiastical causes to the judges of the Court of High Commission. Could the queen legally empower the High Commission? What was the extent of the queen's 'imperial' prerogative by the common law of England? Could her 'imperial' prerogative override statute and common law? The judges ruled that 'by the ancient laws of this realm this kingdom of England is an absolute empire and monarchy'. Citing *ipsissima verba* of the Act in Restraint of Appeals, they adjudged Elizabeth's rule to be Caesaropapalist, although to clinch their case they used weasel words. The phrase the 'ancient laws of this realm' did not refer to common law, but instead was 'code' for the Anglo-Saxon 'laws' given by Edward the Confessor and his predecessors—kings who were theo-crats, since they legislated by words spoken from their own mouths. This is why the same phrase was deleted from the coronation oath in 1689, when William III and Mary swore to govern the people of England according to the 'statutes in Parliament agreed upon, and the laws and customs of the same'. They also swore to maintain 'the Protestant reformed religion established by law'. In 1689 the reson-ances of the theory of sacral monarchy were still the hottest of hot topics.

# The theory of 'counsel'

Henry VIII's ideas of sacral monarchy sparked off a series of critiques from humanist-classical writers like Sir Thomas Elyot and Thomas Starkey, and from common lawyers like Christopher St German, who advocated social and political reconstruction, but who were not Prot-estants. They held 'conciliarism' to be the antidote to 'imperialism'. The theory of 'counsel' was rooted in classical and scholastic litera-ture. If kings were to rule virtuously and effectively, they needed advice and information. The 'will' of the king was the prerequisite for legitimate acts of government, but only if he were suitably (and virtuously) counselled. The 'king counselled' was incomparable, whereas the 'uncounselled' king was a tyrant. It followed that the ideal of 'good counsel' was a model for the orderly conduct of politics.

The theory of 'counsel' was pan-European. Emphases and slants varied, but Aristotle's influence was pervasive. Classical literature depicted unbridled 'will' as 'passion' or 'disease', which is why the 'counsel' of 'friends' was seen as 'physic' for the ruler's soul. Accord-ing to Elyot's *Book Named the Governor* (1531), 'the end of all doctrine and study is good counsel . . . wherein virtue may be found'. Since 'one mortal man cannot have knowledge of all things done in a realm or large dominion . . . it is expedient and also needful that under the capital governor be sundry mean authorities, as it were aiding him in the distribution of justice in sundry parts of a huge multitude.' The defect of monarchy could be averted if government were to be undertaken by councillors who are both good men and good citizens. The 'friends' of the ruler were his 'eyes and ears' and 'hands and feet'. They secured his power, while subduing his autocratic instincts. Conciliarism was a safeguard against despotism. Monarchy rested on another paradox: the more the functions of kings are restricted, the longer their power will last unimpaired.

Quasi-republican implications were etched into this argument. Aristotle, himself a former tutor of Alexander the Great, had constructed his discussion of the king's 'friends' primarily to undermine the legitimacy of monarchy based solely on the king's 'will'. Conciliarism, when stretched to its limits, could mutate into resistance theory. For this reason, 'counselling' was held to be a duty and not a right. As Henry VIII answered the leaders of the Pilgrimage of Grace, and as Elizabeth reminded Mary Stewart, monarchs were free to choose their own councillors and could not be bound by their advice. As Elizabeth told Mary, councillors were 'councillors by choice, and not by birth, whose services are no longer to be used in that public function than it shall please her Majesty to dispose of the same'. If the ruler's 'will' could be voted down by his advisers, the regal power would be no more than that of the doge of Venice. Worse still, the government of the realm would fall into confusion, since the single 'will' that was essential for the formulation of common policy would be absent.

Just as influential in Europe and Scotland was ecclesiastical conciliarism, which was turned against the papacy's claim to the exercise of temporal as well as spiritual power. The papal 'plenitude of power' was attacked from within the Church itself by conciliarists who defined the Church as a community of believers entitled to secure their own good government. The politics of the Great Schism (1378–1415) underpinned their stand. It was argued that the General Council of the Church was superior to the pope and that the pope was an officer of the Church charged with specific duties and responsible to the whole Christian people (including the laity) through their representative General Council. Some conciliarists (including Thomas More) maintained that in the last resort an unworthy pope could be deposed by the Council. Their viewpoint formed the basis of a 'populist' thesis of government and politics in the Church.

The leading centres of ecclesiastical conciliarism were Paris and Padua. It was the close intellectual ties between Scotland and Paris that enabled John Mair (1467–1550) to open the debate later continued by John Knox and George Buchanan, when he argued that the authority of rulers derived from the consent of the community and that the community might withdraw their consent if the ruler abused his power. Mair learned these ideas from Pierre d'Ailly and Jean Gerson, the leading conciliarists at the University of Paris. While his influence over Knox and Buchanan should not be exaggerated, both were his students and the radical theories of resistance and popular sovereignty that emerged in the second half of the century derived at least partly from his teaching at the universities of Glasgow and St Andrews.

Henry VIII drew on conciliarism, when he claimed that the pope was no better than another human legislator who had exceeded his authority and was inferior to the General Council, which could depose him. What Henry could not foresee was that similar, if not identical, arguments would be taken up by his critics and realigned against the theory of sacral monarchy. Moreover, key elements of these arguments spilled over into the controversies over minority and female rule in England and Scotland under Edward VI and Mary Tudor and during the regency of Marie de Guise, when conciliarism and the critiques of papal authority and the powers of monarchy underwent subtle—or not so subtle—transformations, to be seized upon by Calvinist theologians and Protestant exiles to construct a theory of resistance to unlawful or tyrannical rule. In evolving a theory of resistance that was applicable to both England and Scotland during the 1550s, the Protestant exiles on the Continent took 'conciliarism' as the template for the things they were attempting to say and do.

The earliest English exponents of conciliarism were Starkey and St German, who wrote before 'resistance' theory was on the agenda. Starkey had spent almost a decade in Paris and Padua. His intellectual genes were classical, but ecclesiastical (and baronial) conciliarism underpinned his argument at crucial points. His *Dialogue between*

*Reginald Pole and Thomas Lupset* was begun about 1529 and completed between 1532 and *c.*1535. It mingled Venetian secular conciliarism, ecclesiastical conciliarism, and notions of representation in Parliament to define the limits of monarchy. St German's acknowledged mentor was Gerson, and in a draft submitted to Thomas Cromwell as a blueprint for the Reformation Parliament in 1530 or 1531, he aimed to subordinate the functions of the King's Council to those of Parliament in an attempt to restrict the king to a regime that was limited by the 'consent of the realm'. In *A Little Treatise Called the New Additions* (1531), he annexed to the 'King-in-Parliament' the supremacy that his earlier writings had located in parliamentary statute. The 'King-in-Parliament', he said, was 'the high sovereign over the people, which hath not only charge on the bodies, but also on the souls of his subjects'. By locating sovereignty in the 'King-in-Parliament', St German implied that the king was incorporated in the parliamentary trinity and was not the sole legislator. It was a highly contentious argument, which prefigured the parliamentary clashes of 1642 and the concepts of sovereignty and constitutional monarchy validated by the Revolution of 1688.

If this were not enough, St German argued that the assent of the 'kingdom' (defined as 'the king and the estates of the realm') was the touchstone of ecclesiastical and secular legislation. In *An Answer to a Letter* (1535), he invoked 'populist' language to ask, 'Why should not the Parliament then which representeth the whole catholic church of England expound scripture?' All human law, secular or ecclesiastical, was properly made in Parliament, 'for the Parliament so gathered together representeth the estate of all the people within this realm, that is to say of the whole catholic church thereof'. The legitimacy of government rested on the consent of the community. Henry VIII was to exercise the royal supremacy in Parliament, and not as an act of *imperium* as the model of sacral monarchy presupposed.

Neither Starkey nor St German was politically effective in Henry VIII's reign. Starkey's *Dialogue* was not published until the nineteenth century. His influence on his contemporaries was restricted to a circle of Italian and English humanists. St German was widely read by students of common law during their training exercises at the Inns of Court. His arguments made a deep impression on the mindset of the parliamentary gentry by a process of accretion, and in the late 1590s his critique of the royal supremacy was incorporated into

Richard Hooker's *Of the Laws of Ecclesiastical Polity*. Although Book VIII was unfinished when Hooker died in 1600, the crux is the rejection of Caesaropapalism. If Church and commonwealth were one, he argued, Parliament must 'represent' the Church. All laws including ecclesiastical ones 'do take originally their essence from the power of the whole realm and church of England'. The power of making laws belonged 'to the whole, not to any certain part of a political body'. Power was 'derived' to rulers by the 'consent of the people' and should be applied for the benefit of the whole community.

## Theory of resistance and popular sovereignty

The effect of conciliarism was to create a latent ambiguity, or binary opposition, within the idea of monarchy. 'Official' pronouncements claimed that the king was armed with *imperium*. In reply, the critics stressed the role of councils, councillors, and representative institutions if tradition and custom were to be preserved. The extent of this schizophrenia should not be overdrawn, but the potential existed for conflicting positions to reify. In the hands of the Protestant exiles in the 1550s, conciliarism mutated into forms of resistance theory which justified regicide or the deposition of kings. This was a significant change, since rebels such as the Pilgrims of Grace in 1536, or the supporters of Robert Kett in East Anglia in 1549, had avoided direct threats to the monarchy. They had professed their loyalty to the person as well as to the office of the king, and merely attacked those 'evil councillors', flatterers or favourites who misadvised him. When the Pilgrims swore an oath to defend the Catholic Church, to strive for the suppression of 'these heretics', and to expel 'villein blood' and 'evil councillors' from the royal Court and Privy Council, they followed the pattern of medieval dissent, which combined a rising of the commons with protestations of loyalty to the king and the established order.

The shift to resistance theory was confessionally driven and was a 'British' and French Huguenot development. (It is noteworthy that after Elizabeth's accession, a number of the 'English' exiles found life more congenial in Scotland than in England, while others assisted the Protestant cause in France or the Netherlands.) Mary Tudor, and to a lesser degree Marie de Guise, were assailed with objections to their rule on the grounds of religion and gender, encouraging ideas of 'mixed polity' and popular sovereignty that were corrosive of the idea of monarchy. Of the 800 or so Protestants who left England between 1554 and 1558, many went to Frankfurt, Strasbourg, Zurich, and Geneva. From the safety of these exile communities, a crusade of subversive literature was directed against the Marian regime, which it was obliged to suppress or refute as best it could.

Writing from Geneva, Christopher Goodman was explicit. His tract *How Superior Powers O[u]ght to be Obey[e]d of their Subjects* (1558) argued that the covenant (or contract) between God and Israel described in the opening books of the Old Testament was a model for all Christian nations. God's Will was revealed in Scripture: the Mosaic Law condemned idolatry and established the rights of the people. At baptism, individuals entered into a covenant with God. Their responsibility to uphold the covenant was both communal (i.e. vested in the whole community) and individual. It could be enforced against rulers, since political obligation was conditional. Like Henry VIII when confuting the pope, Goodman adopted the most extreme position that the logic of his position could support, moving directly from the identification of an offence against God's law to its redress. A ruler could be deposed by her subjects (and he did not distinguish between ordinary private persons and magistrates) if she violated divine or human law, in which case she was a tyrant.

John Ponet's *Short Treatise of Politike Power* (1556) blended the idioms of biblical fundamentalism and Old Testament prophecy with classical republicanism and conciliarism. By making a firm distinction between the office and the person of the ruler, he could appeal to patriotism and civic duty, but excoriate the ruler as an individual. Power lay in the whole community and the ruler was merely an officer or 'minister' of the law, and not the 'law' itself. Although more nuanced than Goodman, Ponet held that anything which conflicted with the Protestant interpretation of Scripture (and thus 'divine law') was not 'lawful', but rather 'bondage' and 'cruel tyranny'. Once again, a priori logic was central. In a chapter entitled, 'Whether it be lawful to depose an evil governor, and kill a tyrant', Ponet justified regicide. Unlike Goodman, he stopped short of action by private individuals, but this may have been a rhetorical device. An exception was in cases where the magistrates had failed to act, which it is likely he meant to apply to the Marian polity.

In a final chapter, Ponet delivered a prophetic 'Exhortation' to the nobility and people of England. It had been 'prophesied' in Edward VI's reign that 'miseries' and 'plagues' would afflict the land if God's Word were taken away: such omens (along with prodigies and 'monstrous births') were the signs (as Ponet claimed) of God's providence and a scourge to punish England for its idolatry. Here he hit the jackpot. Between 1555 and 1559 an influenza epidemic swept through the lowlands of England and Wales and killed around 200,000 people. Moreover, the epidemic was accompanied by a severe dearth and price rises which were the results of harvest failures in 1554–6 and of the collapse of trade caused by the Habsburg–Valois wars into which England was reluctantly dragged in 1557.

John Knox's *First Blast of the Trumpet against the Monstrous Regiment of Women* (1558) is conventionally read as a misogynist diatribe, but is actually far more sophisticated. It pivots on the idea of 'covenant' as a way of imagining Scotland and England as 'godly' commonwealths and did not preclude the possibility of union between them. Just as the Jewish commonwealth had comprised Judah and Israel, so Scotland and England might unite to form a 'British' people blessed in the sight of the Lord. Primarily, the *First Blast* was informed by the Mosaic covenant, from which Knox went on to develop a justification of aristocratic rebellion, the part of his thought which relied on conciliarism. Unlike Goodman, he did not endorse the right of inferior magistrates or private individuals to act. The responsibility of individuals was to stay free of idolatry themselves. The crux is Knox's distinction between the application of his model to an 'uncovenanted' Scotland and a 'covenanted' England. He held that by officially embracing Protestantism in the reign of Edward VI, England had entered into a pact with God which was irreversible and bound its magistrates and people to depose and destroy an 'idolatrous' ruler. Knox's ideas were still too extreme for most people, but strictly did not apply to the Scots until the Reformation was proclaimed by the Lords of the Congregation and civil war began (May 1559).

Knox is notorious for his denunciation of female rule. With Mary Tudor predominantly in mind, he urged the subjects of women rulers to civil disobedience: to 'repress her inordinate pride and tyranny to the uttermost of their power'. A woman ruler was a 'monster in nature'. If any man feared to violate an oath which he had taken to her, he should be persuaded that oaths rooted in 'ignorance' were a sin; 'so is the obstinate purpose to keep the same nothing but plain rebellion against God'. His polemic was published at Geneva in the spring of 1558; copies reached the streets of London shortly before Elizabeth's accession. She was incensed, and Knox's attempts to wriggle out of a corner by justifying her monarchy as 'exceptional' and a 'miracle' worsened his position. When he wrote a truculent letter from Dieppe suggesting that he be allowed back into England to continue God's work, his request was refused and he embarked instead for Scotland.

So far, resistance theory was ad hoc. A systematic model of popular sovereignty awaited George Buchanan's *De jure regni apud Scotos* and *History of Scotland*, which formed a 'pair' and were published between 1579 and 1582. By the 1560s, Buchanan was the leading humanist and classical scholar north of the Alps. He recognized the philosophical limits of biblical fundamentalism and shunned the extreme ideas of Goodman, Ponet, and Knox in favour of a return to classical humanism. While in France he encountered the conciliarist tradition at first hand. He met Jean Bodin, whose *Six livres de la république* (1576) was the first comprehensive account of the theory of sovereignty. He was exposed to Huguenot resistance theory, which was more classical in its idioms than the writings of the Marian exiles. Conceptually, he held republican Rome in esteem, with its tradition of the *civitas libera* ('free state'). He was consistently repelled by the 'tyranny' represented by the idea of empire. He abhorred ideas of sacral monarchy, dismissing the Emperor Constantine in the *History* as the bastard of a Roman general's concubine. He showed a particular distaste for the colonial idea of 'empire' in the New World, which he had first encountered while teaching at the University of Coimbra in Portugal. His dislike of the 'imperial' iconography that the Stewart monarchy had cultivated under James V and Marie de Guise, partly in reaction to English claims of feudal suzerainty, but mainly to promulgate royal power more effectively, and especially in the Highlands and Islands, was pronounced.

Buchanan's central premiss was that kings were chosen by the people to perform a set of defined functions. If they failed to carry out their obligations, they broke the terms of the contract laid down in their coronation oath. If this happened, the people had the right to depose them and appoint someone better qualified to fulfil the duties of the royal office. Prima facie this was conciliarism, based on the notion that the pope was an officer of the Church charged with specific duties and accountable to the whole Christian people in their representative General Council. Buchanan, however, reworked the entire argument in a classical idiom to define an elective form of monarchy and make it axiomatic that kings were accountable to those who elected them. One of his theses was that kings were subject to the law as promulgated by the people in the interests of the whole community. To achieve this, he collapsed the dogma in Roman civil law which held that, even if the emperor's authority originally derived from the acclamation or consent of the people, once he was 'acclaimed', the emperor was 'sovereign' and the laws which he enacted were his own. In Buchanan's model, the king, far from being above the law by the prerogative of his *imperium*, was subject to the law at all times: not as an act of grace or concession, but because the subordination of the king to the law was justified by the dictates of reason, nature, and the divine will. To flout the law was not merely to oppose the will or welfare of the people, but to declare oneself a tyrant and an enemy to God. Once identified as a tyrant by a public assembly of the people, it was legitimate for the king to be deposed and for any responsible citizen to kill him.

This marked the zenith (or the nadir from the viewpoint of rulers) of the process whereby classical and conciliarist theory fused with Protestantism to create a quasi-republican model which demystified the legal and charismatic status of monarchy. In the *History*, Buchanan introduced the idea of an 'ancient' Scottish constitution which he moulded to illustrate the truth of the claims he had expounded in the *De jure regni apud Scotos*. The irony is that he was tutor to the young James VI, to whom the *History* was dedicated. As he openly remarked, in composing the *History* he was sending his pupil 'faithful advisers from history, whose counsel would help you in your affairs, and whose virtues you might emulate in the business of your life'. In reality the *History* is as eloquent as it is implausible. Its crux is its treatment of the personal rule of Mary Stewart, where the aim is to defend the Protestant rebellion and justify the actions of the earl of Moray (the leading Protestant noble) and the anti-Marians. Facts, where necessary, are invented and speeches put into the mouths of the protagonists. While this conforms precisely to the genre of history defined by several of the Greek and Roman rhetoricians, it is not a methodology which would be recognized as valid today. The quality of 'truth' depends upon the art and conscience of the writer, while its correct understanding depends on the literary and rhetorical skills of the reader.

Buchanan's description of David Rizzio, for example, is that of the archetypical 'Machiavell'. In real life, Rizzio was one of Mary's court musicians, whom she promoted to be her French and Italian secretary, and whom she possibly (but far from certainly) seduced. In Buchanan's *History*, he is low-born, foreign, ambitious, subtle, vainglorious, and physically deformed; he is a papist, a spy, a sycophant, and a voluptuary. His plans are hidden from all except the Devil. As soon as Moray's defeat leaves them free, Mary and Rizzio 'lay the foundations of a tyranny'. They create a bodyguard of foreign mercenaries. They conspire to oust Lord Darnley, Mary's husband, from the business of government and try to starve him to death. When Rizzio becomes Mary's lover, the scandal reaches Darnley's ears. He returns to Court, only to discover the door of the queen's bedchamber bolted against him with the queen and Rizzio inside. Darnley resolves to rid the country of this 'base-born villain'. An assassination plot is devised, which is successful. Mary is overcome by grief and anger, but has to wait for the punch line. Immediately after Rizzio's murder committed in her presence, she is given a lecture on political thought: 'The authority of Scottish kings derived from the law: the kingdom was not accustomed to be ruled by the whims of one person, but according to written law and the consent of the nobility. Any kings who attempted to overthrow this practice had paid dearly for their rashness.'

It is said that when the Scots forded the Tweed at the outbreak of the British Civil Wars in 1640, almost every minister (and there was one in every regiment) could produce Buchanan's *History* as readily as the Bible. Whether or not this is true, the work was repudiated by its dedicatee. When he became king, James VI proscribed both the *De jure* and the *History*, and in his own *Basilikon Doron* (1599, revised in 1603) advised his son to suppress 'such infamous invectives as Buchanan's or Knox's Chronicles'.

# The Elizabethan Privy Council and the 'mixed polity'

In 1559 Knox's attack on female monarchy was answered by the Marian exile, John Aylmer, later bishop of London, whose *An Harborowe for Faithfull and Trewe Subiectes* was an apology for Elizabeth's rule. Often cited as a 'defence' of her regime, it is unlikely that Aylmer was an 'official' apologist or that his pamphlet won her approval. Not only was it backhanded in its compliments, it argued that the 'gift' of a female ruler was proof of God's 'secret purpose' and 'wonderful works'. Aylmer invoked the Old Testament heroines of Deborah and Judith as regal prototypes, but his slant was closer to Knox's polemic than is often acknowledged, and still closer to the stance Knox took in his defence of the *First Blast* in a letter to Cecil in which he held that Elizabeth might be queen, but only if she 'shall confess' that it was the 'extraordinary dispensation' of God's mercy that legitimized her rule.

Elizabeth never accepted that her monarchy was the result of a 'miracle' or an 'extraordinary dispensation' of God. She fulminated against this opinion for decades. Her reasons were not feminist but dynastic. Her case was summarized in 1563 or 1566 by Thomas Norton in a paper that put in capsule form the exchanges of 1559. Close to Cecil and 'forward' in religion, Norton was a leading political figure of the second rank, who had translated Calvin's *Institutes* for publication in 1560–1. As he set out Elizabeth's objections: if her title were to be established 'by God's special and immediate ordinance' without any regard to her hereditary right and title, it 'setteth all her subjects at liberty, who acknowledge no such extraordinary calling'. Furthermore, a title established solely by an 'extraordinary miracle' of God left the validity of the dynastic title unresolved. 'It carrieth a present title to the next heir male, and so an evident means to destroy allegiance, to advance ambition, rebellion and treason.' Elizabeth would be left with 'no defence by law but an ostentation of God's dispensation against law, in which case the pope and papists may as easily say that the queen ought not to be queen though she have right'.

If this were not enough, Aylmer had argued in the *Harborowe* that the 'regiment' of England was not a 'mere' or unrestrained 'monarchy', but a 'mixed polity'. The queen shared her sovereignty with Parliament. 'If the Parliament use their privileges, the King can ordain nothing without them. If he do, it is his fault in usurping it, and their folly in permitting it.' This was a proposition so close to St German's model of parliamentary conciliarism that the cracks are scarcely visible. From the viewpoint of sacral monarchy, one can only say that with friends like this, who needed enemies? About the same time as he published the *Harborowe*, Aylmer wrote an obsequious letter to Robert Dudley (later earl of Leicester) seeking ecclesiastical preferment. When he obtained it, he turned conservative. By the 1570s, it was not Alymer who would invoke the thesis of 'mixed polity' to describe the Elizabethan state, but Thomas Cartwright, the Presbyterian leader and scourge of the conformist establishment. Cartwright claimed that the regime was a 'mixed estate'. By this he meant that Elizabeth was not an 'imperial' queen, but shared her sovereignty with the Privy Council and Parliament, an opinion tantamount to heresy in Elizabeth's eyes. The irony is that it was a heresy shared by Cecil (later Lord Burghley) until 1587. Elizabethan politics are sometimes surreal: the most powerful and subversive critiques of the monarchy did not emanate from parliamentary puritanism or the literature of exile, but from the heart of the Court itself. It is almost as if leading privy councillors were sometimes closet republicans.

The critical issues were the queen's marriage, the Protestant succession (and in particular the claim to the English throne of the Catholic, Mary Stewart), foreign policy (especially in Scotland, France, and the Netherlands), and the alteration of the Religious Settlement of 1559. Whenever these topics were raised, Elizabeth attempted to limit or (in the case of the succession) forbid discussion, or else professed herself unable to follow her councillors' advice, either because the matters were so complex that she needed to be 'further advised' or because her councillors were in apparent disagreement. She redefined these topics as 'matters of state': they became *arcana imperii*. If discussed without her permission, the veil of 'majesty' was pierced. She threatened Cecil with dismissal, and fumed against the earls of Leicester and Pembroke, for furthering the debates over her marriage and the succession in Parliament. She exiled Leicester and Sir Francis Walsingham from Court in 1579 for their opposition to her proposed marriage with Francis, duke of Anjou. In the privacy of her secret lodgings, she denounced those 'wrangling subjects' who challenged her judgement on marriage and the succession, and impugned those in Parliament 'whose ears were deluded by pleasing persuasions of common good'.

The radicalism of Elizabethan politics should not be exaggerated. The quasi-republican and conciliarist stances of the Privy Council were shaped as emergency responses to the need to ensure the queen's 'safety' and the 'security' of the Protestant state against the threat of international Catholic conspiracy and Mary Stewart's claim to the throne. Burghley felt this so strongly, he referred to it in the Latin inscription on his tomb in Stamford parish church in Lincolnshire. No one seems to have noticed that his recurrent references to the 'safety' of the queen and the kingdom stem from his classical education, and specifically the maxim *salus populi suprema lex esto* ('let the safety of the people be the supreme law'), which was the primary duty of magistrates in republican Rome according to the Twelve Tables, the earliest code of Roman law, which Livy described as 'the source of all public and private law'. Burghley drew on Cicero's injunctions that the rights of citizens (for which read Protestants) must be defended by magistrates against the tyranny and injustice (for which read Mary Stewart) which had enabled Julius Caesar to reduce freemen into slaves.

Until 1585 or thereabouts, the Cecilian political creed may be summarized thus: England was a 'mixed polity' in the terms defined by St German; the prerogative of the ruler was limited by the advice of the Privy Council; and the 'assent of the whole realm' in Parliament was required to effect significant political or religious change and in particular to resolve the issue of the succession to the throne.

The model pivots on the subject of 'councils' and counselling. Was the 'sovereignty' of the ruler to be limited by the advice of the Privy Council in a case of emergency? The implications did not become apparent until the collision between queen and Privy Council in 1587 over regicide, when the signed warrant for the execution of Mary Stewart was despatched on Burghley's instructions without Elizabeth's knowledge. Following the Babington plot, when she refused either to settle the Protestant succession or to sign the death warrant for the Scottish queen, Burghley told Walsingham, 'We stick upon Parliament, which her Majesty mislikes to have, but we all persist, to make the burden better borne and the world abroad better satisfied.' When push came to shove, he took a position extremely close to a view of Parliament as the 'court' of Protestant public opinion, a standpoint far removed from the 'official' model of Parliament as the Crown's instrument of government for securing legislation and taxation.

In February 1587, when the warrant for Mary's execution was signed but Elizabeth (as was later claimed) ordered her secretary William Davison to show it to no one other than Walsingham, who lay sick in bed, and the Lord Chancellor, who was to seal it, Burghley convened a meeting of ten privy councillors in his private chamber at Court which ordered the immediate despatch of the sealed warrant to commissioners at Fotheringhay. He drafted letters appointing the commissioners on his own initiative. A further covering letter, to which Walsingham added his signature from his sick bed, justified their action as taken 'for [the queen's] special service tending to the safety of her royal person and universal quietness of her whole Realme'. In this affair, Burghley appropriated a vocabulary of necessity linked to 'the safety' and 'preservation' of the 'queen' and 'state' in his attempt to emasculate the fact that the Privy Council acted clandestinely, a blatant act of republicanism (or more accurately a syncretism of republicanism and conciliarism) for which Elizabeth sought to hang Davison by royal prerogative for allowing the warrant to leave his possession. When a majority of the judges pronounced this course of action imprudent and almost certainly illegal, Davison was tried and sentenced in the Court of Star Chamber.

It has been said of the Privy Council's actions, they were 'akin to touching the sceptre'. Faced with the threat of Catholic conspiracy and Mary's title to the throne, the conciliar elite chose to 'preserve' and 'protect' the Protestant 'state' at the expense of the monarchy. Not only were their initiatives predicated on Aylmer's (or Cartwright's) view of England as a 'mixed polity' (a phrase also used by Ponet in the *Short Treatise of Politike Pouuer* where regicide was defended), a closer look at Burghley's contingency plans exposes his belief that, in the event of Elizabeth's death, the Privy Council and Parliament should not fail to act despite the lapse of their authority. His drafts for the settlement of the succession and the exclusion of Mary Stewart variously imagined a 'Council of State', 'Great Council' or 'Grand Council', which would form a provisional government in the absence of a Protestant monarch and which would adjudicate the claims of candidates for the succession in conjunction with

Parliament. Whether or not these plans were politically feasible, they marked yet another resurgence of aristocratic conciliarism. One wonders how, if at all, these schemes differed from the initial stages of the Revolution of 1688, when a committee of peers and privy council-lors formed themselves into a provisional government in the absence of the king. Of course, Burghley's plans became redundant after Mary's execution, when the succession of her son, the Protestant James VI, became (at least theoretically) assured.

Under pressure of these events, the binary opposition latent in the theory of monarchy since the death of Henry VIII was played out: the tension between an 'imperial' monarchy and the conviction of Burgh-ley and the Privy Council that acts of quasi- or outright republican-ism were defensible if the Protestant state were to be preserved, and most especially when the ruler declined to follow her (male) council-lors' advice. On the other hand, Mary's execution was followed by a swing to the right. No longer was the 'mixed polity' in vogue, and the theory of sacral monarchy re-established itself as the political norm. This was partly due to changes in the composition of the Privy Coun-cil. Between 1588 and 1590 the earls of Leicester and Warwick, Sir Walter Mildmay, and Sir Francis Walsingham died. All were cham-pions of Protestantism. Their deaths altered the balance of opinion. Burghley was increasingly a Polonius-type figure in the 1590s: a polit-ical survivor until 1598, he lacked the energy and sense of mission he had earlier displayed. The running was made by men like John Whitgift, archbishop of Canterbury (1583–1604), who entered the Privy Council in 1586 at Burghley's nomination, but was not close to him. They differed over the archbishop's anti-puritan campaign, enforced by the Court of High Commission, which Burghley compared to the 'Romish' or 'Spanish Inquisition'. When in 1591 Hatton and Whitgift arranged the Star Chamber trials of Cartwright and the Presbyterian leaders, Burghley was a conspicuous absentee. Whitgift outlived him and was secure in royal favour until the queen's own death. His favour reached its height when his private troops played a crucial role in the defence of Whitehall during the earl of Essex's revolt.

Whereas until 1587 the idiom of 'mixed polity' had reflected the prevailing patterns of Elizabethan politics, by the 1590s careerists were arguing that the queen wielded an 'imperial' sovereignty, that she alone enacted the laws, and that she was above the law by the prerogative of her *imperium*. This was the beginning of a shift of

opinion later seen as sacerdotalist: its pioneers, men like Richard
Bancroft, John Bridges, Thomas Bilson, and Hadrian Saravia, were all
avant-garde conformist clergy. In Scotland the lead was taken by
James VI himself, when he went spectacularly into print to refute the
legacy of Buchanan. These publicists had a double target, since the
models of 'mixed polity' and popular sovereignty were propagated
not only by Scottish and English Calvinists, but also by Catholics
eager to frustrate James's succession to the English throne. The Jesuit
Robert Parsons held that the ruler's prerogative was strictly limited by
law and that, whereas the pope derived his powers directly from God,
kings drew theirs from the people.

At one level this was familiar, at another deeply unfamiliar. A profound alteration of pitch and tone can be discerned in British political culture after 1603. The (mainly historical) arguments that had
justified sacral monarchy in the reign of Henry VIII gave way to an
intense rhetoric of patriarchalism and advocacy of royal and clerical
authority *jure divino* ('by divine right'). Whereas kingship was justified in the sixteenth century as much by the maxims of the common
law as by Roman civil law or the theory of sacral monarchy, it was
shrouded in mystery after 1603. Its attributes were not to be discussed;
they were an aspect of divinity rather than law. In a speech in Star
Chamber in 1616, James went considerably beyond his remarks to
Parliament in 1610. He put the point explicitly: 'It is Atheism and
blasphemy to dispute what God can do . . . So, it is presumption and
high contempt in a Subject, to dispute what a king can do', for which
reason the king's mystical 'absolute' power was 'no subject for the
tongue of a lawyer'. It has been the argument of this chapter that the
monarchies of Henry VIII and Elizabeth were conceptually sacral at
base, but each of these rulers had still allowed the *arcana imperii* to be
discussed with their permission. Elizabeth had several times allowed
her privy councillors to discuss her marital status, notably during the
Anjou marriage negotiations, and the scope of the royal prerogative
had been openly disputed in the House of Lords in the 1540s, when
Lord Chancellor Audley had explained and redefined the law of
*praemunire* and its relationship to the rights of the monarchy and the
Church.

# Classical literature and the idea of monarchy by 1600

Despite the rise of *jure divino* models of kingship and authority, the subliminal effect of resistance theory and the regicide of 1587 could never be erased. Just when the theory of sacral monarchy seemed to have been vindicated in Cawdrey's case, the claims of the Crown were further circumscribed by the resurgence of the classical-republican idea of the 'state': the thesis that had underpinned the Cecilian drafts for the exclusion and execution of Mary Stewart, and which now reappeared in less politically strident but more insidious and widely distributed forms.

The new lexicon stemmed from the classicization of language and politics in Europe and Britain by 1603. The beginning of the shift is discernible in Elyot and Starkey, and was accelerated in the circle around Sir John Cheke and William Cecil in Cambridge and at the Court of Edward VI. In the 1550s, Roger Ascham, Sir Thomas Hoby, and Sir Thomas Wilson were in the vanguard of a project of vernacular acculturalization and linguistic purification, aiming to standardize English, which (in Wilson's resonant phrase) would become the 'King's English'. (Hoby's translation of Castiglione's *The Courtier* belongs to this phase, and led to Ascham's claim that Castiglione was more valuable if read in English than Italian.) Although partly aimed at purging English of imported foreign words, the project was classical in inspiration, because its thrust was to centralize and 'civilize' a national community by the power of eloquence. Wilson's *Rule of Reason* (1551) and *Art of Rhetoric* (1554) marked his initial forays into the links between classical language and political ideas. In *Three Orations of Demosthenes* (1569), he began to conceptualize the classical idea of the 'state'. In his *Discourse on Usury* (1572), the term is explored in the contexts of governors, magistrates, and ambassadors, plainly differentiated from the use of the vernacular 'common weal', which is depoliticized and reserved for discussions of the welfare of the community.

Wilson did not have a partisan political agenda. He was testing the boundaries of rhetoric. The metamorphosis began in the 1590s, when a commercial market arose in translations of classical texts (and especially Roman histories) for gentry consumption. Before the 1590s, the works of the leading authors were available in Latin editions, mainly from the great printing centres of the Continent, but their circulation was limited. Only two translations of Cicero's *De officiis* were published in England or Scotland before 1600. Robert Whittinton's parallel-text edition was issued in 1534, almost certainly for pedagogical uses. Nicholas Grimald's translation appeared in 1556 and was reissued (as a parallel-text edition) seven times between 1558 and 1600, but print runs were small before the editions of 1596 and 1600. In 1598 Aristotle's *Politics* was translated from a French edition. Extracts from Sallust had appeared in small print runs between 1520 and 1557: the first mass edition had to wait until 1608, when Thomas Heywood's version reached the bookshops. Brief extracts from Livy had appeared in 1544, but a more comprehensive edition of the *Roman History* was not planned until 1598 and took two years to complete.

The crux is the vogue for Tacitus, which developed at Oxford in the 1580s and spread to the earl of Essex's circle at Court. The key figures were the earl's secretary, Henry Cuffe, a professor of Greek, and Henry Savile, warden of Merton College. In 1591 Savile published his translation of the first four books of *The Histories* alongside the life of Agricola. There followed his reconstruction of the lost final chapters of the *Annals*. Finally, the complete extant text of the *Annals* was translated by Richard Greneway. This edition included *The Germania*, and appeared in 1598. With the arrival of these works, the spotlight was on two topics: the troubles that afflicted Rome after Octavian's victory at the battle of Actium, and the process by which a weak monarchy disintegrated after the rebellion which toppled Nero and extinguished the Claudian dynasty. It is a story of the displacement of civic virtue, 'friendship', and 'good counsel' by flattery, autocracy, and violence, as Tiberius and his councillors corrupted one another and the state degenerated into tyranny. The relationship between military and civic virtue is also revealed as deeply ambiguous in these translations.

Tacitus was the historian for the times. In the case of Essex's circle, his writings functioned as a handbook for courtiers subjected to 'tyrannical' rule: they had convinced themselves that Elizabeth fell into this category in her last decade. More generally, the atrocities of the French Wars of Religion and Dutch Revolt led readers to locate in

Tacitus the source of a 'private' prudence that complemented the concept of prudence found in Cicero. The Dutch commentator Joost Lips, whose *Six Books of Politics* were translated in 1594, defended a 'mixed prudence' or deceit by rulers for public ends. Three types of deceit were distinguished: light, middle, and great. Lips justified a resort to the first, which included dissimulation. He was willing to tolerate the second, if it were profitable to the state. Only 'great deceit' which included treachery and pure malice was condemned.

By 1603, all the primary texts of the classical-republican tradition were available in English translations. Their precise impact is elusive, but the culture was moving in two directions. One involved nostalgia for the model that Elyot had expounded in the *Book Named the Governor*, with its emphasis on 'counsel', virtue, and 'friendship'. The other was towards an investigation of the *arcana imperii*. The concepts of 'mysteries of state' and 'reason of state' were put under the lens. The Italian phrase *ragione degli stati* was familiar in Europe; the classical tradition was the arena in which politics and 'state' power were defined. Beyond this, it was the classical (and especially the Roman) tradition which underpinned ideas of constitutionalism and republicanism. Whether in a monarchy or a republic, the 'active citizen' set the standard for the councillor or civil magistrate, and would continue to do so as long as the texts of Aristotle and Cicero formed the backbone of the educational curriculum. The British Isles were not immune from these European trends, as is evidenced by the reading habits of the Jacobean Court circle and the increasing number of translations of writings by Continental political theorists after 1610.

In the speech to Parliament with which this chapter began, James VI and I did not simply declare monarchy to be 'the supremest thing on earth', he put the *arcana imperii* out of bounds. They were too high for rational (or legal) comprehension. He cited three 'similitudes' to illustrate the 'state' of monarchy. None was drawn from law, and yet the common lawyers utterly rejected his argument that there were *arcana imperii* beyond the limits of legal or rational debate. The danger was that a moment would arrive at which the idea of liberty would come to be imagined in terms of the 'rights' of individual 'subjects' or 'citizens' rather than in relation to the 'kingdom', 'realm', 'commonwealth', or 'state' as an entity. The common law tradition posed fewer difficulties for the Crown as long as its vocabulary was informed by ideas of feudal tenure rather than proprietary ownership. On the other hand, the classical lexicon makes it virtually impossible to discuss the 'liberty' of the 'kingdom' or 'realm', and yet 'state' or 'commonwealth' were each rendered *respublica* in the Latin literature, with obvious republican connotations. As the powers of the monarchy and the 'state' were examined and deconstructed in the politics and literature of the Stewart period, it was these connotations that came to the fore, whereupon the debate snowballed. As Hobbes remarked in *Leviathan* (1651):

we are made to receive our opinions concerning the institution, and rights of commonwealths, from Aristotle, Cicero, and other men, Greeks and Romans, that living under popular states, derived those rights, not from the principles of nature, but transcribed them into their books, out of the practice of their own commonwealths, which were popular.

By reading classical literature 'from their childhood', men had 'under a false show of liberty' acquired the habit of 'favouring tumults, and of licentious controlling the actions of their sovereigns'. It was a viewpoint with which James VI and I would have wholeheartedly concurred, but by then his opinions were irrelevant.

# Sources

The principal sixteenth-century authors and works discussed and cited in this chapter are John Aylmer, *An harborowe for faithfull and trewe subiectes, agaynst the late blowne blaste, concerninge the government of wemen* (London, 1559); George Buchanan, *The History of Scotland*, ed. and trans. J. Aikman (Glasgow, 1827); idem, *The Powers of the Crown in Scotland*, ed. and trans. C. F. Arrowood (Austin, Tex., 1949); idem, *The Art and Science of Government among the Scots*, ed. and trans. D. H. McNeill (Glasgow, 1964); Sir William Cecil, *A Collection of State Papers ... left by William Cecil, Lord Burghley*, ed S. Haynes and W. Murdin (2 vols.; London, 1740–59); Sir Thomas Elyot, *The Book Named the Governor*, ed. S. E. Lehmberg (London, 1962); Sir John Fortescue, *De laudibus legum anglie*, ed. S. B. Chrimes (Cambridge, 1949); idem, *The Governance of England: Otherwise Called the*

*Difference between an Absolute and a Limited Monarchy*, ed. C. Plummer (Oxford, 1885); Edward Foxe, *Opus eximium. De vera differentia regiae potestatis et ecclesiasticae, et quae sit ipsa veritas ac virtus utriusque* (London, 1534); Stephen Gardiner, *Obedience in Church and State*, ed. P. Janelle (Cambridge, 1930); Christopher Goodman, *How Superior Powers O[u]ght to be Obey[e]d* (Facsimile Text Society; New York, 1932); John Hooker, *Parliament in Elizabethan England: John Hooker's 'Order and Usage'*, ed. Vernon F. Snow (New Haven, 1977); Richard Hooker, *Of the Laws of Ecclesiastical Polity*, ed. A. S. McGrade (Cambridge, 1989); James VI and I, *Political Writings*, ed. J. P. Sommerville (Cambridge, 1994); John Knox, *On Rebellion*, ed. R. A. Mason (Cambridge, 1994); John Ponet, *A short Treatise of Politike Pouuer and of the true Obedience which subiectes owe to kynges and other civile Gouernours, with an Exhortacion to all true naturall Englishe men* (Strasburg, 1556); Christopher St German, *An Answere to a Letter* (London, 1535); Thomas Starkey, *A Dialogue between Pole and Lupset*, ed. T. F. Mayer (Camden Society, 4th Series, 37; London, 1989).

Figure 7  Wollaton Hall, Nottinghamshire.

# 5

# The Renaissance in Britain

## Greg Walker

All their plays be neither right Tragedies, nor right Comedies ... [they] thrust in clowns by head and shoulders, to play a part in majestical matters, with neither decency nor discretion, so as neither the admiration and commiseration, nor the right sportfulness, is by their mongrel tragi-comedy obtained.[1]

Thus Sir Philip Sidney (1554–86), the archetypal Renaissance man, excoriated contemporary dramatists in his *Apology for Poetry* (published posthumously in 1595). What annoyed Sidney most was the playwrights' lack of decorum, their failure consistently to apply classical precepts, resulting in a hybrid product, neither one thing nor another. In fact this charge might be levelled at most of the artistic disciplines in Britain in the sixteenth century. Yet it was this very 'mongrel' failure to conform to pure generic categories which was to produce most of what is now seen as characteristic of the Renaissance in Britain.

The Renaissance, in reality not one movement but a number of related pan-European phenomena, was largely initiated by Italian humanists in the fourteenth century. Humanism, a term derived in the nineteenth century from the *studia humanitas*, was essentially an academic reform movement dedicated to the rediscovery of Greek and Roman literature and culture in their original languages and forms, and the cultivation of classical style as the informing principle

---

[1] Philip Sidney, *An Apology For Poetry*, ed. Geoffrey Shepherd (Manchester, 1973), 135.

behind a new educational curriculum. But the words 'humanism' and 'Renaissance' have acquired wider connotations, coming to stand for a fundamental reappraisal of the nature and ends of human existence and a new appreciation of the potential dignity of human achievement. In the course of the sixteenth century there were in effect two distinct kinds of Renaissance in Britain and two distinct periods during which they made their presence felt. There was the scholarly Renaissance of the pre-Reformation period, conducted in the universities and filtered down into the schools, and there was the artistic, or practical Renaissance of the last third of the century, implemented primarily by architects, musicians, poets, and playwrights, and characterized by the creative use of classical materials in the construction of new forms and the reworking of old ones. The second Renaissance was in many ways the heir of the first, but like many an heir, it used its inheritance in ways that those who, like Sidney, saw themselves as trustees of the estate, felt were profligate and irresponsible.

The sixteenth century cannot claim exclusivity in the history of the Renaissance in Britain. Veneration of the work of classical authors was a feature of the fourteenth century. Geoffrey Chaucer had travelled to Genoa and Florence in the 1370s and had been inspired to imitate the work of Boccaccio, Dante, and Petrarch. Yet, when one talks of the Renaissance in Britain, one usually means the sixteenth century, and probably the products of the last two decades of the century in southern England. Where the Netherlands looks to the paintings of Rembrandt for the epitome of its own Renaissance, and France to the chateaux of the Loire valley and the writings of Rabelais, Ronsard, and Montaigne, for Britain it has always been the literature of the Elizabethan period, the repertoire of the London theatres, and especially the work of Shakespeare that provide the pinnacle of domestic cultural achievement, the fullest reception of the Renaissance in these islands.

For a full appreciation of the state of the arts in the sixteenth century, it is necessary to take into account two major phenomena dealt with more exhaustively elsewhere in this volume, the development of a bourgeois, metropolitan culture, particularly in London, but also in Edinburgh, Dublin, and the larger provincial cities of England and Scotland, and the religious changes of the Reformation. Each contributed to cultural developments in Britain in the period, running alongside the reception of continental classical culture, complementing or qualifying it.

As we shall see, the Renaissance in Britain was in many ways a limited and circumscribed affair, derived by indirect and uncertain paths. As elsewhere in Europe, its reception was marked by the adaptation to and absorption of classical notions by older vernacular traditions in a productive dialogue, and this process left neither element unaltered. Even in Italy itself, Renaissance neo-classicism built upon older, medieval forms.

# Literature and learning: the humanist Renaissance

This first, humanist phase in the Renaissance aimed at allying scholarship to the service of the commonweal. In England its monuments were educational treatises such as Sir Thomas Elyot's *Boke Named the Governor* (1531) (itself inspired by Castiglione's *Courtier*, which was circulating in England in the late 1520s) designed to fashion virtuous princes and public servants. Even such ostensibly playful works as Sir Thomas More's *Utopia* (first published in Latin in 1516) were part of this process. Freed from the medieval distrust of the things of the world by their encounters with Roman civic virtue, the humanists were able to move away from the ideal of the contemplative life to revitalize the notion of active public service as the true goal of human aspirations. Through the work of scholars such as William Grocyn (*c.*1446–1519), Thomas Linacre (*c.*1466–1524), and primarily John Colet (*c.*1467–1519), Renaissance principles were introduced into England and put into practice in the universities and in new schools such as Colet's foundation, St Paul's. A second generation of educated laymen, among them Thomas More, was able, in the years before Henry VIII's Break with Rome, to build upon the methods pioneered by Colet, and further the exploration of classical culture through textual editing and translation, historiography, literary imitation, and innovative methods of language teaching.

The translation of influential classical texts began early in the century. In Scotland, Gavin Douglas (*c.*1475–1522) translated Virgil's

*Aeneid* into vigorous Middle Scots verse between 1512 and 1513, thus pre-empting the earl of Surrey (who borrowed significantly from Douglas's text) by some two decades. In 1533 John Bellenden (1495–1587), archdeacon of Moray, translated the first five books of Livy into Scots, and George Buchanan (1506–1582) translated Euripedes from Greek into Latin while he was in Paris in the 1530s. The systematic attempt by academics to translate the classics, however, began in earnest from the mid-century onwards. The dramas of Seneca were each translated during the 1560s by a group of scholars inspired by Jasper Heywood (1535–1597), and were republished together in the omnibus *Ten Tragedies* of 1581. Ovid's *Metamorphoses* was translated by Arthur Golding (1536–1605?) between 1565 and 1567. In 1579 Thomas North's version of Plutarch's *Lives of the Greeks and Romans* appeared, like many of the works, translated not directly but via a French intermediary.

Alongside translation came imitation. Robert Henryson's *Moral Fables* (finally printed in 1571) dressed Aesop in distinctly Scottish garments. George Buchanan's Latin paraphrases of the Psalms owed much to his reading of Horace's *Odes* and *Epodes*, and Gavin Douglas's *Pallice of Honour* (*c.*1501) rehearsed material from Ovid and Virgil with confident familiarity. The Comedy of Plautus was brought to English audiences in plays such as Nicholas Udall's *Ralph Roister Doister*, while Senecan tragedy was domesticated, first in Norton and Sackville's *Gorboduc* (1562), and later on the public stage in Thomas Kyd's *Spanish Tragedy* and Shakespeare's *Titus Andronicus*. Ovidian erotic narrative poetry found its English counterpart in Christopher Marlowe's *Hero and Leander* (printed posthumously in 1598) and Shakespeare's *Venus and Adonis* (1593) and *The Rape of Lucrece* (1594).

This enthusiasm for translating the classics and leading continental texts was not, however, common across Britain. In Wales, although Gruffyd Robert (pre-1532–post-1598) began to translate Cicero's *De senectute* into Welsh, the task was never completed, and his compatriots concentrated upon more immediately useful projects. The polymath William Salesbury (*c.*1520–1584?) published a Welsh primer for English speakers (in 1550), an Anglo-Welsh Dictionary, in 1547, and, in the same year, an introduction to the wryly entitled anthology of proverbs, *Oll Synnwyr Pen Kembero ygyd* ('The Whole Sense of a Welshman's Head') of Gruffudd Hiraethog. Similarly, in Ireland, although writers were aware of the models offered by classical

literature (Riocard do Búrc, for example, was to produce a free translation of a narrative from Ovid's *Amores*), the majority of scholars
were involved in more pragmatic linguistic projects, such as the
Gaelic primer produced for Queen Elizabeth by Christopher Nugent,
5th Baron Delvin (1544–1603). This is not to say, however, that Wales
and Ireland were without authors capable of writing in good
humanist Latin. Sir John Prys (*c.*1502–1554), John Owen (1564–1628),
and John Davies (*c.*1567–1644) enjoyed a European reputation, as did
the Dublin poet and scholar Richard Stanihurst (1547–1618) and
Scotsmen such as Hector Boece (*c.*1465–1536) and Buchanan.

It is, then, possible to chart the gradual reception of classical ideas
into Britain through an account of such translations and imitations.
But this would be only half of the story, and perhaps the less interesting half at that. What such an account would not reveal is how far this
scholarly passion for translation actually influenced cultural practice
on a wider scale. What follows will examine this question in detail.

# Discipline and virtuosity: the literary Renaissance

George Puttenham, writing in *The Arte of English Poesie* (1589),
identified a clear break with the literary past in the reign of Henry
VIII brought about by the encounter with Renaissance ideas.

In the latter end of the same king's raigne sprong up a new company of
courtly makers, of whom Sir *Thomas Wyatt* th'elder and *Henry* Earle of
Surrey were the two chieftaines, who having travailed into Italie, and there
tasted the sweete and stately measures and stile of the Italian Poesie as
novices . . . greatly pollished our rude and homely maner of vulgar Poesie.[2]

Puttenham neatly summarizes the standard model of the English
Renaissance. Its spirit was something located abroad, specifically in
Italy, that had to be imbibed *ad fontes* by pioneering individuals who
then spread its influence at home. The conflation of the ideas of
travel and labour in the word 'travailed' conveys neatly the debt to

---

[2] George Puttenham, *The Arte of English Poesie (1589)* Scolar Facsimile Edition
(Menston, 1968), 48.

foreign inspiration—the need to journey to Italy as 'novices' in order to find examples of true poetic excellence—with a sense of the hard work necessary to plant and cultivate its fruits in the barren domestic soil. Here also baldly stated is the long-standing sense of cultural inferiority felt by Englishmen, whose language, 'rude and homely' was considered ill-suited to the expression of refined subjects.

There is no doubt some truth in each of these claims, but to accept them at face value would be unwise. The history of the Renaissance in Britain has often been written as if it were the story of the reception of Italian culture, with the moment at which a 'medieval' cultural heritage which looked to France and Burgundy for inspiration was replaced by a 'modern' spirit which looked to Italy marking the decisive break with the past. A closer look at the state of British culture at the mid-century, however, suggests a more complex situation in which continuity has as important a role to play as change. French culture exercised a deep and contradictory fascination for the English and Scots throughout the medieval period and deep-seated debts and obligations were not easily uprooted. Indeed, rather than being replaced by Italian influences, French culture was itself the channel through which the Italian Renaissance reached Britain in the early sixteenth century, as a French vogue for the culture of the Peninsular city states was first observed and then imitated by patrons in England and Scotland. The general debt to France is reflected in specific cases, not least those highlighted by Puttenham as initiating the move towards Italy. Wyatt did indeed travel to Italy, and toured the country on embassy, but only after he had first been to France, where he was reported to have showed 'as much wit to mark and remember everything he seeth as any yong man hath in England'.[3] It may well have been the contemporary vogue for Italianate poetry that he encountered in France, where the work of Serafino dè Ciminelli (1466–1500) was much admired and copied, and men like Clemont Marot (1496–1544) were introducing Italian forms into French verse, that prompted him to journey to Italy in 1527.

But, however it was encountered, Italian—and specifically Petrarchan—poetry did have a profound effect upon Wyatt and subsequent lyric poets. In experimenting with the sonnet form, first

[3] K. Muir, *Life and Letters of Sir Thomas Wyatt* (Liverpool, 1963), 6; all quotations from his verse are from Sir Thomas Wyatt, *The Complete Poems*, ed. R. A. Rebholz (Harmondsworth, 1978).

devised in Provence in the twelfth century, and by fusing universal themes with the quotidian details of his own feelings for his beloved Laura, Francis Petrarch (1304–1374) had established a poetic scenario, register, and vocabulary which were to provide the essential grammar of secular lyric verse for the next 300 years. The devoted suitor and his cool, cruel mistress, the sublime possibilities and mundane frustrations of human love, the physical and emotional contradictions to which passion and desire drive the thinking, feeling subject, and the capacity of poetry to express, accommodate, and seek to transcend all these things: these were to be the subject of lyric poetry in every major language of Western Europe.

In its wide emotional range and the opportunities for the witty expression of sensibility it provided, coupled with the rigorous discipline demanded by its fourteen-line form, the sonnet offered a challenge against which aspiring poets could test their mettle. Like Chaucer one hundred and fifty years earlier, Wyatt and Surrey found in Petrarch's work, not only an arsenal of rhetorical devices, but a range of new emotions and states of mind which were now licensed as the subject of courtly poetry. The poetic subject—and, as they were courtiers, the courtly subject—could now express itself not merely in moral certainties, but in paradox and contradictions.

> Love and Fortune and my mind, rememb'rer
> Of that that is now with that that hath been,
> Do torment me so that I very often
> Envy them beyond all measure.
> Love slayeth mine heart. Fortune is depriver
> Of all my comfort. The foolish mind then
> Burneth and plaineth as one that seldom
> Liveth in rest, still in displeasure.
> My pleasant days, they fleet away and pass,
> But daily yet the ill doth change into the worse,
> And more than the half is run of my course.
> Alas, not of steel but of brickle glass
> I see that from mine hand falleth my trust,
> And all my thoughts are dashed into dust.

The divided self, conditioned by emotional turmoil, evident here in Wyatt's sonnet translated from Petrarch's *Rime* 124, could now be the subject of verse in a way which the lyric, previously conditioned by moral and religious sententiousness, had not enunciated in English before.

After this brief period of intense poetic creativity, however, there was a long hiatus. The return to sonneteering is usually attributed to the influence of Sir Philip Sidney's *Astrophil and Stella*, the publication of which in 1591 prompted the 'sonnet craze' of the 1590s. But later Elizabethan lyricism did not emerge fully formed from Sidney's head. The resurgence of sonneteering began in Scotland, and was inspired by James VI's *Essayes of a Prentise, in the Divine Art of Poesie* (1585). James was no stranger to continental trends or the tenets of humanist educational theory. He was taught for a time by the great Scottish neo-classicist George Buchanan, and later complained that his tutors had 'gart me speik Latin or ar [i.e. before] I could speik Scottis'. He was to inspire a coterie of court poets dubbed 'the Castalian band' (after the fountain of the Muses on Mount Parnassus), many of whom were, like Alexander Montgomerie and Sir William Fowler, to follow their sovereign's lead in writing sonnets, although most of their endeavours were not printed until the seventeenth century, if at all.

This reluctance of the Scottish sonneteers to publish their work in printed form alerts us to a crucial feature of literary culture in the northern kingdom, where, despite the existence of a healthy print industry, manuscript production remained the crucial means of preserving and circulating texts. Our knowledge of sixteenth-century Scottish literature is largely the result of the survival of a number of the major manuscript anthologies, the best known of which is the Bannatyne Manuscript, compiled by George Bannatyne between 1565 and 1568. It, along with other collections such as the Asloan manuscript, and the Gaelic anthology commonly known as *The Book of the Dean of Lismore* (which contained many verses of Irish origin), preserved medieval poems alongside contemporary work in the same idiom, and poems of a more modish stamp, demonstrating that manuscript production at this time was neither a sign of a backward-looking culture, nor a coterie affectation, but a means of recording and circulating a diverse and vigorous body of indigenous verse.

In Wales and Ireland too, the manuscript tradition prospered during the sixteenth century, reflecting in part a conscious effort to preserve and expand the indigenous literary heritage in the absence of a well-developed native print culture. The fact that the sonnet, like the other characteristic Renaissance forms the pastoral and the epigram, found few imitators in Wales and Ireland in the period suggests strongly that they were not seen to answer any pressing need for native writers. For Welsh poets in particular, the kind of challenge to their virtuosity offered by the sonnet had long been a feature of their repertoire. The *cynghanedd*, the complex and demanding rules of alliteration and internal rhyme governing the structure of Welsh formal verse, had since the fourteenth century determined the composition of forms such as the *cywydd* (based upon lines of exactly seven syllables, arranged in rhymed couplets, in which one rhyme must be a stressed syllable, the other unstressed). Still more complex was the four-line *englyn* (consisting of exactly thirty syllables, distributed between the lines in the precise ratio 10, 6, 7, and 7, with all four lines repeating the same rhyme, although in the first line it must not be in the final syllable). A fine example is the anonymous meditation upon longing from Moslyn manuscript 131.

> *Dos ymaith hiraeth orig o'm calon,*
> *cilia i ffwrdd ychydig;*
> *dywed i'm gwen felenfrig*
> *fod dyn ac arno fyd dig.*

> [Longing, leave my heart for an hour
> and turning away awhile
> to tell my yellow-haired girl
> that here is a man for whom the world is vile.][4]

The fact that traditional Welsh verse was resistant to the new poetic influences at work in England and the continent has prompted allegations of parochialism and regression. This charge was initially levelled by the poets' own humanist compatriots. The scholar Edmwnd Prys of Mentwrog (1544–1623), himself a gifted poet, conducted an extended verse controversy with the bard William Cynwal in the 1580s, arguing that traditional verse was becoming an introverted and merely nostalgic form. But to condemn bardic poetry for being too formulaic is to misunderstand its nature (no doubt wilfully in the case of Prys and the humanists), and to mistake its greatest strength for a weakness. It was the very rigour of its rules that created the

---

[4] Gwyn Williams (ed.), *The Burning Tree: Poems from the First Thousand Years of Welsh Verse* (London, 1961), 156–7.

productive tensions that enlivened the *cywydd, awdl* (ode), and *eng-lyn*. Like the rules governing the production of the sonnet, the strictures of *cynghanedd* enforced a liberating rather than a stultifying discipline upon the best practitioners. Ironically, of course, the humanists were driven to criticize the bards for following indigenous medieval conventions, not because they themselves prized innovation, but because they thought that they should be following the even older rules of the classical theorists. Like Sir Philip Sidney, they were seeking to impose an inappropriate classical model on native practice, prescribing a straitjacket as a cure for alleged immobility.

# Dramatic developments: English theatre in the Renaissance

One of the most important developments in the artistic culture of the sixteenth century—and one which colours our whole sense of the Renaissance in Britain—began not as a response to continental ideas, but as a purely pragmatic alteration in the commercial operation of an acting company. In 1576 a businessman, James Burbage, built a playhouse, called simply The Theatre, in Shoreditch. Coming exactly one hundred years after Caxton set up his press in Westminster, Burbage's decision arguably had an equally significant influence, both in shifting cultural paradigms and in advancing the cultural dominance of the metropolis.

Prior to the building of the Theatre and its successors, professional acting in Britain was a largely peripatetic activity. Rather than its audience going to the theatre, drama travelled the country in search of audiences, performing wherever the physical conditions permitted and paying customers could be found. The chief 'theatrical' spaces were thus, not theatres at all, but the great halls of palaces, manor houses, and the Inns of Court, town halls, inn-yards, urban streets, churches, and open spaces. The acting companies took their wares to potential buyers in much the same way that other peddlers did, and consequently endured the same social stigma, being liable to prosecution under the legislation restricting the movements of sturdy beggars if they could not secure the patronage of a friendly aristocrat who would offer them his name and vouch, however nominally, for their integrity.

With the creation of the commercial playhouses, the fortunes of the acting companies improved considerably. For a large proportion of the year, they were able to stay in the capital and avoid the arduous and risky business of continual touring. The playhouses also profoundly altered the career pattern of poets. In an age when royal patronage was a precarious and unreliable commodity, writing for the theatre provided a measure of financial security for anyone prepared to submit to its rigours. It also provided a forum for the exploration of ideas independent of the direct control of Church and State—a fact which troubled both of these institutions to differing degrees. And finally, in an age when literature was still burdened with a moral utilitarian dimension, the theatres gave playwrights a reason to write. In the days of regular touring, a company might eke out a career with only a small number of plays to perform, certain that their wares would find a fresh welcome in every new town. Once the companies settled in London, they had continually to court the same, albeit large audience with fresh wares, and hence needed a constant stream of new plays. The commercial playhouses thus created an insatiable demand for novel matter, and drama became self-justifying for the first time. We know the titles of some 436 plays performed in London between 1560 and 1600 (probably only part of the dramatic output in the capital in the period), but the rate at which demand was accelerating can be judged from the fact that 266 of those titles date from the final decade of the century.

The playhouse itself quickly became a favoured, indeed overworked metaphor for human existence in the wider world. Theatrical imagery had always been useful for discussing the transitory and illusory qualities of worldly existence from a Christian viewpoint. But, as the theatrical experience itself took on a new and vibrant form, the nature of the metaphors and the experience of thinking about life 'through theatre' shifted also. Within twenty years a fundamental paradigm shift had occurred in the ways in which informed observers discussed human existence. The idea that 'all the world's a stage' may have been around for as long as there were stages, but with the building of the playhouses it took on crucial new resonances. By 1600 *homo ludens* had become *homo histrionicus*. When Thomas More compared the pretences of princely politics to stage plays in his

*History of King Richard III* (written *c.*1514–18), he described a situation in which the actors inhabited an exclusive world, and the common man stepped onto the stage at his own peril. 'And so they said that these matters be King's games, as it were stage plays, and for the more part played upon scaffolds. In which poor men be but the lookers on. And they that wise be, will meddle no further.'[5] When Sir Walter Ralegh (1552–1618) revisited the life-as-theatre metaphor in his meditation 'On the Life of Man', he assumed a wholly different theatrical scenario. Not only had the material conditions of performance changed—he imagined the performance played out in a playhouse, equipped with curtains and a tiring-house, rather than as a pageant presented in the streets as in More's anecdote—but the players were no longer the keepers of a dangerous mystery, but the humble purveyors of a commodity. The 'lookers on', now transformed into a sophisticated, fee-paying audience, could make or break the actors' fortunes with their verdict on the performance.

> What is our life? A play of passion;
> Our mirth the music of division;
> Our mothers' wombs the tiring-houses be
> Where we are dressed for this short comedy.
> Heaven the judicious sharp spectator is,
> That sits and marks still who doth act amiss;
> Our graves that hide us from the searching sun
> Are like drawn curtains when the play is done.
> Thus march we, playing, to our latest rest,
> Only we die in earnest—that's no jest.[6]

With this change in the business of playing, drama, which had been a vehicle for a moral and religious critique of worldly life and what we would identify as a consumer society, became unmistakably an integral and compromised part of that same commercial culture. Playgoing had always been only problematically related to sober living and moral improvement, but with the development of the playhouses, it could no longer seriously be maintained that it was primarily a pious activity, akin to attending a sermon or reading a work of improving literature. The very geography of the theatres proclaimed their

---

[5] R. Sylvester (ed.), *The Complete Works of Thomas More, Volume Two* (New Haven, 1963), 81.

[6] M. H. Abrams, et al. (eds.), *The Norton Anthology of English Literature*, 5th edn. (2 vols.; New York, 1986), I, 783.

proximity to those other centres of licentious indulgence and 'waste', the cockpits, bear-baiting rings, bowling alleys, and brothels. And in the plays of Kyd and Marlowe the links became all too obvious.

The work of Thomas Kyd (1558–1594) introduced Senecan principles to the public stage. In a now lost *Hamlet* and *The Spanish Tragedy* (1587) he established a rhetoric of tragic theatre (the quest for revenge, the hero's madness, a scheming villain, the conscious exploitation of theatricality in a play-within-a-play) which was profoundly to influence later dramatic practice. But it was Christopher Marlowe (1564–1593) who was to exploit the opportunities opening up for the professional dramatist most obviously and radically. In a characteristic gesture, Marlowe used the Prologue to *Tamburlaine the Great* (1587) to announce the superiority of both his theme and his method to all that had gone before him:

> From jigging veins of rhyming mother wits
> And such conceits as clownage keeps in pay,
> We'll lead you to the stately tent of war
> Where you shall hear the Scythian Tamburlaine
> Threatening the world with high astounding terms
> And scourging kingdoms with his conquering sword.[7]

After Kyd's experiments, playwrights were freer to employ explicitly immoral heroes in their drama, prompting a vogue for plays focused on men of ambition, tyrants, and Machiavells, Shakespeare's Richard III, Jonson's Sejanus, and, quintessentially, Marlowe's Tamburlaine, Duke of Guise, and Barabus (the eponymous *Jew of Malta*). The last named makes the link with Machiavellianism (at least as it was currently understood in England) explicit by having 'Machiavell' speak the Prologue, and appal conventional morality by declaring: 'I count religion but a childish toy, / And hold there is no sin but ignorance.'

The Senecan mode allowed secular, pre-Christian notions of morality and civic conduct to enter the theatre. Marlowe took that secularization a stage further, appropriating the still-potent didactic vehicle of moral drama, freeing it from its capacity to teach, and cavalierly asset-stripping it of its most affective theatrical features for his own use. The result was a play like *Faustus* which, unlike the clear-cut Moralities characteristic of the tradition, gives full value to both

---

[7] All quotations from Marlowe's work are taken from Roma Gill (ed.), *The Plays of Christopher Marlowe* (Oxford, 1971).

the exhilaration and the horror of the protagonist's pact with Mephistopheles and the very tangible benefits which it seems to offer him.

> Was this the face that launched a thousand ships
> And burnt the topless towers of Ilium?
> Sweet Helen, make me immortal with a kiss.
> Her lips suck forth my soul—see where it flies!
>
> (v. i. 98–101)

Along with the evident delight in exploiting the potential of the stage to represent such wonders as Helen of Troy, Marlowe adds to his narrative a powerful element of irony—at times savagely comic, at others merely savage—which unsettles any sense of stable moral orientation.

The audacious challenge which Marlowe threw down to both conventional morality and dramatic practice can be felt in the anxious response to his life and work from both the authorities and his fellow writers. The accusations of atheism and pederasty, the suggestions that he was involved in dark conspiracies, the hint of danger and excitement still attached to his name, all speak eloquently of a man who was provocatively out of step with the mainstream of his age. But it is a telling reflection of the pace at which the *avant-garde* was advancing in the theatre at the end of the century, and of the continuing demand for novelty generated by theatre audiences, that, within a decade, Marlowe's 'high astounding terms' were being burlesqued by Shakespeare in the sub-plot of *Henry IV, part I* and *Henry V* (even as he used them more conventionally to underpin his hero's speeches before Harfleur and at Agincourt). Simultaneously, the kind of radical challenge to conventional morality that had driven plays like *Tamburlaine* and *The Jew of Malta*, was being domesticated in the mouth of Falstaff. 'What is honour?', the latter asks, offering the unsettling answer: 'a word ... a breath ... nothing'.[8] Yet, such anarchic sentiments had become so unexceptionable that Elizabeth I herself (if tradition is to be believed) asked for more of the same, prompting the playwright to resurrect Falstaff in *The Merry Wives of Windsor*. The shock of the new had rapidly faded into the comfort of the familiar.

---

[8] All quotations from Shakespeare's plays are taken from P. Alexander (ed.), *The Complete Works of William Shakespeare: The Alexander Text* (London, 1951).

The contribution of the Renaissance to this new theatrical culture was considerable. For the playhouse dramatists and their audiences, classical literature provided a fund of historical and mythical figures, stories, and ideas that could be called upon to evoke moral, philosophical, political, or emotional themes and situations. So much is evident from the plays themselves. The theatres could fill houses with plays based on classical material: not simply the well-known stories of Julius Caesar or Mark Antony and Cleopatra, but also Coriolanus, Timon of Athens, and Catilina. The stages played Roman and Greek history almost as frequently as they played English. Clearly Elizabethan audiences were not alienated by material that modern audiences would consider highbrow and exclusive. But the common currency which the classics provided for those who had enjoyed any sort of professional schooling in the period is still more evident from the less obvious, almost casual allusions which consistently punctuate the plays, from the passing references to the myths of Actaeon and Arion in the first sixty-five lines of *Twelfth Night*, to the allusions to Hyperion, gods, and satyrs that litter Hamlet's upbraiding of his mother.

The pedagogic techniques of the humanist grammar schools, in which boys learnt by rote stories and adages from the classics, imitated them in their own compositions and in exercises in disputation, produced playwrights grounded in the skills necessary to write the highly rhetorical, disputatory, and allusive drama of the Elizabethan stages, and audiences predisposed to understand and appreciate its qualities. The dangers of all 'religions of the book', however, is that they can breed fundamentalism. In the case of Renaissance humanism this came in the form of an overly precise regard for the decorum in artistic forms which was thought to be characteristic of classical practice.

It was primarily, as we have seen, the heterogeneous quality of Renaissance drama that alarmed neo-classicists such as Sidney, whether their anxieties were social or aesthetic or both. The Elizabethan theatres were socially diverse institutions, but more importantly for their critics, they were tonally and thematically diverse. Sidney's criticisms of 'mongrel tragi-comedy', quoted at the head of this chapter, had a powerful influence on subsequent writers, critics, and playwrights alike. John Florio in his *Second Fruites* (1591) repeated them almost word for word, while in 1597, Joseph Hall rephrased the complaint, describing the 'goodly hoch poch' that results 'when vile Russetings / Are match't with monarchs'.[9] Some playwrights attempted to correct these assumed abuses and produce a drama characterized by decorum and classical principles. Sackville and Norton's *Gorboduc* (notably the only contemporary play for which Sidney expressed any enthusiasm) adopted the consistent seriousness of tone as well as the five-act structure and choruses of what its authors took to be 'pure' Senecan drama. And, most famously, Ben Jonson brought to the public stages a drama based on the unities of time, place, and action, and sought to remove the frivolous gestures and anachronisms which he felt marred the work of contemporaries like Shakespeare. Yet, even in the most successful 'classical' experiments of Jonson, such as *Volpone* (1606) and *The Alchemist* (1610), disparate matter is brought into explosive combination.

Hamlet bemoaned the fact that 'The toe of the peasant comes so near to the heal of the courtier, he galls his kibe' (v. i. 136–8), but these were clearly not the sentiments of his creator. The disorientating juxtaposition of high and low which so outraged Sidney and offended the archetypal university wit, Hamlet, clearly delighted Shakespeare. And, in the Globe theatre, if not the peasant, then at least the petty bourgeois, the artisan, the de-mobbed soldier, and the truant apprentice, all could rub shoulders (and heels) with courtiers, lawyers, and gentlefolk, witnessing a drama in which clowns and commoners, whores and drunkards, vied with revered icons of high culture such as Caesar and Brutus, Henry V, and Henry VIII for attention and sympathy, and in which all were played by actors who were themselves low-born artisans.

Throughout his career, Shakespeare explored such incongruities with relish, not least the sort of radical material and metaphorical transformation that might translate great Caesar, dead and turned to clay, into a bung to stop a privy wall. Throughout the plays the resonant names of the great are subjected to comic metamorphoses in the mouths of his clowns and fools. Alexander the Great becomes Alexander the Big, and thus in the Welsh accents of Llewellyn (in *Henry V*), 'Alexander the Pig'. Pompey the Great, played by the clown Costard in *Love's Labour's Lost*, becomes likewise, Pompey the Big, via the still more belittling malapropism 'Pompion the Great' (literally 'a

---

[9] A. Davenport (ed.), *The Poems of Joseph Hall* (Liverpool, 1969), 5.

pumpkin', but also slang for a fat oaf), a transformation brought to a climax in *Measure for Measure* in the crushing bathos of giving the name Pompey to the bawd, Master Bum:

ESCALUS. What's your name, Master Tapster?
POMPEY. Pompey.
ESCALUS. What else?
POMPEY. Bum, sir.
ESCALUS. Troth, and your bum is the greatest thing about you; so that, in the beastliest sense, you are Pompey the Great.

(II. ii. 202–8)

With such a spirit presiding, there was little room for the kind of classical decorum advocated by Jonson.

An alternative history of British drama—and owing to the limited nature of surviving texts, this will inevitably be largely a history of English drama—would thus chart, not only the vernacular play-wrights' gradual reception of classical elements from abroad, but also their continued resistance to them. A distinctly mongrel quality had also characterized medieval vernacular drama. The northern cycle plays brought Yorkshire shepherds and carpenters (in the guise of soldiers) into the action of the Nativity and the Crucifixion, and gave their contemporary complaints full dramatic value, even among the highest mysteries of the Christian story. The moral interludes of the late fifteenth and sixteenth centuries similarly mixed kings and commoners, philosophical questions and the broadest scatological comedy without any apparent sense of impropriety. This robust, indecorous, and accommodating vernacular tradition was not universally hostile to the spirit or methods of Renaissance classicism: it simply took from them what it wanted and adapted it to local practice. Thus, in the 1520s, John Heywood had adopted material from the French farces and *sotties* ('fool's plays') in his interludes. When British dramatists adapted classical material, they did so creatively, turning it into something rich and strange. When they looked to Greek and Roman writers for their inspiration, they unsurprisingly favoured the more accommodating, mongrel sort of author whose work suited their own disposition and practice. They looked to Eurip-ides, Plautus, and the protean spirit of Ovid over Sophocles, Terence, or the precepts of Aristotle. And, even when they adapted Seneca, they did so in ways that compromised his universal seriousness and

Figure 8  The mongrel drama: classical and contemporary costumes mixed in a performance of Shakespeare's *Titus Andronicus*.

gravity of tone, reducing the ghost in Hamlet to an old mole in the cellarage. However much he might mock the pedantic generic confusions of the 'pastoral, tragical comical' theatre of his predecessors, Shakespeare was their heir. He was in one sense a classical, Renaissance playwright, but his was a classicism that used and abused the classics rather than felt itself hidebound by them.

In *Hamlet*, written at the very end of our century, Shakespeare offered an implicit summation and critique of its cultural and intellectual achievements. Hamlet himself is frequently cited as the archetypal Renaissance man: prince and poet, duellist and drama critic, he is the definitive product of the humanist dream to fashion a governor in the image of the man of letters. Yet he is also the bearer of the burden of guilt and doubt that the century had created. Self-aware, he voices the uncertainties that seem to characterize humanity on the cusp of modernity. Humanism, with its positive reassertion of human dignity is subjected to devastating qualification: 'What a piece of work is man! how noble in reason! how infinite in faculties . . . in action, how like an angel! in apprehension, how like a god! the beauty of the world! the paragon of animals! And yet, to me, what is this quintessence of dust? Man delights not me—no, nor woman either' (II. ii. 300–8). The individualistic turn of humanism is turned back upon itself, as the rational mind rejects the tendency to venerate itself ('And yet, *to me*, what is this quintessence of dust?'). The spiritual anxieties born of sixty years of Reformation and Counter-Reformation are also powerfully evoked. Barred by Protestant theology from freely indulging his instinctive belief in his father's ghost, Hamlet is forced to doubt its credibility and thus bring upon himself the guilt-inducing delay. Yet the play itself seems to endorse the Catholic interpretation of the spirit's purgatorial origins. And Hamlet, although a graduate of Luther's own university at Wittenburg, is still haunted by a very unreformed sense of his own sinfulness, a product of his own works rather than of predestination. 'I am myself indifferent honest, but yet I could accuse me of such things that it were better my mother had not borne me . . . What should such fellows as I do crawling between earth and heaven?' (III. i. 121–8). The Machiavellian notion that politics was, beneath the new clothes of moral conduct, a matter of naked self-interest, also haunts the play in the figure of Claudius, an eloquent politician who has come to power through the murder of his brother. Here Shakespeare began mining a theologically sceptical, tragic seam which would ultimately lead to the nihilism of *King Lear* (1605), in which Gloucester's declaration 'as flies to wanton boys are we to th'gods—They kill us for their sport' (IV. i. 37–8) proves to be an over-optimistic reading of the human condition. In such a world, the humanist dream of improving the world through the power of eloquence is reduced to the inarticulate despair of Lear's 'howl, howl, howl' (v. iii. 257), which acts as a terse summation of the play's philosophy. But *Lear* was a Jacobean rather than an Elizabethan play. It is to the histories rather than the mature tragedies that we should look for the most characteristic concerns of Shakespeare at the *fin de siècle*. For, in turning to English history and chronicle for his material, the playwright was part of a far wider trend.

# National histories

Humanist historiography was introduced into England with More's *History of King Richard III* and the *Anglica Historia* of the Italian scholar Polydore Vergil (?1470–?1555). These works brought a new and critical approach to the material they represented. Although they were not as thoroughly free of the mythologies of the past as they sometimes claimed, their authors nonetheless sought to apply standards of evidential scrutiny and analytical rigour closer to what they saw as the practice of classical historians such as Livy and Tacitus than to the medieval chroniclers. Edward Hall's *Union of the Two Noble and Illustre Families of Lancaster and York* (the first edition of which was printed in 1542), and Raphael Holinshed's *Chronicles* (1577), derived in great part from Hall, took this process further. They produced synoptic histories of England (and in Holinshed's case, Britain) which incorporated documentary sources and eyewitness accounts (Hall was himself a member of the House of Commons during the Reformation Parliament) into a teleological narrative in which the accession of the House of Tudor fulfilled the nation's destiny, bringing an end to the 'calamitous' civil wars of the fifteenth century and uniting the English people in a single, powerful, Protestant nation. This version of English history was given a still more strident embodiment in John Foxe's *Actes and Monuments*, the Latin edition of which was published in 1559, with the first English text following in 1563. Again a powerfully deterministic Protestant version of history was combined with a careful consideration of the relevant documentary sources, diligently gathered from bishops' registers, correspondence, and the testimony of surviving witnesses. North of the Tweed, John Knox's *History of the Reformation* (written *c*.1556–7 and printed in 1586) offered a similar, if more personally aggrandizing genealogy for Scottish Protestants, bringing Knox's infamously combative prose style to the task of forging a national history.

The mixture of political polemicism and concern for documentary accuracy which characterized Foxe's work was the basis for the new sense of nationalism characteristic of the last decades of the century. When under pressure to justify their own dissenting positions, British Protestant polemicists sought to establish the authenticity of their own claims and positions by looking to history. The result was, if not the invention, then at least the conscious rethinking of the national heritage, a process that found expression not only in the political and religious narratives of Hall and Foxe, but also in the creation of literary histories such as John Bale's *Scriptorum Illustrium Maioris Brittanicae Catalogus* (1557–9), or Puttenham's *Arte of English Poesie* and, most powerfully, in legislation. As Henry VIII's Act of Appeals (1533) declared, 'by diverse sundry old authentic histories and chronicles, it is manifestly declared and expressed that this realm of England is an Empire'. Similarly, this attempt to document a national identity was reflected at a local level in the rise of regional and civic histories, of which John Stow's *Survey of London* (1598) is perhaps the best known example.

The renewed interest in historiography was not, however, a unified movement. At the heart of the enterprise lay the humanist desire to rescue the true origins of the nation from the myths which clouded earlier accounts (as George Buchanan put it, 'to free our ancient history from the uncertainty of fable, and rescue it from oblivion'), but, as one writer's myth is another's authentic early history, this led inevitably to disagreement. Different agenda dominated practice in the different nations of Britain, and correspondingly diverse versions of historical truth were advanced. The founding myths of Welsh nationhood, chiefly the 'British History', promulgated by Geoffrey of Monmouth, in which Britain was founded by Brutus, great-grandson of the Trojan hero Aeneas, came under sustained attack from

Polydore Vergil, and were criticized to differing degrees by subsequent English historians such as William Camden. The resurgence
of Welsh history writing in the later sixteenth century was in great
part a response to this attack. In the 1540s, Sir John Prys had drafted
his *Historiae Brytannicae Defensio* (eventually published posthumously by Prys's son Richard in 1573), a direct defence of
Geoffrey's account. In 1584, Dr David Powel of Ruabon (1552?–1598)
completed the *Historie of Cambria now called Wales*, which built upon
the medieval chronicler's claims and brought his narrative up to date.

The Scottish historiographical tradition was, however, far less
closely wedded to the 'British History', and was consequently freer
to follow the sceptical line advanced by Vergil. The Latin *Scottorum
Historiae*, of Hector Boece, published in Paris in 1527, and the Scots
translation made by John Bellenden in 1531, consciously employed
Latin models, reading domestic events in the light of Livy's account
of the Roman kings and early Republic. In their narratives, as in
George Buchanan's magisterial *Rerum Scoticarum Historia* (1582),
the Brutus story was given short shrift. The equally mythical alternative, however, in which Scotland owed its origins to a Greek hero,
Gathelus, and his Egyptian bride Scota, was treated with greater
sympathy. Even humanist objectivity, it seems, would bow to
national pride.

In Ireland, history writing had a still more overtly political agenda,
inextricably linked as it was to the defence of traditional culture
against the imposition of English rule. After the Dissolution, a number of the more significant monastic annals were continued by lay
scribes, and these, with the histories of the great provincial families
formed the bulk of Irish historiography in the period. Something of
the humanist impulse can be detected in the *Life* of St Colum Cille
produced around 1532 under the direction of Maghnus Ó Domhnaill,
Lord of Tír Conaill (*c*.1490–1564). Ó Domhnaill, a poet as well as a
historian and hagiographer, attested to the educational agenda
behind the *Life* in his preface, describing how he had taken pains to
collate material from disparate manuscripts, translating from Latin
and 'hard Gaelic' into colloquial Gaelic in order to reach the widest
possible audience.

The most obvious arenas for the popularization of national history, were, however, not scholarly tomes, but poetic 'histories' such as
*The Mirror for Magistrates* (first published in 1559) and Edmund

Spenser's *Faerie Queene* (1589–96), which freely incorporated myth-ical material into its chivalric genealogy of England's Protestant heri-tage, and most powerfully, the work of the London theatres. Chief among the latter were the history plays of Shakespeare, in which a powerfully affective mimetic dimension complemented the potent rhetoric of the chronicle texts. In the first part of *Henry VI*, the playwright had fed the popular taste for heroic national drama with the figure of Talbot, whose martial exploits in France were the sub-stance of the play. Thomas Nashe (1567–1601) offered some idea of the popularity of this enterprise, when he described how 'ten thousand spectators at least, at several times' wept for Talbot, because 'in the tragedian that represents his person they imagine they behold him fresh bleeding'.[10]

The strong association between nation-building and history writ-ing was clearly appreciated by Shakespeare. The way that the crude matter of past events, could be selected, shaped, and given meaning in a satisfying narrative, itself became the subject of drama. In *Henry V* the whole enterprise was carefully reappraised. The play famously divides its attention between two distinct time frames—the historical time of the Agincourt campaign and the contemporary time in which those events are represented to the audience as drama, a process commented on in a highly self-conscious way by the Chorus. The latter makes sport of apologizing for the limited resources with which the Elizabethan theatre could attempt to bring the French campaign, like the long-dead Talbot, back to life.

> . . . pardon, gentles all,
> The flat unraised spirits that hath dar'd
> On this unworthy scaffold to bring forth
> So great an object. Can this cockpit hold
> The vasty fields of France? Or may we cram
> Within this wooden O the very casques
> That did afright the air at Agincourt?
>
> (8–14)

But he also brings to the audience's attention the ways in which that necromantic enterprise involves an inevitable shaping of the events.

---

[10] Thomas Nashe, *Pierce Penniless his Supplication to the Devil*, most readily access-ible in Thomas Nashe, *The Unfortunate Traveller and Other Works*, ed. J. B. Stearne (Harmondsworth, 1972), 113.

On your imaginary forces work.
Suppose within the girdle of these walls
Are now confin'd two mighty monarchies
...
Piece out our imperfections with your thoughts
...
For 'tis your thoughts that now must deck our kings . . .
(18–20, 23, 28)

Subsequent scenes do not, however, fully live up to the Chorus's high expectations. Rather than seeing mighty monarchies and clashing armies, the play gives us two clerics, Canterbury and Ely, plotting to deflect a parliamentary assault on church property by inciting Henry to invade France. The motives for the great patriotic war are thus called into question before the king has even appeared on the stage. Each subsequent act similarly juxtaposes a triumphalist Chorus with more bathetic action. The question is not whether Henry is or is not a hero—that is left unresolved, or rather he both is and is not heroic by turns in the course of the plot. Similarly it is not possible to say whether the English are shown to be a nation vindicated by the god of battles or a band of disputatious mercenaries who simply get lucky. The material is there to support both interpretations, what matters is who is doing the interpreting.

# The architectural Renaissance

As we have seen, literature in English failed to follow a simple narrative in which the humanist 'rediscovery' of Greek and Roman principles led to a steady and enthusiastic development of classical styles in vernacular practice. In domestic architecture and the visual arts the story was similar. In architecture, of course, tradition and history come in the very concrete and visible form of existing structures which the designer has to incorporate into any new work. Only rarely did an early modern patron have either the luxury of a bare site on which to indulge his or her imagination, or the wealth and liberty completely to level an existing building and start afresh. Hybridity and compromise were thus inevitable features of most sixteenth-century buildings.

In architectural terms the century was one of considerable activity. The Dissolution of the English and Welsh monasteries in the late 1530s and (far more gradually) the Scottish Reformation after 1560, released a large amount of land onto the market, land that was snapped up by old and new families who saw opportunities to make a financial killing and enhance their status in their local communities. The natural recourse was to build new 'power houses' on the acquired lands, to show that they were literally there to stay. This relative boom in secular domestic building did not, however, lead to any major shifts in design. Not until the seventeenth century and the renewal of royal patronage on a significant scale under the Stewart kings was there any consistent application of neo-classical principles to English architecture.

There were individuals who appreciated the theoretical foundations of the continental Renaissance: the importance of proportion, symmetry, and the classical orders in the construction of buildings, for example, and the sparing use of classical ornament in their decoration. One could thus—just about—chart a 'history' of Renaissance building in Britain, in which the reception of continental ideas could be traced from the reign of Henry VIII, when men such as Sir William Sharrington at Lacock Abbey, Wiltshire, and Sir Richard Weston at Sutton Place, Surrey, built or rebuilt their houses using ideas that they had encountered on the continent. Such a history would then notice with satisfaction the enthusiastic and more thoroughgoing adoption of classical principles by the circle around Protector Somerset in the late 1540s which was to produce Syon House, Middlesex, and Somerset House on the Strand, before moving on to chronicle the employment of Renaissance motifs in the prodigy houses of the Elizabethan period, and features such as the classically proportioned gatehouse and storeyed porch added at Beaupré (St Hilary, Glamorgan) between 1586 and 1600. But to isolate these houses as the significant elements in the history of domestic architecture would be entirely to misrepresent the bulk of building activity at the time. Renaissance ideas and values were only rarely comprehensively applied in practice (at Beaupré, for example, a late gothic archway was also added in this same period), and, even when they were, the results were not always appreciated and imitated by contemporaries. When Sir William Thynne reworked his house at Longleat in Wiltshire along classical lines, replacing late medieval

irregularity with a comprehensively symmetrical design, his aspirations were derided by his neighbour William Darnell of Littlecote,
who clearly saw them as ludicrous, and wrote a satirical poem to
demonstrate the point.

Evolutionary narratives based upon the gradual development of
Renaissance sensibilities in Britain also face difficulties accounting for
the evidence of funerary sculpture. Although examples of work
clearly influenced by classical style can be noted, such as Bishop
Gardiner's chantry chapel in Winchester Cathedral, or the Vaughan
monument in Llanddwywe in Wales, a clear developmental model is
difficult to apply. Generally speaking, the fruits of the continental
Renaissance were plundered piecemeal by British builders and their
patrons, and applied in an often apparently haphazard manner to
projects conceived in traditional medieval terms. And in this the
crown tended to lead the way. Significantly, given the doubts surrounding the origins of the literary Renaissance, it was again through
French example rather than directly from Italy that the inspiration
frequently came.

Nonsuch Palace, begun in 1539, is perhaps the pinnacle of the architectural achievements of Henry VIII's reign. The building itself (of
which only the foundations survive), centred on a symmetrical
double-courtyard pattern and was largely unexceptional. It was the
decorative scheme that justified its claim to the title of nonpareil. On
the inner and outer elevations, images of the liberal arts and cardinal
virtues, of the Roman emperors and the labours of Hercules, turned
the building into a bravura display of humanist learning, an architectural equivalent of the handbooks for governors of men such as
Castiglione and Elyot. The decorative work was borrowed from the
designs for Francis I's palace at Fontainebleau, where Italian craftsmen such as Rosso Fiorentino and the Mantuan Francesco Primaticcio were at work. Henry's ambassador, Sir Henry Wallop was kept
busy writing reports of the progress of the French project, and when
Henry initiated work at Nonsuch, he imported the Fontainebleau
spirit at second hand, luring the Italian stuccoist Nicholas Bellin of
Modena, who had worked under Primaticcio, and others to add the
decorative programme to a structural frame erected by English
artisans. The other great palace building project of Henry's reign, the
extension of Hampton Court (acquired from Cardinal Wolsey after
1525 and happily still standing) shows a similar parasitic spirit. Wolsey

had built a palace fundamentally gothic in design, albeit constructed on a grand scale. To these traditional foundations, a smattering of Renaissance chic was added in the form of the terracotta medallions on the courtyard turrets. These were the work of the Florentine sculptor Giovanni da Maiano. Again, continental workmen had been imported to produce the classical flourishes to a work constructed on traditional lines.

Future reigns did little to alter this trend. The sheer volume rather than the quality of Henry's building projects won him the palm as the century's leading British royal builder. But, after his death no further palaces were built in Tudor England. The political instability of the mid-Tudor years was followed by a reign characterized by Elizabeth's tendency to progress around the palaces of her leading subjects rather than build any new homes of her own. This lack of royal patronage had a decisive effect upon domestic fashions. Had Elizabeth planned a new palace, she would have been forced to match her fellow princes in both the scale and the design of the building. The result would almost inevitably have been something recognizably classical in inspiration. Her courtiers would then have been likely to follow suit. As it was, the situation did not arise. The queen remained in the essentially gothic palaces designed by her father, leaving her courtiers free to continue to experiment with traditional forms in the houses they built in the last third of the century.

The Elizabethan prodigy houses mark a return to medieval conceptions of taste rather than a confident striding forward into the full implementation of earlier Renaissance experiments. William Cecil's houses at Burghley and Theobalds, Sir Christopher Hatton's Holdenby, and Sir Francis Willoughby's Wollaton Hall, Nottinghamshire, all show a remarkably productive mingling of Renaissance ideas with older gothic notions of style (the latter a product of the chivalric revival fostered by the Queen's Accession Day tilts and the vogue for Chaucer and medieval romance at court which was reinvigorated by Spenser's *Faerie Queene*). Wollaton Hall, designed by Robert Smythson (1534/5–1614) between 1580 and 1588, is a splendid example of this mongrel spirit at its most fantastic. Based upon a regular rectangular design with towers in all four corners, it employs the classical orders with confidence on each of its elevations, yet the end result is not a monument to classical decorum but a *jeu d'esprit*, in which bravura decorative details and walls of windows overwhelm the eye, while the roofline suggests sketches towards an Arthurian castle. The overall effect is one of virtuosity in action, as in the best of the sonnet sequences, the creative interplay between the self-discipline of the symmetry and the flamboyant display of the decoration creating a whole far greater than the sum of its parts. Clearly employing the fruits of a classical education for its own ends, Wollaton is nonetheless 'classical' in only the most tenuous of senses: a creation which is distinctly vernacular, both in effect and inspiration.

As in England and Wales, so in Scotland: a dearth of palace building after the death of James V deprived the Scots of the sort of inspirational royal patronage necessary to impose and popularize an imported style on the nation at large. During James's lifetime a number of experiments with Renaissance techniques had hinted at a more thoroughgoing flirtation with continental style. Again, as was the case in the literary sphere, the closer relations with the continent, especially France, enabled Scotland to appreciate and investigate European fashions rather more fully than was possible in an increasingly isolated England. Like Henry VIII, James had imported French craftsmen to work on his royal palaces, most notably on Falkland Palace, which was reworked between 1537 and 1541 for Mary of Lorraine. The palace consequently represents an injection of French Renaissance aesthetic taken pure and from the source, rather than mediated at second hand through the observations of visitors or via pattern books. The combination of attached columns and paired portrait medallions on the upper storeys presents an imposing classical façade reminiscent of the contemporary work on the palaces of the Loire. Characteristically, though, as was the case in England, the Renaissance façade is attached to a pre-existing, and very Scottish palace structure. A similar spirit of inspired improvisation and compromise suffuses the work on Stirling Castle, begun in 1540 and unfinished on James's death, which combined twisting columns reminiscent of contemporary German and Spanish work with Moorish-looking cusped arches, and gargoyles and statues in a northern European idiom, the whole ensemble adorning an otherwise solid, vernacular grey-stone building.

With the King's death, and the onset of another period of unstable minority government, royal patronage effectively ceased, and the initiative passed to the gentry and aristocracy, whose preoccupation with security against English invasion and civil disorder coloured their building plans. Once the return of Mary, queen of Scots seemed to herald a degree of domestic stability, however, an upsurge in domestic building projects followed. The characteristic medieval towerhouse that dominated Scottish and Irish medieval architecture—defensively strong and relatively economical to build and maintain—began to be modified to include slightly more exuberant features, extra wings and greater elaboration of decoration on the safer, upper stories, such as the ornate corbels at Fyvie Castle, Aberdeenshire, the playfully nostalgic gargoyles in the form of cannons at Castle Fraser and Craigievar (both again in Aberdeenshire), or the conical cap-houses of Crathes castle. The result was a rather more uneasy compromise between disciplined construction and expressive decoration than was evident in the English prodigy houses. But again, while it clearly drew upon French motifs and sensibilities, the result would hardly be recognized as a product of the Renaissance by anyone schooled rigorously in the Palladian principles. A fine example is Fyvie Castle, which was remodelled at the very end of the century for Alexander Seton, first earl of Dumfermline. The south front presents a striking symmetrical design, centred on a breathtaking roof-line archway, but the overall style of the construction, evident especially in the three non-symmetrical sides, resembles in most other respects a traditional castellated house in the local Aberdeenshire style.

In Scotland and England alike, royal building was hampered by a lack of finance, or of the will to employ the available wealth in major building projects. But it was also held back by the lack of a secure notion of the role and status of the architect. Like the writer of plays, the designer of buildings struggled in this period to overcome a social stigma which placed his profession among the craftsmen rather than the artists. Only in the seventeenth century did the role acquire, chiefly through the career of Inigo Jones, a status commensurate with the nature and scale of the work it involved. There were men whose work can now be recognized as encompassing the responsibilities and skills of the modern architect, chiefly Robert Smythson, the designer of Wollaton, and William Schaw (1550–1602), James VI's Master of Works in Scotland, both of whom were dubbed with the new-fangled term 'architect' by their contemporaries. The former, however, never really shook off his artisanal roots, and is buried in the modest parish church of St Leonard's, Wollaton, within view of perhaps his greatest achievement. Schaw, by contrast, a scion of the laird class, had the advantages of gentle birth and a place at court, and thus could more legitimately claim to foreshadow Inigo Jones as a designer rather than a builder. He also had the opportunity to travel abroad and imbibe directly the continental ideas which inform his decorous neo-classical designs. Yet the relative obscurity which even Schaw enjoyed when contrasted with the celebrity of Jones only a generation later provides a sobering reflection on the status of the architect in the sixteenth century.

# The impact of the Reformation on the arts

As Chapter 3 of this volume reveals, the Renaissance and the desire for religious reform were initially allied in Erasmian humanism. But the alliance was short-lived. The reception of Lutheran ideas into Britain divided the scholarly community, and Henry VIII's break with Rome widened and complicated the divisions. Thus, Thomas More and William Tyndale, fellow scholars with interests in the Greek language and biblical translation became implacable enemies, both ultimately dying for their beliefs. In Wales, both Gruffyd Robert and John Davies of Brecon were forced to flee the country, the latter ultimately to Milan, where he wrote his Welsh Grammar. Still more striking were the large numbers of Irishmen who, alienated by the religious changes imposed by the English administration, flocked to the new colleges at Douai, Louvain, and elsewhere.

The Dissolution of the English, Welsh, and Irish monasteries between 1536 and 1540 destroyed centres of scholarship that had flourished for centuries. In Wales, the Cistercians had been particularly active in the patronage of the arts, especially vernacular poetry, and the loss of their influence was sorely felt. An equally grave blow to education was dealt by the suppression of the Welsh friaries, chantries, and religious guilds, albeit some reforming bishops attempted to rectify the loss in the medium term through the establishment of new grammar schools, such as that founded by William Barlow in Brecon in 1541. In England, it was the loss of the Benedictine houses and the colleges for the regular clergy at Oxford and Cambridge which dispersed priceless book collections and removed sources of livelihood for authors and scholars alike. In Ireland, it was a similar story, although, again, humanist schools like those run by Peter White in Waterford and Alexander Lynch in Galway, attempted to fill the gap, while the founding of Trinity College, Dublin, in 1592, belatedly provided education at a higher level on Irish soil.

The suppression of English religious drama by zealous Protestant bureaucrats wiped out over the course of a generation a communal art form which had characterized the cities of the north and elsewhere for more than two centuries. The play cycles of York, Chester, and Wakefield were only the most prominent representatives of a dramatic culture which flourished across the midlands and northern counties of England and much of Scotland. It has been claimed that the plays were the victims of concerted governmental censorship, but in reality the initiative came at a lower level of local administration, as Protestant activists used their influence to purge practices which they thought superstitious, or about which they were dubious, on their own initiative. Crucially, however, they produced nothing substantial enough to replace it. The experimental Protestant dramas of John Bale and his successors were too exclusive and too obviously imposed from above to gain popular acceptability. And this, as we have seen, left the field clear for the professional, secular theatre of the London playhouse companies to stake its claim to be the provider of drama to the nation. The second half of the century saw increasing hostility to drama and to travelling players across Britain, and in the mid-1570s the more advanced Protestants in the City of London turned their attentions to the new commercial playhouses, whose trade they thought godless and licentious. Only the protection of the Crown and influential court patrons such as the earl of Leicester saved the theatres from going the same way as the York cycle, but the acting companies had to endure withering salvos of invective from their detractors in texts such as Stubbes's *Anatomy of Abuses* and Gosson's *Schoole of Abuse*.

It was, however, the visual arts that suffered most immediately from the Reformation. The wholesale destruction of 'popish' images in parish churches ended a rich visual culture that had flourished for over 600 years, dominating both elite and popular consciousness in ways which were never matched or recovered. The consequences involved not only the long-term aesthetic impoverishment of the people, but also the immediate practical diminution of opportunities for the countless sculptors, printers, glaziers, and woodcarvers who had been responsible for constructing, beautifying, and maintaining the church fabric, icons, images, windows, roods and roodlofts. This and the disappearance—or partial suppression—of a whole series of festive practices such as mayings and folkplays, gave rise to a powerful sense of nostalgia among many of those who recalled the old ways, or resented the new. Thus was born the idea of a lost paradise, not merely of Merry England, but of Merry Scotland, Merry Ireland, and Merry Wales too, in which things had been better, before, as Thomas Howard, 3rd duke of Norfolk, had grumbled, 'the new learning came up'.[11] In Scotland, Sir Richard Maitland of Lethington (1496–1596) expressed similar sentiments a generation or more later, eloquently lamenting the destructive effects of Reformation discipline on the festive culture he recalled from his youth.

> Quhair [i.e. where] is the blyithnes [jollity] that hes beine,
> Baith in burgh and landwart sene,
> Amang lordis and ladyis schene,
> Daunsing, singing, game and play?
> Bot now I wait [i.e. know] not quhat thay meine,
> All merines is worne away.[12]

The impact of the Reformation on the visual arts was not, however, entirely negative. Efforts were made to replace lost festivals with new ones, notably the annual celebrations of Elizabeth's Accession Day and the defeat of the Armada. And the Reformation provided a massive stimulus to the print industry through the production of works of controversy and instruction. Three works in particular had an immeasurable impact upon subsequent cultural life. The Tyndale and Coverdale Bibles and Cranmer's *Book of Common Prayer* introduced into English a simple yet numinous prose style that reverberates through subsequent literature throughout the British Isles. A similar impact and influence was exerted upon Welsh by the biblical translation of William Morgan (*c*.1541–1604), published originally in 1588, then newly edited and revised in 1620. This Welsh Authorized Version provided the Welsh language with an enduring example of formal

[11] J. S. Brewer, et al. (eds.), *Letters and Papers, Foreign and Domestic of the Reign of Henry VIII* (21 vols. in 33 parts; London, 1862–1920), XVI, 101.
[12] W. A. Craigie (ed.), *The Maitland Quarto Manuscript*, Scottish Text Society (Edinburgh, 1920).

style and vocabulary that, in the absence of a native royal court or university to set and maintain the linguistic gold standard, did much to foster a unified, high literary Welsh in the centuries that followed.

The stress upon the Word did not wholly eradicate the powerful effectiveness of the image. In elite society, aristocratic funerary sculpture quickly replaced religious imagery with heraldic and symbolic devices. More popularly, the sensationalist prints in John Foxe's *Actes and Monuments* provided on a far more limited scale something of the communal religious culture that the icons and images of the Catholic Church had offered. The memorable scenes of martyrdom had a profound effect upon Foxe's readers and at least in part account for the enduring popularity of the *Actes and Monuments*. Many of the prints may even have been detached and pasted upon walls to provide improving decoration for godly households. This new Protestant iconography was, however, poor recompense for the destruction done to the rich visual culture of medieval Britain by the advocates of reform.

# Music in the sixteenth century: Reformation and Renaissance

Nowhere in the arts were the Dissolution and the Reformation felt more fundamentally and to such devastating effect than in music, specifically in the ecclesiastical sphere, where an entire medium— Catholic liturgical music—was almost completely dismembered. Of the other two major cultural phenomena stressed in this chapter, the neo-classical revival and the rise of the metropolis, the former was of only limited importance for music, and the latter was itself intrinsically linked with the course of the Reformation.

With the Dissolution of the larger monastic houses after 1538 went many of the institutions capable of sustaining substantial choirs, and as a result the career and training opportunities for subsequent generations of choristers and composers were drastically diminished. With the Edwardian Reformation in England and Wales and the Scottish Reformation, the Latin liturgical music composed for choral performance was denounced as popish, and a sparer, less adorned idiom which foregrounded the text (without stretching a verbal syllable over many notes) was favoured in its place. Archbishop Cranmer had stressed the importance in the new dispensation of rescuing the sacred Word from the accompanying music in a letter to Henry VIII in 1544. 'The song that shall be made for the English service would not be full of notes, but, as near as may be, for every syllable a note, so that it may be sung distinctly and devoutly.' It was a principle which the Elizabethan Injunctions of 1559 were to reiterate, establishing that the music should become wholly subservient to the sense of the verbal text: 'that the same should be as plainly understood as if it were read without singing'.[13]

Prior to the Reformation, composers such as Thomas Tallis (c.1505–1585) and John Taverner (c.1490–1545) in England and Robert Jones (c.1485–1535) in Wales had specialized in an intricate, flamboyant, polyphonic style in which the complexities of the interweaved melody lines had dominated the work, often threatening to obscure the words that were being sung in the process. This distinctly insular style owed little to continental trends and was the source of considerable admiration from foreign visitors. In 1515, for example, a Venetian diplomat noted of Henry VIII's choristers that their 'voices are more divine than human . . . they probably have not their equal in the world'. In Scotland, Robert Carver (c.1490-post 1546) wrote in a similar idiom, but with greater apparent debt to continental styles, as his *Missa l'homme armé*, based upon a French *chanson*, demonstrates. With the Reformation composers had to curb their more flamboyant instincts and subordinate melody to the text in the approved Protestant fashion.

The destruction of the monasteries, chantries, and religious colleges had the effect of reducing the ecclesiastical musical profession to a few strongholds, in England chiefly in the major cathedral schools and those royal establishments that clustered around London. Outside these, the lot of the chorister was a bleak one. Indeed, it is safe to say that only the enlightened patronage of musicians by Elizabeth's Chapel Royal kept English sacred music alive in the latter part of the century, providing the safe haven for men like William Byrd (1543–1623) and Tallis who would otherwise have fallen foul of the reformist suspicion of complex polyphonic music. The, so-called, golden age of Elizabethan church music was thus built upon very small and precarious foundations.

[13] Bruce Patterson, *Music and Poetry of the English Renaissance* (London, 1948), 84.

The role of the Chapel Royal in protecting men whose instincts were more conservative than the current climate allowed is most dramatically demonstrated in the career of Byrd, the most gifted English composer of the period. A committed Catholic, Byrd was able to make his living, and his reputation, writing anthems and services in the vernacular spare style for Anglican worship. Outside his official employment, however, he composed Latin motets and settings of the mass and liturgical music. In the wake of the execution of the Jesuit Edmund Campion and his fellow missionaries in December 1581, Byrd composed a setting of the seventy-eighth Psalm: 'They have reduced Jerusalem to ruins. They have left the corpses of your servants to the birds of the air for food, and the flesh of your devout to the beasts of the field.' It was a fitting epitaph for Catholic musical culture in the period as well as a plangent lament for the courageous sacrifice of Byrd's co-religionists.

Lower down the social scale, there was a great expansion later in the century in playing and singing for pleasure and edification. Metrical psalms for the godly and lute songs, consort songs, and airs for the more worldly, became popular, fuelling a growing market in printed scores. From the late 1580s onwards, the 'craze' for the madrigal, scored for a cappella voices or accompanied by one or more lutes, almost exactly mirrored the contemporary enthusiasm for the sonnet. Like the sonnet, the madrigal, and the music for consorts of viols, pleasurably linked intense discipline (in the highly structured vocal line) with opportunities for virtuoso display (in the subject matter of the lyrics and the free play of the viols). Thomas Morley's *Plain and Easy Introduction to Practical Music* (1597) made plain the principles behind the madrigal, showing how the music must closely follow the sense or mood of the lyric, ascending or descending, for example, to accompany allusions to height or depth, exultation or dejection. 'If the subject be light, you must cause your music [to] go in motions, which carry with them a celerity or quickness of time, as minimes, crotchets and quavers; if it be lamentable, the note must go in slow and heavy motions, as semibreves, breves, and such like.'[14]

By the end of the century, English composers such as Byrd, John Dowland (1563–1626), Orlando Gibbons (1583–1625), and Thomas

---

[14] Thomas Morley's *Plain and Easy Introduction*, quoted in B. Patterson, *Music and Poetry of the English Renaissance* (London, 1948), 105.

Morley (1557/8–1602) had re-established an international reputation for English music. But, again it is important to note the limits of the new, continental influences upon domestic practice. Beyond the high-profile music of the social elites, a whole subculture of musical activity flourished which was less directly influenced by the Italianate culture of the madrigals. The tradition of urban music, embodied in the groups known as the town waits continued throughout the century, despite the efforts of reformers to limit and prescribe their activities. Originally created by their civic employers as nightwatch-men, the waits quickly became municipal musicians-in-residence, gracing 'feasts and solemn meetings' with their diverse repertoire.

# The arts and politics

It was a central tenet of the humanist educational programme that the true nobleman, like the true courtier, needed to combine the martial virtues of the knight with the intellectual refinement of the scholar and poet. Hence the sixteenth century saw a marked increase in the number of aristocrats who exercised the pen as well as the sword. In this they were only following the example of their sover-eigns, for Henry VIII was a musician, composer, and lyricist, James VI a poet and literary critic, and Elizabeth I a musician, translator, and poet of considerable accomplishment. Their own creative endeavours set the tone for the wider political culture. And, in the reign of Eliza-beth, literary accomplishment became a still more functional political asset, as a conscious reinvigoration of the poetry of *fin amour* estab-lished a culture and discourse which enabled members of the male political elite to relate comfortably to an unmarried, female ruler.

Such men as Wyatt or Sidney used literary forms to express their political ambitions and anxieties, confident that this was both a fitting form of expression for a gentleman and an effective means of gaining and influencing an audience for their views. When Wyatt sought a means of expressing his dissatisfaction at his lack of favour at court in the mid-1530s, he looked to poetic satire as the most affective and dignified way of making the point. Using the tenth *Satira* of Alamanni as his model, he characterized his absence from court, in 'Mine Own John Poyntz', as a stoic retreat into rural retirement, where he could find true virtue 'in Kent and Christendom / Among the Muses where I read and rhyme'.

A still more effective way of addressing an elite audience was through courtly drama, in which an author could be assured of a captive royal audience for the duration of the two or so hours traffic of an interlude. Even so influential a politician as Sir David Lindsay, Scotland's chief herald and a close confidante of James V, saw virtue in Hamlet's dictum that, 'The play's the thing / To catch the conscience of the king'. He produced his most eloquent and enduring appeal for religious and social reform in the form of a drama, *Ane Satyre of the Thrie Estaitis*, first produced before the king at Linlithgow in 1540, and subsequently much reworked and expanded for public performance at Edinburgh and Cupar (Fife) in the 1550s. That, in this case at least, art had a direct and immediate impact on politics is clear. Immediately following the 1540 performance, King James (who may well have encouraged Lindsay to write in order to provide just such an opportunity) summoned the bishop of Glasgow and 'diverse other bishops' to him and 'exhorted them to reform their factions and manners of living, saying that unless they so did, he would send six of the proudest of them unto his uncle of England [Henry VIII], and as those were ordered, so he would order all the rest that would not mend'.[15]

Examples such as these suggest both the importance of literature and drama to the life of the early modern court and the negotiative quality of the political culture to which they contributed. The courtly arts of the period were not all about prince-pleasing and sycophancy, even during the reign of Elizabeth I. Rather than the temple of a secular religion, the court was an arena for dialogue and debate, especially when, as was the case with James VI in Scotland, the sovereign actively encouraged robust discussion on important political issues. But, even where courtly protocols were more rigidly adhered to, the traces of debates can be detected, provided one knows where to look and how to decode the subtle language of counsel and the nuances of praise in which they were conducted. Even panegyric itself, the most overtly fulsome of literary forms, had its negotiative element. As Erasmus wrote to Jean Desmarais, such hymns of praise

---

[15] Douglas Hamer (ed.), *The Works of Sir David Lindsay of the Mount* (4 vols.; Edinburgh, 1936), II, 2–3.

were invented not simply to flatter. Their role 'consists in presenting princes with a pattern of goodness, in such a way as to reform bad rulers, improve the good, educate the boorish . . . and cause even the hopelessly vicious to feel some inward stirrings of shame'.[16] The eulogaic poetry of the Welsh and Irish bards, frequently condemned for its sycophancy, can also be read in this light, and was employed for direct interventions in the affairs of its recipients, as revealed by the *cywydd* written by Tudur Aled (*fl.* 1480–1527) in an attempt to bring Humphrey ap Hywel of Ynys Maengwyn to a peace with his kinsmen.

The court was the centre of a thriving literary and artistic culture, but it was not completely isolated from the other cultural centres and communities which surrounded it. In London and Edinburgh royal households rubbed shoulders with civic, legal, parliamentary, and ecclesiastical communities each with their own favoured cultural forms and political imperatives. In such circumstances cultures interpenetrated and interacted with each other in varied and often productive ways, some formal and carefully planned, others more spontaneous and unlicensed. One of the most obviously formal of these was the ceremony of the royal entry, in which allegorical pageants, *tableaux vivants*, verse, and music combined to welcome a sovereign or royal spouse into the capital or major city of the realm. Such spectacles combined festivity and celebration with panegyric in the Erasmian vein, in which the civic community took the opportunity, not only to welcome their royal guest, but also to let them know what was expected of them. When Mary, queen of Scots, ceremonially entered Edinburgh in 1561, she was greeted with a gift of 'ane bybill and ane psalme buik' which, she was informed, revealed 'the perfytt waye unto the heavens hie', and was forced to endure a number of speeches and pageants condemning idolatry and supporting 'the putting away of the Mass'. Clearly her Protestant subjects were keen to impress upon their Catholic queen the nature of the religious settlement they wished her to support.

More radical were the verses of the Irish poets in support of the rebellions against English rule during the latter half of the century. Given the integral part played by the poets in Irish society, it is no surprise that successive English administrations sought to outlaw and

---

[16] R. A. B. Mynors and D. F. S. Thomson (eds.), *The Correspondence of Erasmus: Letters 142–297* (Toronto, 1975), 81.

suppress their activities. But the poet's position was too deeply embedded in the culture of Gaelic Ireland to be legislated away by a 'foreign' government, and rhymers continued to speak out against any compromise with England, as in the anonymous verses written in response to the capitulation of the nobles to Henry VIII's Royal Supremacy.

> Fúbún fán ngunna ngallghlas,
> fúbún fán slabhra mbuidhe,
> fúbún fán gcúirt gan bhéarla
> fúbún séanadh Mhic Mhuire.
>
> A uaisle Inse seanAirt,
> neamhmaith bhur gcéim ar gclaochlúdh;
> a shluagh míthreórach meata,
> ná habraidh feasta acht 'faobún'!

[Shame for the grey foreign gun [gown?], shame for the golden chain, shame for the court without language, shameful the denial of Mary's son.
O nobles of the Island of Art of old, ill is the change of your dignity, O weak, cowardly crowd, hereafter say nothing but 'shame'! Translation adapted from that of Brian Ó Cúiv.][17]

---

# The visual arts: politics and propaganda

Closely analogous to the relationship between literature and politics was that between the visual arts, and especially portraiture, and politics. Both poetry and painting are material traces of social relationships, the products of negotiations between patrons and clients, of attempts to record aspirations in enduring, concrete forms, or of interventions in contemporary debates.

The conventional view of the Renaissance in the visual arts in Britain in the sixteenth century is a simple one: it did not happen. The impact of new ideas in the period was minimal, and where it did occur it was largely the work of non-native artists. Consequently, England had to wait until the seventeenth century for its artistic Renaissance, Scotland, Wales, and Ireland considerably longer. There may be some truth in these assertions from a purely stylistic

[17] Brian Ó Cúiv, 'A Sixteenth-Century Political Poem', Éigse, XV (1975), 261–76.

viewpoint, but this is as much a reflection of the inappropriateness of applying neo-classical aesthetic principles to British practice as it is of any failings on the part of native art. Henry VIII may have drawn his best artists, like his best secular musicians, from abroad, relying upon long-term visitors such as Holbein, and immigrants like the Horenbout family, for the bulk of the extant portraits from the reign, but this does not mean that there was not a distinctly English employment of paintings.

The most conspicuously politicized class of paintings from the period are those royal portraits, chiefly of Henry VIII and Elizabeth I, that still colour our sense of the Tudor monarchy today. These powerful and seemingly eulogistic images of Henry and Elizabeth have often been seen as pieces of governmental propaganda, aimed at promulgating particular images of the sovereign to a mass audience. But, the closer one looks at these pictures, their contexts, and provenance, the less plausible that suggestion seems. Paintings did not address a wide audience. Often kept behind curtains when not being actively viewed, they were accessible to only a select few, and thus ill-suited to propagandistic uses. Nor was the Tudor monarchy able to police and control all the artistic representations of the sovereign or images created in his or her name. Individuals might comment pointedly on the long reach of princes, but the crown had neither the resources nor the will to employ its corrective powers consistently. Subjects were thus free, provided they kept within certain limits, to experiment and manipulate royal imagery for their own ends. Consequently, representations of the monarch were always also part of an ongoing negotiation *with* monarchy over its nature and limits, or the direction of policy.

Holbein exploited the themes and motifs of traditional sacred art to celebrate Tudor kingship in works such as *Henry VIII and the Barber Surgeons* (a variation on the themes of Christ in Majesty and The Adoration) and *Solomon and the Queen of Sheba*. Such images, and the famous Whitehall Privy Chamber mural of Henry and his father, Jane Seymour and Elizabeth of York grouped around a monolith bearing eulogistic verse, clearly serve a political function, but they are not propagandistic in the true sense of the word. These images are visual panegyrics in the Erasmian spirit, designed to persuade the sovereign to emulate the symbolic role that the images portray. Thus, the depiction of Henry as the reforming, Protestant

prince in the portrait by Joos van Cleve of c.1535 and the frontis-
pieces to the Coverdale and Great Bibles (1535 and 1539, respectively)
are best read as attempts to encourage the king to live up to the role
of Protestant Solomon rather than as reflections of his settled will to
do so. Similarly, those portraits of Elizabeth conventionally interpreted as official icons crafted to foster a 'cult of Eliza' might more
effectively be read as interventions in political debates over religious
policy and royal marriage plans, inspired by her counsellors and
advisers.

If the reign of Elizabeth did not see a change in the function of
royal portraiture, however, it did witness a major shift in its style,
from the naturalistic mode of Holbein and William Scrots to a more
stylized, symbolic style. In part the shift reflects a Protestant desire to
produce works that appealed to the intellect rather than seduced the
senses, but it was not a purely reactionary move. It drew in equal
measure from positive stimuli, the Renaissance fashion for the aphor-
istic symbolism of the emblem books and the older, native traditions
of heraldic and iconographic art. How far Elizabeth herself was in
control of the new iconography is unclear. Both personal vanity and
political calculation probably stood behind the draft proclamation of
1563 which sought to prohibit the reproduction of any images of the
queen not based upon an approved exemplum to be produced 'by
some special person, that shall be by her allowed'. But the order was
never issued, and it was not until July 1596 that the Privy Council
intervened officially to regulate the circulation of royal portraits. By
this stage the impulse was not a desire to launch a new 'approved'
icon, but merely to destroy any images thought unacceptable to a 62-
year-old queen who was having increasing difficulty living up to her
royal motto *Semper eadem* ('Always the same').

# Conclusion

It might, then, be possible to portray the British Isles in the sixteenth
century as the passive subject of revolutionary pressures beyond their
control, a fragile promontory battered into new and alien shapes by
successive waves of continental influence (humanism, Protestant

reformation, neo-classicism). This model of indigenous cultures suc-cumbing to external forces could in turn be applied to the constituent regions within Britain, to show how the forces emanating from the south-east of England, and London in particular, extended into the provinces. But such a model of cultural change grants too passive a role to the 'victims' of these processes. In reality the subjects were dynamic and the process more symbiotic. If the encroachment of English government and the English language changed Welsh and Irish culture, so the versions of Englishness exported to those areas were in turn changed by their encounter with indigenous cultures. English culture in Dublin or Caernarfon was as distinct from the culture of York, Durham, or Exeter, as the culture of those cities was from that of London. In the sixteenth century, regionalism remained a powerful cultural force, despite the growing influence of London in most spheres of public life. The Irishness of Spenser's *Faerie Queene*, for example, is at least as important as its Englishness, and the poem reflects more vividly the politics of Anglo-Irish government under Arthur, Lord Grey of Wilton, than it does the situation in an English royal court that the poet could not experience at first hand and had to reconstruct from the resources of his memory and imagination.

Similarly, the nature of continental neo-classicism (itself a gross simplification of a diversity of regionally-influenced trends and prac-tices) was everywhere altered by the traditional cultures with which it interacted. Where the inroads of the Renaissance were less obvious, traditional forms and practices continued to dominate, and new ideas were experimented with on a strictly pragmatic basis by artists and craftsmen who thought that they could use them to their own advantage. The results in almost every case were the kinds of dis-proportionate hybrids to which Sir Philip Sidney took such excep-tion. The 'mongrel' quality of the Renaissance in Britain, as evident in the Italianate façades and details grafted onto medieval buildings as in Shakespeare's commonwealth of styles, was the result, not of cru-dity or ignorance on the part of the artists, but of a fruitful and productive use of selected imported ideas in a vernacular context. Practice everywhere softened the harsh dictums of even the sternest neo-classicist theorist. Had Sidney's fundamentalist view prevailed, of course, we would have been denied not only the buildings of Smythson and Schaw, the drama of Shakespeare and Lindsay, and the poetry of the Welsh and Irish bards, but also Sidney's own romantic prose hybrid, *Arcadia*. The resulting Renaissance, while purer in spirit, would have been infinitely poorer in substance than the indecent 'hoch poch' that actually emerged.

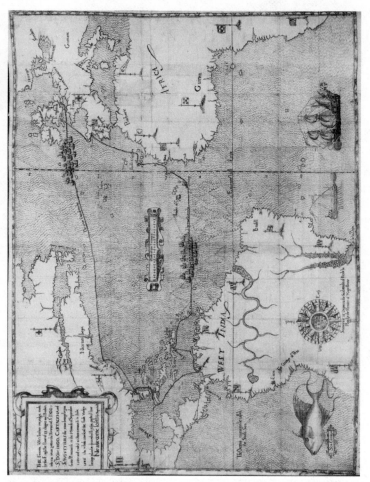

**Figure 9** Elizabethan seapower in action. *The Famous West Indies Voyage*, drawn by a cartographer on the expedition, Baptista Boazio, and published in 1589. Although nowhere as successful as was hoped beforehand, Drake's 1585–6 West Indies Voyage frightened Philip II into launching the Armada.

# 6

# Britain, Europe, and the world

## Simon Adams

There are few greater myths in British history than 'our island story', not least because 'Britain' is not an island, but an archipelago. In 1603 the union of the crowns between England and Scotland combined with the successful imposition of effective English military control throughout Ireland created for the first time—on a governmental level at least—a single relationship with the outside world. Before 1603 the position was far more complex. In 1500 England's relations both within and without the British Isles were still defined by what were essentially feudal relationships of considerable antiquity. The most important of these was the English crown's substantial if fluctuating interests in France. In 1340 Edward III had laid claim to the crown of France itself, a claim revived by Henry V in 1420 and not abandoned by his successors until 1801. It was to prevent an English succession that the 'Salic Law', which barred claims to the French crown by the female line, had been invented. In 1453 the French possessions had been reduced to the Pale of Calais and the Channel Islands, but the pretensions remained, even if Edward IV and Henry VII were prepared to barter them for a pension, whose symbolic value as tribute was more important than regularity of payment.

Within the British Isles, the authority of the English crown in Ireland rested ultimately on the grant of the lordship of Ireland to Henry II by Pope Adrian IV in the alleged breve *Laudibiliter* of 1155. The crown's claims to suzerainty over Scotland had been formulated classically by Edward I in 1290. These claims were not uncontested. The grant of the lordship of Ireland could be interpreted as leaving the papacy as ultimate feudal overlord and thus make possible a native appeal against the king of England. Nor was it entirely clear whether the lordship extended to the whole of the island or merely to those parts where the king's writ ran, and therefore whether Gaelic chieftains could legitimately consider themselves independent. Suzerainty over Scotland had been effectively repudiated in the Wars of Independence of 1296–1357 and the ancient independence of the kingdom of Scots sustained by the precociously nationalist school of Scottish historical writing of the fourteenth and fifteenth centuries. The striking difference between Scotland and Ireland was the early success of the Scots in forming an effective community of the realm, which could negotiate abroad as a body politic, even in the absence of a king, as the making of the 'Auld Alliance' with France in 1295 had demonstrated. In Ireland, with the fleeting exceptions of the Geraldine League of 1538–9 and the earl of Tyrone in the 1590s, it was not until the 1640s that the opponents of English rule were able to form a recognizable political entity.

There were major transformations in the nature of these relationships during the course of the sixteenth century, but there is no consensus over what they were. In historiographical terms we are only just emerging from a teleology formed in the nineteenth century in which the union of 1603 was the first stage in the creation of Great Britain, the Westward Enterprise and the founding of empire. The key development of the sixteenth century was the supposed Tudor creation of an English nation state. J. A. Froude, the most influential Victorian historian of sixteenth-century England, argued that in breaking with the papacy, Henry VIII also broke with the 'medieval past', a process concluded with the defeat of the Armada. Not only did England win the 'dominion of the seas' in 1588, but it was also the victory of the forces of modernity over the medieval Spain of Philip II. The decades after the 1888 Armada tercentenary saw a new interest in the Elizabethan navy, maritime expansion and the origins of empire. Long forgotten Spenserian names of Elizabethan warships—*Dreadnought, Warspite, Ark Royal*—were deliberately revived for those of the Fisher era. For the late R. B. Wernham, author of the standard modern history of Tudor foreign policy, the century was one in which England felt 'her way towards an insular policy based on sea power and regarding herself as an island "off" rather than "of"

Europe—the foreign policy that was to be characteristic of modern England'.[1]

The Anglocentricity of this approach is perhaps most striking today, but it does reflect the fact that for Scotland and Ireland the primary relationship was that with England. England had a far greater range of interests, and Britain was not always the most important. If the Reformation was the single greatest agent of change both of relations within Britain and between the various parts of Britain and the outside world, it was not the only one. The rise of the Habsburgs was no less important during the first half of the century, and the presence of two queens regnant on one island together with the long minority of James VI was a major shaping force in the second. If the course of the century was to confirm England's dominance over the British Isles, the nature of that dominance was itself transformed.

# The end of the Hundred Years War

It has recently been argued that as a young man Henry VIII saw himself as a new Henry V, destined to regain the Plantagenet domains and even the French crown. These ambitions are revealed most clearly in the grandiose plans he made with Charles V for the partition of France in 1520–3 and 1543–4. If he found himself at war with both France and Scotland simultaneously in 1544–6, this was not intentional. From the British perspective the parallel to be drawn is possibly less Henry V than Edward I, for it was in Edward's reign that the difficulties faced by an English government in conducting major wars in France and ambitious policies within Britain simultaneously had been encountered most dramatically. There is much to be said for seeing the period 1286 to 1547 as a unit, defined by the absolute priority the English crown gave to its claims in France. Edward III's abandoning of Scotland for France after 1337 was the effective cause of Scottish success in the last phase of the Wars of Independence. The issue was not whether an English king possessed the resources to dominate the British Isles, but that he preferred to spend them in

[1] *Before the Armada: The Growth of English Foreign Policy 1485–1588* (London, 1966), 11.

France. This priority also shaped Scottish and Irish foreign relations, for it made France the obvious ally, even if the French crown was more concerned with countering immediate English pressure than in formulating a British policy of its own.

The apparent exception to this rule was the Wars of Roses, when it appeared that the English had effectively turned inwards. But these civil wars were not conducted in a vacuum, for the French, the Scots, and the Irish dabbled in them extensively. For the French crown, the motive was clear: there was no guarantee that 1453 was conclusive and that the English might not return to Gascony. Alexander Grant has recently suggested that the last battle of the Hundred Years War was in fact Bosworth Field. Within Britain the most dramatic interventions occurred after 1485. In Dublin in May 1487 the earl of Kildare crowned the pretender Lambert Simnel Edward VI. In 1491 the second pretender Perkin Warbeck was recognized by the earl of Desmond and subsequently by James IV of Scotland. The Fitzgerald backing for the pretenders is usually seen as the precipitant of a new approach to the government of Ireland by Henry VII. With Scotland the solution was a dynastic alliance: the 'Treaty of Perpetual Peace' of 1502 and the marriage in the following year of James IV and Henry VII's daughter Margaret, the first voluntary Anglo-Scots royal marriage since 1328.

By bringing the Stewarts into the English succession, the Treaty of Perpetual Peace was the effective cause of the regal union a century later. Its immediate significance, however, was to make Henry VIII the nearest male relative of the offspring of James IV and his sister Margaret. Yet despite this novelty many aspects of the first years of Henry VIII's reign read almost like recycled fourteenth-century history. Having joined the Papal Holy League against France in 1511, Henry sent an expedition to encourage a revolt in Gascony in 1512 and then led an invasion of France himself the following year. If the 'Battle of the Spurs' (16 August 1513) was not in the Crécy league, it was still a victory and crowned by the occupation of Tournai. James IV behaved no less to type, and at Flodden on 9 September suffered a disaster that put Halidon Hill (1333) and Neville's Cross (1346) in the shade. Flodden also created a Scottish regency crisis in which Henry dusted off the old Edwardian claims to suzerainty and combined them with his own avuncular relationship to James V to claim the regency for his sister. The community of Scotland offered it instead to John Stewart, duke of Albany, who was then residing in France.

What was different was Henry's VIII's more cynical or more mercurial approach to foreign policy, which he demonstrated by making a separate peace with France in 1514. His assumption that Albany was a French creature led him to the apparently sophisticated yet ultimately dangerous conclusion that the easy way to deal with Scotland was through Paris. However, the real novelty of these years was the inheritance of the Emperor Charles V, which effectively brought the politics of the Hundred Years War to an end. Henry initially embraced Catherine of Aragon's nephew with the same heavy-handed benevolence he showed to James V. But the Habsburg alliance of 1520, under which the Great Enterprise against France was launched, came to a sharp end in 1525 when he grew suspicious of Charles's ambitions. As in 1514, he swung back to an alliance with France. This lasted until the mid-1530s, when he came to appreciate that Francis I would not support his repudiation of the papacy.

Henry's rejection of papal authority was undoubtedly the great revolution in England's foreign affairs during the century. It left England potentially isolated, with the awkward exception of the Schmalkaldic League of Lutheran princes and cities. It also threatened to transform relations within Britain. Thanks to his belief that France was the key to Scotland, Henry was surprised by the coup in 1528 under which James V (then aged only 12) obtained his majority. A period of tension ensued, settled by a new Treaty of Perpetual Peace in May 1534, and Henry then encouraged his nephew to follow his ecclesiastical policy. James, however, took an independent course. His visit to France in 1536 and his two French marriages coincided with the breakdown of Henry's alliance with Francis, and in 1539–41 Henry grew increasingly suspicious that James had joined a Catholic alliance against him. The 1530s saw similar trends in Ireland. In his appeal to Charles V during his rebellion in 1534, the earl of Kildare's son, Lord Offaly, first linked the fate of the Church in Ireland to the Geraldine cause. The Geraldine League, headed by Con O'Neill of Ulster, was a potentially more serious exercise. Although rendered stillborn by its defeat in August 1539, the League's offer of the lordship of Ireland to James V was the first association of the Catholic cause with the Scottish–Ulster connection. How far James contemplated turning Edinburgh into the orthodox rival of a schismatic Westminster is an interesting question, but the surviving evidence suggests he was more concerned with siring his army of bastard children.

In 1537 the Dublin administration proposed to resolve the residual issue of papal overlordship by proclaiming Henry king of Ireland. This resulted in the Act for the King's Title or Declaratory Act of 1541. The Act was accompanied by the policy of surrender and regrant and those Gaelic chieftains who accepted their new titles could be said to have accepted symbolically the legitimacy of the new crown over them. The Act also inspired a novel response by the papacy: the attempt to keep an Irish Catholic hierarchy in being through papal provision. This policy got off to a rocky start when the Jesuit mission to Ulster in 1542 reported that Con O'Neill's recent acceptance of the earldom of Tyrone suggested that there would be little support for it. But it initiated a unique feature of the Counter-Reformation.

The new policy in Ireland was overshadowed by events in Scotland, which owing to a series of accidents made Britain a major international issue during the middle decades of the century. The outbreak of war between Francis I and Charles V in July 1542 was followed in the autumn by the outbreak of hostilities on the Borders—though precisely who started them remains unclear. In November James took the still-unexplained decision to raid the West March of England, only to have his army trap itself at Solway Moss and surrender with minimal bloodshed on the 24th. The king's sudden death on 14 December (six days after the birth of his daughter and heir) created a replay of the events of 1513. Henry now saw the opportunity to resolve 'the British Problem' in a conclusive manner by assuming the regency for the infant Mary and arranging a marriage with the young Edward, prince of Wales. However, once again he was pre-empted when the earl of Arran (heir to the Stewart succession) was proclaimed governor of Scotland on 3 January 1543. Henry decided to make the best of things, given Arran's Protestant sympathies and apparent willingness to proceed with the marriage, and the marriage alliance was concluded in the treaties of Greenwich in July 1543.

It was in the belief that Scotland had been neutralized that in February 1543 Henry agreed to a new alliance with Charles V (the Treaty of Mutual Aid) under which they would mount another Great Enterprise against France in the following year. What threw everything out of gear was Arran's repudiation of the English marriage and return to the Auld Alliance in the last months of 1543. The best explanation for his volte-face was the willingness of Cardinal Beaton and the queen mother, Mary of Lorraine, to confirm him as heir apparent. Henry's commitment to the invasion of France in 1544 now forced him to engage in a major war on two fronts. In Scotland it was believed that the deliberately brutal devastation raids of 1544 and 1545 were an attempt to impose the marriage by force (though the popular description 'The Rough Wooing' was actually coined by Sir Walter Scott). Their real purpose was to damage the Scottish economy to such an extent that the Scots would pose no threat to England while Henry was in France. The priority he gave to France was underlined by the one success of the 1544 campaign, the capture of Boulogne. He spent £1,300,000 of the proceeds of the dissolution of the monasteries on fortifying the town, the main concern of the last two years of his life.

# The British priority

The financial dangers of a military effort on this scale were fully appreciated by Henry's councillors, many of whom were prepared to return Boulogne to France in the summer of 1546. But Henry was succeeded by a no less obsessed figure in the duke of Somerset, Lord Protector for Edward VI. Somerset was the one Tudor statesman for whom Britain was the primary concern, and he reformulated the marriage of Edward and Mary as a Protestant union project in 1547–9. Emboldened by the success of his invasion of Scotland in 1547 and the defeat of a large Scottish army at the battle of Pinkie on 10 September, he attempted to impose the union by force. Somerset's refusal to accept the wider implications of what became an open war with France over Scotland (and rumours that he was prepared, if necessary, to sacrifice Boulogne and Calais) was the basic cause of his overthrow in 1549. The peace treaties with France and Scotland in 1550–1, which included the surrender of Boulogne and the garrisons in Scotland, marks a major turning point in Tudor government. For the junior members of Edward's government, many of whom later served Elizabeth I, the dangers of military overextension had been learned the hard way.

The 1550 settlement created rather than resolved 'the British Problem', and led to some strange continuities during the following decade. 1548 had seen the marriage treaty between Mary and the Dauphin Francis. After 1550 there was a French-dominated administration in Edinburgh, with Arran surrendering the governorship to Mary of Lorraine in 1554 in exchange for the duchy of Châtellerault. Edinburgh was now in a position to intervene in Ireland, and Ulster once again became the centre of attention. The last years of Edward's reign saw the emergence of two policies that would reshape the Anglo-Irish relationship: English colonization in the Irish midlands and the imposition of military control over Ulster. Despite Mary Tudor's restoration of Catholicism, the continued Scottish threat to the security of Ireland gave her little option but to retain her brother's policies. The re-establishment of the Church also meant that Rome, which had recognized the crown of Ireland following Mary's reconciliation, lost interest in the immediate government of Ireland.

Yet Mary's reign also introduced a novel element that would reshape decisively the relationship between England and Scotland. Scottish Protestantism had undoubtedly suffered from its Anglophile taint in the 1540s. It overcame this disability thanks to the greater fear of dynastic absorption into France following the marriage alliance of 1548. Despite Mary of Lorraine's caution on the religious front, her discreet but deliberate policy of placing reliable Frenchmen in key positions in the Scottish government so transformed the position that by 1559 only a minority of Scots remained loyal to the French alliance. Mary Tudor's decision to ram through a marriage to Charles V's heir Philip in 1553 brought home the reality of dynastic absorption to the English at the same time. The duke of Northumberland had raised fears of a foreign marriage in 1553 and Sir Thomas Wyatt had played to them in his rebellion in early 1554. The frosty reception Philip received on his arrival in England in July 1554 and the equally frosty reciprocation by his escort from Spain was the product less of some deep Anglo-Spanish antagonism than of the resentment both sides felt at a marriage imposed by Mary and Charles V. Major efforts were made to limit Philip's powers and authority, but his informal influence with Mary exposed the weakness of the marriage treaty. This point was underlined in 1557–8, when having been bounced into a major war by Philip, England both lost Calais and had to face a possible invasion from Scotland without assistance from him.

English relief at their deliverance from 'foreign rule' in 1558 created a novel fellow feeling for the Scots in 1559–60. This is brought out vividly in Sir Henry Percy's report of a conference he had with Châtellerault at Norham Castle on the Borders in January 1559. Percy brought up the 'subjection our realm was in by our late marriage with the king of Spain and what inconvenience thereof did follow, as by the entangling us in wars and other like things, and in like case your realm, which at this present is not avoided of the encumbrance as now ours clearly is'. To this Châtellerault replied, 'as for the encumbrance that you had by your marriage and now presently we have, it is a thing we would gladly have avoided, and yet it is not in our power, until such time as God hath sent the same fortune unto us as hath lighted upon you, although we would much rejoice if God would send us the same hap'.[2] Although the English played no direct role in instigating the Scottish 'revolution' of 1559, despite its nationalist inspiration it only succeeded with English military aid. Few episodes in the century could have been as symbolic as the meeting on 2 April 1560 at Inveresk, on the edge of the old battlefield of Pinkie, between Châtellerault, now nominal head of the Lords of the Congregation, whose incompetence in 1547 had cost the lives of thousands of Scots, and the commander of the English relief army, William, Lord Grey, his face heavily scarred by the nasty wound he had received then. When the allied camp was set up at Restalrig several days later one Scottish account noted that it was 'with such quiett and peaceable entertainment betwixt English and Scots that wes a wonder'.[3]

Elizabeth's government did not place a high price tag on this assistance and restricted English aims effectively to Scottish home rule. Sir William Cecil certainly kept suzerainty on hand as a possible justification for intervention and later for the right to try Mary in England in 1568 and 1587, but it was not advanced publicly. In turn the leaders of the Lords of the Congregation, John Knox and the Lord James Stewart, the future earl of Moray, saw 1560 as the beginning of

---

[2] BL, Cotton MS Caligula B. x, fo. 6ᵛ, Sir Henry Percy to [Sir Thomas Parry?], 22 Jan. 1559.

[3] 'Historie of the Estate of Scotland', *Wodrow Miscellany I* (Wodrow Society; 1844), 83.

what Moray described as 'ane mutual reciproque luif and benevolence betwix the twa nations'.[4] The new amity with Scotland had the
added bonus of isolating Ulster. The apple of discord was the return
of Mary Stewart to Scotland in 1561. Not only did she threaten to
overturn the new Scottish status quo, but she also posed a challenge
to Elizabeth's right to the English throne, as only the illegitimate
daughter of Henry VIII. The Treaty of Edinburgh in July 1560 had
given Elizabeth what she wanted, the renunciation of that claim, but
Mary refused to ratify the treaty—an issue that dominated relations
between the queens for the rest of Mary's life. In the short term Mary
attempted to barter the rival claim for recognition as Elizabeth's heir
apparent, a proposal that triggered a public debate over the English
succession. Mary's place in the succession contributed to pressure on
Elizabeth herself to marry, while the experience of Philip and Mary
undoubtedly inspired the desire for her to marry within the realm.
However, Elizabeth's refusal either to marry or settle the succession
by legislation effectively left both issues unresolved.

Fortunately for Elizabeth, Mary Stewart's reign in Scotland turned
out to be almost as short as Mary Tudor's, though Elizabeth was then
left with the problem of dealing with her as a refugee after 1568. There
has been much debate over Mary's intentions as queen of Scotland,
specifically whether she was willing to operate within the 1560 settlement, or whether she was biding her time to overturn it. The murder
of David Rizzio (who among other things handled her correspondence with Catholic Europe) in March 1566 effectively brought her
independence to an end, but in the six months prior to it, the English
had become increasingly concerned about contacts between her and
Shane O'Neill in Ulster. Mary's demission or abdication (24 July 1567)
was the effective confirmation of the 1560 settlement. As a result
England and Scotland under the regencies of the earls of Moray
(1567–70), Lennox (1570–1), Mar (1571–2), and Morton (1572–8) grew
closer than they had been since 1357. Yet Mary's influence was not
entirely dead and the Anglophile policy had its limits, as the assassin-
ations of Moray and Lennox in 1570 and 1571 and the execution of
Morton in 1581 dramatically illustrated.

Nevertheless, Mary's failure effectively reduced hopes for the
Catholic cause within Britain to Ireland and England. In the Irish

---

[4] BL, Egerton MS 1818, fo. 21, to Lord Robert Dudley, 25 May 1562.

Parliament of 1560 Elizabeth's government returned Ireland to the constitutional position of 1547, and the papacy in turn revived the policy of maintaining an Irish hierarchy. This time it was more successful, thanks to the nunciature of the Jesuit David Wolfe between 1561 and 1565. A number of archbishops and bishops were provided, but many of them were subsequently either apprehended or driven into exile. By the early 1590s it was accepted that a full hierarchy was impossible and a more ad hoc system of vicars apostolic adopted. Nevertheless, Rome's efforts to keep an Irish Catholic Church alive inspired the foundation of numerous communities of exiled Irish clerics, who began to play an active role in the diplomacy of Irish Catholicism.

## The Enterprise of England

Support in the Catholic world for the Irish cause was tempered by a number of considerations. Much has been made recently of the Elizabethan identification of Gaeldom as savages, yet Catholic Europe regarded the 'Wild Irish' in the same way, however impressed they were by their devotion to the faith. A no less effective inhibitor was the Enterprise of England, the restoration of the Church there. A restored Catholic monarchy in England would mean one in Ireland too, and that monarch's rights could not be abrogated in the meantime. Only if the Enterprise of England were abandoned would an Enterprise of Ireland make sense. This dilemma came home to Philip II as early as the summer of 1559, when a surprise landing in England was proposed in the course of his return to Spain, while at the same time his ambassador in London received an emissary from a shadowy Irish league wishing to repudiate Elizabeth.

With only two exceptions (the Ridolphi Plot of 1571 and the Fitzmaurice Smerwick expedition of 1579–80), Philip II treated the Enterprises of England and Ireland with great caution until the end of 1585. While the restoration of the Church in Britain was devoutly to be wished for, until it could be accomplished successfully, provoking Elizabeth was dangerous. Much has been made of Mary Stewart's place in this equation, on the assumption that Philip was not prepared to put a French candidate on the English throne. This may have been true for the years 1559–60, when she was queen of France, but after 1561 Mary's negotiations for a marriage with Don Carlos showed that her allegiances had shifted. The real issues were more complex. First, although his ambassadors regularly reported that the majority of the English population remained loyal to the old faith, only a few members of Mary Tudor's court had actually gone into exile in 1559 and the Enterprise was too risky unless there was clear evidence of significant internal support. Secondly, and even more importantly, in the early 1560s Madrid's primary concern was the Mediterranean. Stability in northern Europe was essential.

After 1566 Philip's main concern was the Netherlands, and the Netherlands-English equation posed possibly the most difficult dilemma of his reign. From the beginning there were those like Cardinal Granvelle who argued that London was the source of the heresy spreading into the Netherlands, thus making the Enterprise of England the key to defeating the Dutch Revolt. On the other hand, it was doubtful whether the Enterprise was militarily practicable without a firm base in the Netherlands, a case argued cogently by the duke of Alba in 1568–73 and the prince of Parma in 1583–6. Until the Revolt was defeated every effort should be made to pacify Elizabeth. Ireland posed a further problem. Given Elizabeth's probable hostile intentions, supporting the Irish cause was the most effective means of keeping her from meddling in the Netherlands. On the other hand, if Elizabeth was to be persuaded to abstain from aiding the Dutch rebels on grounds of political morality, the example had to be set by abstaining in Ireland as well.

France did not provide an alternative. For all the supposed sympathy in France for Mary Stewart, Catherine de Medici had little love for her daughter-in-law, and saw the issue primarily as one of maintaining the prestige of the French crown in Scotland. But this had to be balanced against English involvement with the Huguenots, a very real parallel to Philip II's dilemma over the Netherlands. Good relations with Elizabeth were vital to maintaining the civil peace in France. Moreover, the possibility of a marriage between Elizabeth and the dukes of Anjou, which ran on for over a decade between 1570 and 1581, offered a potentially more fruitful means of restoring French influence in Britain.

The paralysis of the greater Catholic powers left the field open for the papacy and enthusiastic individuals. The papacy felt a clear sense of moral responsibility to the oppressed members of the Church, and it was the recipient of appeals from a number of British clerics as well as partisans of the Irish cause like Thomas Stuckeley and James Fitz-maurice Fitzgerald. But it lacked the resources to act independently. Pius IV was willing to follow Philip's lead, but Pius V (1566–72) and Gregory XIII (1572–85) found his caution frustrating. The Enterprise of England also attracted a number of junior royals and nobles in the 1570s, especially Don Juan of Austria and Henry, duke of Guise, but their finances were even weaker. Catholic 'policy' thus amounted to a series of dangerously amateurish fits and starts. Pius V published the bull of excommunication of Elizabeth in 1570 to aid the Rebellion of the Northern Earls, but deliberately without informing Philip first. Philip gave Roberto Ridolphi's plan to depose Elizabeth in 1571 cautious support, but this was discovered by the English. Gregory XIII's encouragement of Don Juan was leaked to the English by the prince of Orange in 1577. The most dangerous conjunction was Gregory's support for both the Jesuit mission to England and Fitzmaurice's Irish Enterprise in 1579. The shipping Philip provided for the Fitzmaurice expedition was the one clear exception to his policy of avoiding provocation, but his purpose was primarily to conciliate Rome in order to assure papal consent to the union with Portugal. Philip was far more cautious about the Guise–Robert Persons plan for the invasion of England in 1582–3, a plan also dis-covered by the English when the 'Throckmorton Plot' was broken at the end of 1583.

## The English response

For all the myths about its intelligence service, the greatest weakness of the Elizabethan government in formulating its foreign policy was its failure to appreciate the divisions within the Catholic world. Cer-tainly the 'plots' were broken with some success, but they simply reinforced an existing belief that there was a broad Catholic alliance behind the Enterprise of England. Sir William Cecil expressed his concerns on this score at the beginning of the reign and this appreci-ation underlay the consensual approach Elizabeth's government gen-erally took towards foreign policy. Thus, the mission of David Wolfe in Ireland in 1561 was viewed as evidence of the wider plan, not for the papal initiative it was. If at times scepticism was advanced, events like the Massacre of St Bartholomew's undermined it. Only in the last decade of the reign, following the public royalist–*ligueur* debates in France and the Archpriest or Appellant controversy, was there any real understanding that the Catholic world was by no means united and that there might be a 'moderate' wing to do business with.

If defence against the Enterprise was the central aim of Elizabethan foreign policy prior to 1588, where the precise threat was located was more debatable. Fears that the house of Guise was planning to make Mary Stewart queen of Britain inspired the English intervention in the First French War of Religion in 1562 and the occupation of Le Havre. The compromise settlement of that war in February 1563 had a paradoxical effect. Even though Le Havre had to be evacuated, the entrenchment of a powerful Protestant minority in France initiated a definite amelioration in Anglo-French relations. The French crown was never entirely trusted before 1589, but the Huguenots made it impossible to launch the Enterprise from France. Spain posed a more awkward problem, for the relative proximity of Galicia to Munster and south-western Ireland made a landing there a very real danger. Yet an invasion of England itself was more likely from the Netherlands than Spain. Thus, English debates over the Netherlands were a curious mirror image of the Spanish, for apart from the moral debate between the religious imperative and the supporting of rebels, the strongest argument for backing the Orangeist cause was that a friendly Netherlands was the most effective defence against invasion. This issue came to a head at the end of 1575 when the States of Holland and Zealand offered their joint countship to Elizabeth.

This offer was refused politely on the ground that to accept it was tantamount to a declaration of war against Spain. But simultaneously the more complicated issue arose of a possible alliance with France to support the Dutch cause, which might counteract the dangers of a war with Spain. This, however, had to be balanced against distrust of the French crown's motives and the suspicion that, if it was serious, its intention was to annex the Netherlands itself. It is no coincidence that some of the stormiest debates over foreign policy during the reign took place over the distinctly ambiguous Netherlands enterprise of the duke of Anjou in 1578–79, combined as it was with Anjou's proposal of marriage to Elizabeth. Nearly a century ago Conyers Read portrayed these debates as a struggle between two factions, one strongly puritan, masterminded by Sir Francis Walsingham, though headed by the earl of Leicester, which advanced an interventionist Protestant foreign policy, the other conservative and cautious in foreign policy and headed by Lord Burghley and the earl of Sussex. The conservatives supported the Anjou marriage and the alliance with France; the puritans opposed it and had their ultimate victory in 1585 when Elizabeth did at last intervene in the Netherlands independently.

This interpretation is based on a superficial and partial reading of the debates. The only strong supporter of the marriage was the earl of Sussex, and his arguments were extreme—the claim for example that the marriage between Philip and Mary had shown that a foreign Catholic consort would pose no problems. The marriage was never a serious proposition except in the overheated imaginations of Anjou's agents, because the religious terms Anjou demanded would never be granted. But it was in both his and Elizabeth's interests to keep the pretence going, for he needed the English negotiations to maintain his credibility in the Netherlands, while she believed them to be a means of controlling him. Matters were greatly simplified by the death of Sussex on 9 June 1583 and then Anjou himself on 31 May 1584. Although there was still a period of uncertainty surrounding the possible cooperation of Henry III over the winter of 1584–5, Elizabeth's government undertook the protection of the United Provinces with remarkable smoothness in August 1585. The argument that carried the day was the established one that the Netherlands was the first line of defence against the Enterprise.

## The maritime context

Ironically, it was the Netherlands intervention that persuaded Philip II to abandon his caution and agree to the Enterprise in the form of the Gran Armada at the end of 1585. Yet his change of strategy was caused less by the Netherlands intervention itself than by the simultaneous launching of Sir Francis Drake's West Indies Voyage and the fear of a war at sea with the English. The growth of English maritime power during the century has become so well known that its nuances have been overlooked. The creation of the Tudor navy can be attributed to the need to replace the cross-Channel frontier zone the crown's possessions in France had provided before 1453. It was believed after 1453 that Calais and Dover gave England control of the Narrow Seas, but the steady silting of Calais's harbour meant that by the first decades of the sixteenth century it had lost any serious commercial or strategic importance. More importantly, the defence of any enclave was an expensive if not impossible task against a major power determined to regain it. For all the myths of its invincibility, the very survival of Calais as an English possession until 1558 can be attributed to the French crown's greater interests elsewhere.

The Channel was not a 'moat defensive to a wall' for the crossing was a short one and the English coastline lay open. Although there were only a limited number of estuarial harbours capable of sheltering a large fleet (the subject of exhaustive study in 1587–8), successful landings were frequent. Most recently, Henry VII had landed unopposed in Milford Haven in 1485 and Lambert Simnel in Lancashire in 1487. The weather was a more effective defence, for it restricted the period within which an invasion was practicable to a few summer months. It was the weather that prevented the French from reinforcing their garrison in Scotland during the winter of 1559–60. Yet the weather also made it impossible for the English fleet to control the seas round the British Isles. In 1548 the navy failed to prevent the French sending a large expedition to Scotland and Mary Stewart from escaping to France. There was never any question of patrolling the approaches to Ireland effectively, the best the navy could do was cut the invaders off from reinforcement after they had landed, as happened at Smerwick in 1580 and Kinsale in 1601.

The 'great ships', frequently described as floating castles, constructed during the first half of the sixteenth century were less symbols of prestige than the instruments of the primarily defensive role of the fleet. Henry VII built the first two great ships, the *Regent* and *Sovereign*, in 1488–9, but Henry VIII has generally been credited with the founding of the modern Royal Navy. This was due both to the dramatic expansion in the size of the fleet (he left nearly fifty warships at his death) and to the modernization of its armament during his reign. Great ships continued to be built until the 1560s, but under Elizabeth a new policy of constructing warships of smaller size but greater manoeuvrability was initiated. This innovation has been traditionally attributed to Sir John Hawkins, treasurer of the Navy between 1577 and 1595, but the first ships of this type were actually launched nearly a decade before he took office. Primarily for reasons of economy, the Elizabethan Navy was smaller in overall size than Henry's, numbering between twenty-five and thirty major warships. The relatively limited number of ships caused major problems after the outbreak of war with Spain in 1585. The fleet was essentially a battle fleet, not a trade protection fleet, and there were insufficient warships to provide adequate escorts ('wafters' was the Elizabethan term) for English trade and fishing. Great Yarmouth had to hire wafters for its fishing fleet in 1585–6.

English naval power was nevertheless a reality by the middle of the century, and gaining the use of the fleet was one of the few attractions Philip found in his marriage to Mary. For this innovations in naval armament were chiefly responsible, a paradoxical legacy of Henry VIII. Henry had a strong prejudice against handguns, and as a result the English lagged behind the continental armies in adopting them. This attitude only changed in the middle decades of the century, when the superiority of firearms over the longbow became irrefutable and professional soldiers entertained serious doubts about the ability of traditionally armed English armies to hold their own against their rivals. A few outspoken advocates of the longbow can still be found late in Elizabeth's reign, but their arguments were chiefly sentimental and moralistic, archery being enshrined by tradition and considered better for the moral fibre. During the 1560s the Elizabethan government finally tackled the problem of the rearming of the militia with firearms, a policy which had actually been initiated by legislation in Mary's last Parliament. This was an expensive process, which at its outset involved large-scale arms purchases from the continent, and demanded a new attention to training and equipment. But it was successfully accomplished by the 1580s, and counts as one of the major achievements of the reign. In both France and Castile efforts to create national militias at the end of the fifteenth century had been effectively abandoned. For all the Shakespearean jokes about the militia (the sixteenth-century precursor of *Dad's Army*), by the end of the century it was possibly the most effective in Europe.

Henry's hostility to firearms did not extend to cannon, however, and in the manufacture of cannon the English made major strides during his reign. Cornish tin provided one of the two main ingredients of brass (or bronze), the primary cannon-making alloy. The search for the other—copper—inspired the chartering of the Company of Mines Royal in 1568, the patentees of which included the leading members of the Privy Council. The company's most successful operation was the copper mine at Keswick in what was then the extremely remote Lake District. No less important was the discovery in the 1540s of a process for making reliable cast-iron cannon (earlier wrought-iron cannon being notoriously as dangerous to their users as their targets). Cast-iron cannon did not replace brass cannon, which remained the preferred equipment of the queen's ships, but they provided a valuable supplement and there was now more than enough artillery to go round. The 'state' of the Ordnance Office for 1574 (one of the few to survive) records 452 brass and 83 cast-iron cannon of various sizes distributed among the ships of the fleet, with a further 109 brass and 7 cast-iron in reserve in the Tower.[5]

England was not only self-sufficient in artillery, but a near-monopoly supplier for Europe as well. It held this position until the 1620s when the cheaper products of the Swedish armaments industry (founded and financed by the Dutch to break the English monopoly) began to undercut it. Cannon were potentially the most valuable English export commodity during Elizabeth's reign. Export was controlled by licence from the crown, but rumours and allegations of a thriving black market were widespread. In 1583 the French ambassador in London reported that the English were supplying cannon to customers as diverse as the Sultan of Morocco and Ivan the Terrible, claims which are confirmed by other sources. Ivan the Terrible's policy towards England can in fact be reduced to two simple aims: to marry Queen Elizabeth or another Englishwoman and buy some artillery.

A neat illustration of the effects of this near-monopoly is supplied by two simultaneous sieges in 1573. Elizabeth supplied thirty-one cannon, transported by sea, to force the surrender of Mary Stewart's supporters in Edinburgh Castle, a small and prominent target. The French crown could only assemble forty-two for the much larger siege of La Rochelle. The heavy armament of English ships was well known throughout Europe, while Philip II had to scour his empire to provide the artillery for the Armada (much of it rumoured to be illicit English exports). The duke of Medina Sidonia himself had

---

[5] BL, Harleian MS 617.

written to the earl of Leicester in 1576 to purchase copper and tin to found cannon. England's allies were the beneficiaries. As early as 1568–9 assistance to the Huguenots took the form of cannon and munitions. The Dutch soon overtook them, and from 1572 onwards there were regular requests from the prince of Orange for English cannon. In 1575, for example, he instructed the Dutch Church in London to purchase one hundred pieces for his fleet. During the making of the treaty of Nonsuch in 1585 many of the members of the Dutch embassy came with shopping lists from their respective towns or provinces. The States of Holland wanted to buy 'eene goedt getal van geschuten' [a good number of cannon] — 200 pieces to be exact.[6] Enkhuisen purchased nine tons of cast-iron ordnance and Harlingen twenty-four pieces. The next decade saw further substantial sales of cannon to the United Provinces: 200 pieces in 1592, 50 in 1594, 16 in 1595. The effects of these sales can be seen in the victorious campaigns of the Dutch army under Maurice of Nassau during the 1590s. These were dominated by sieges, in which Maurice's success was attributed specifically to the unusually large size of his artillery train.

Yet for all the Navy's precocity and the power of its weaponry, England was certainly not 'mistress of the seas' during the sixteenth century. Throughout the century English merchant shipping lagged behind Spanish and Dutch. This was a reflection of the structure of English commerce, which in bulk terms was still dominated by the import of wines from Gascony and export of woollens, neither of which demanded particularly sophisticated shipping. The very narrowness of the Channel meant that, give or take the weather, only short voyages were necessary. If the weather was favourable, the voyage from the Thames estuary to the Scheldt could be made overnight. When he went to take up his command of Elizabeth's forces in the Netherlands, the earl of Leicester left Harwich at 3 o'clock in the afternoon of the 9th of December 1585 and arrived off Flushing at noon the next day.

The export of raw wool was controlled by the Staple at Calais, but by the end of the fifteenth century the export of woollens increasingly took the form of the export of untreated woollen cloth to the market at Antwerp. During the first half of the sixteenth century the export

---

[6] The Hague, Algemeen Rijksarchief, 3.01.04.01.20, *Gedrukte Resolutiën van de Staten van Holland*, 1585, p. 331, letter to envoys, 15/25 June 1585.

of wool dwindled almost to nothing and was yet another reason for the decline of Calais, for under the Act of Retainer of 1473 the custom on exported wool paid for its fortifications and garrison. Antwerp by contrast was a booming market, the English cloth trade being accompanied by the Portuguese spice factory. The Antwerp market was the major reason for the limited construction of large merchant ships during the first half of the sixteenth century for there was no need for costly voyages to the Iberian Peninsula or the Mediterranean. Antwerp also secured the dominance of London—the nearest estuarial port—over the other English ports, which became known by the end of the century simply as the outports.

The key to the politics of trade was the crown's dependence on the customs revenues. This had been masked to some extent by the expansion of the crown estate during the second half of the fifteenth century, but the crown lands declined steadily in relative importance during the first half of the sixteenth century. Possibly only the king of Denmark was proportionately as dependent on customs revenues as Elizabeth. There were in practice only two ways of increasing the revenue, increasing the duties on individual commodities or expanding the overall volume of trade. Manipulation of customs duties by the crown was notoriously unpopular and increases simply encouraged smuggling. Henry VII published the earliest known 'Book of Rates' (which consolidated the duties paid on various commodities) in 1507. This was revised (upwards) in 1558, but not again until the reign of James I. The crown could (and did) add new dutiable commodities—termed impositions—to those in the Book under the prerogative, but by 1603 impositions were themselves the subject of legal and parliamentary challenge.

The crown's encouragement of trade was thus a curious combination of well meaning and self-interest, but it could not overcome some basic economic facts. The most important was the relative lack of interest in England in the two areas that became the key to Dutch maritime expansion in the second half of the century: the North Sea fisheries (particularly the herring fishery) and the carrying trade between northern and southern Europe. This was not for lack of official encouragement. In the 1490s the crown (possibly copying Castilian practice) began subsidizing the construction of ships over 100 tons. In 1563 the Elizabethan government attempted to stimulate the fisheries by creating Wednesday as a second fish day by statute, only to find the market for fish in England stubbornly inelastic. On the other hand, the crown itself was partly to blame for the weakness of the carrying trade. Thanks to the extensive privileges the Hanseatic League of German North Sea and Baltic towns possessed under the Treaty of Utrecht of 1475, Hanseatic merchants paid a lower duty on exported woollens than English merchants while direct English trade with the Baltic was effectively barred. Not surprisingly the Hanseatic privileges were bitterly resented in London and calls for their abolition united the London merchant community. Edward IV had had specific diplomatic reasons for buying the support of the Hanse; what is surprising is that none of his successors (including Henry VII, otherwise so concerned to increase customs revenues) reversed the policy until 1551. This was the work of the duke of Northumberland, acting on the advice of the most influential of the London merchants, Sir Thomas Gresham. At the request of Philip, Mary restored the League's privileges, and it was Elizabeth who finally abolished them.

The middle decades of the century saw substantial changes to the commercial 'system' of the first half, but the reasons were political rather than economic. There was a dramatic slump in cloth exports following the abolition of the Hanseatic privileges in 1551, but they soon recovered. The key factor was the decline in relations with the Habsburgs after 1558. On two occasions (1563–5 and 1569–73), Philip II's government employed embargoes of English trade with Antwerp and Spain as a political weapon, under the belief that the English crown was uniquely dependent on its foreign trade. The embargoes inspired a variety of schemes for diversifying and expanding trade, though once they were ended there was an immediate return to Antwerp. What finally destroyed the Antwerp market was the sacking of the city by Spanish troops in 1576, after which the English migrated to safer staples in the northern Netherlands, particularly Middelburg in Zealand. Ironically, the revolt of the Netherlands also enabled the English finally to break into the north–south carrying trade thanks to the embargoes the Spanish government instituted against Dutch shipping. As neutrals the English could step into the breach and there was a dramatic increase in English trade with Spain and the Mediterranean between 1573 and 1585. Following the outbreak of hostilities in 1585, Elizabeth's government sought to blockade the Iberian Peninsula, only to drive the Spanish government back to tolerating Dutch trade. The Dutch flouting of the joint blockade soured Anglo-Dutch relations to a far greater extent than any other issue

# The wider world

English maritime expansion during the century was characterized less by mercantile considerations than by the complex growth of piracy and privateering. Privateering involved the issuing of letters of marque by a supposedly legitimate authority, but they were not always choosy about the grantees. The wars with France and Scotland in the 1540s and 1550s were accompanied by widespread issuing of letters of marque. The outbreak of the various religious struggles after 1559 brought a number of further participants into play: the Lords of the Congregation in 1559–60, the Huguenots and the English governor of Le Havre in 1562–3, the Huguenots again after 1568, followed by the English government after the embargo of 1569, and the Dutch admiralties after 1572. In the early 1580s the Portuguese pretender Dom Antonío sought to create a private fleet by the lavish granting of letters of marque. It appears that most English privateers in those years were operating under his flag. The seizure of English shipping in Spain in May 1585 initiated the largest single explosion of privateering, which was to last for the remainder of the century. Initially the letters were issued as reprisals for the seizures, but very soon they were granted indiscriminately—in the autumn of 1585 several were even granted to Dutch sea captains. Many of the English skippers previously trading with Spain simply turned to privateering.

No less important was the resentment—shared by the French—of the Hispano-Lusitanian monopoly of the wider world created by the Treaty of Tordesillas of 1494. This was held in check (so far as England was concerned) by the crown's desire to maintain good relations with the Spanish monarchs during most of the first half of the century. However, by the second half the belief that the wealth of Philip II came from the Indies became widespread and this made it a legitimate target once relations deteriorated. English, French, and Dutch Protestants also refused to be bound by a treaty based on papal mediation. Elizabeth's government stated this more or less openly in 1561. Philip II defended his empire with a mixture of diplomatic pressure, commercial reprisals (as in the embargoes of 1563–5 and 1569–73), and periodic despatch of fleets to key areas. Drastic punishment was inflicted on offenders when caught, the most notorious early examples being the destruction of the Huguenot colony in Florida in 1563 and then the attack on John Hawkins's fleet in Vera Cruz in 1568.

The decisive event in Elizabethan western expansion was Drake's Circumnavigation Voyage of 1577–80. The background to it is still murky, but the coincidence of Drake's return to England in September 1580 with the second Spanish-supported landing at Smerwick overcame any qualms about piracy. What made the voyage so important was the impression it gave that the Spanish empire was an easy target. Ironically, Philip II drew the same conclusion and appreciated the need to make serious improvements in imperial defence. It also inspired his decision to launch the Armada. For all the moral pressure behind the Enterprise of England, Philip's concerns in 1585–6 were primarily strategic, in particular the fear that Drake's West Indies Voyage was the beginning of a naval war of attrition in the empire. To avoid this, a short and decisive resolution of the English problem was essential. His strategy for the Gran Armada reflected this priority. It was intended as a single decisive blow at the heart of the English government, and for all the arguments for the greater chances of a successful landing in Ireland or Scotland, the length of time necessary for mounting an effective attack from either militated against them. He almost guaranteed the Armada's failure by attempting to resolve the old debate over a Netherlands base through an overly complicated plan involving a meeting at sea of fleets from both Spain and the Netherlands. Philip's strategic dilemma was also reflected in a surprise outcome of the Armada. By accident and in the worst possible circumstances, the wrecking of so many of its ships on the Irish coast did deposit a large body of Spanish soldiers on the island. When Philip came to appreciate how many had survived, he could not decide whether to reinforce or rescue them.

No less erroneous was Philip's pessimism about the empire for the resources devoted to forts and ships after 1580 paid off and it proved more resilient than he had expected. The effects of the privateering war have been variously debated, but by the end of Elizabeth's reign it did at least produce a large body of English mariners with wide experience of extra-European waters, who would play a crucial role in later English colonization in North America. The Circumnavigation inspired an initial vogue for Western voyaging and planting in the 1580s. Sir Philip Sidney was one of the many interested and his father, the Lord President of Wales, circulated appeals to Chester and Shrewsbury to contribute to a major voyage in 1584. But like the Dutch, actual English overseas colonization would have to wait for the end of hostilities. The 'state' had no interest in colonization, nor was there any mercantile pressure. Drake and Hawkins talked occasionally of planting colonies, but were diverted by the war. Sidney preferred to go to the Netherlands. The most sustained interest was shown by a small but active lobby of enthusiasts, of whom the best known are Richard Hakluyt and Sir Walter Ralegh. In Ralegh's case this approached the borders of obsession in his search for El Dorado in 'the large, rich and beautiful empire of Guiana . . . a country that hath yet her Maidenhead, never sacked, turned, nor wrought'.[7] The only colony actually planted by the English in Elizabeth's reign—Roanoke—was his work entirely. Although he was to gain a posthumous reputation as the last of the great Elizabethans, in his interest in colonization as in so many other things Ralegh was the exception that proves the rule.

The Roanoke colonists were in fact among the victims of the Armada, for a proposed relief expedition in the autumn of 1587 was halted by the ban on long-distance voyaging imposed as a defensive measure. Yet there was one unique feature to English colonization that first appeared in the Elizabethan projects and then became a pronounced characteristic of the plantations of the following century. This was the use of colonies as a combination of exile and refuge for religious dissidents. It emerged first in the discussions for a Catholic plantation in North America in 1583, though the ultimate inspiration may have been the Huguenot colony in Florida. A group of Separatists actually sailed for North America in the 1590s. Had they not been driven back by bad weather the Pilgrim Fathers might have been preceded by twenty years.

[7] *The Discovery of the Large, Rich and Beautiful Empire of Guiana*, in *Sir Walter Ralegh: Selected Writings*, ed. Gerald Hammond (Harmondsworth, 1984), 120.

# The Continental imperative

By a supreme irony, at the very moment the English intervention in the Netherlands initiated the Anglo-Spanish conflict, this conflict in turn was overshadowed by an issue that dominated Europe during the decade 1584–94, the French succession. The greater commitment of Elizabeth and Philip to the Netherlands and the Armada initially limited the support they could give to their respective French allies, and the complex manoeuvrings of Henry III prevented a resolution within France itself. But Henry's assassination on 1 August 1589 brought Henry IV to the throne and open intervention on both sides. It is a debatable point whether it was the greater efficacy of Spanish military assistance to the *ligue* or the basic strength of French Catholic opinion that finally forced Henry IV to seek a political solution by conversion in 1594. Nevertheless, the centrality of the struggle for France made both the war in the Netherlands and the Anglo-Spanish war at sea essentially secondary theatres.

The war with Spain did, however, decisively shape Anglo-Scots relations in the 1590s. It has been argued that James VI's sex and his Protestant upbringing made him an almost unstoppable candidate for the English succession after 1566, but the godly image of James was not as apparent in the 1580s as it was later, and only in 1584 did he finally break with his mother. What worked in his favour was the absence of a serious English rival after the death of Lady Catherine Grey in 1568. The succession and the grant of a pension from England after 1585 gave him, though ostensibly neutral, a vested interest in Elizabeth's success in the war. If the point needed underlining, Philip II provided it in his decision in 1587 that in the event of the Armada's success the English crown was to go to his daughter the Archduchess Isabella. Her claim was publicized by the Jesuit Robert Persons in *A Conference about the Next Succession* in 1595. Frightened that it might win support in Catholic Europe, James informed Rome that he would grant toleration for Catholics once crowned. On the other hand, the dangers posed by Isabella's claim eliminated any real opposition in England to his.

Lord Burghley's often-quoted comment to the earl of Shrewsbury on 27 May 1589, 'My lord the state of the world is marvellous changed when we true Englishmen have cause, for our own quietness, to wish good success to a French king [Henry III, not Navarre] and a king of Scots . . . And this is the work of God for our good . . . for no wit of man could otherwise have wrought it' reflects the novel circumstances of the 1590s.[8] After 1594 the conflict with Spain went through two distinct phases. The first was initiated by Henry IV's declaration of war against Philip II in January 1595 and the attempts to form an Anglo-French-Dutch alliance to drive Spain out of the Netherlands. This appears to have been motivated in part by the belief that Philip's authority in Spain was crumbling, but the effective Spanish defence of the Netherlands broke the French war effort and Henry IV made an independent settlement in 1598. The war also saw a gearing up of major naval expeditions on both sides, with fleets of over one hundred ships assembled. The English made two major naval assaults, the Cadiz Voyage of 1596 and the less successful Islands Voyage of 1597. The Spanish 'second' armada ultimately proved unable to go to sea, but the debates over its target revealed once again the dilemmas of Philippine strategy. The attack on Cadiz had removed any remaining moral scruples about intervention in Ireland and sending an expedition there was proposed, but Philip decided instead to employ the fleet in reinforcing the Netherlands.

The Franco-Spanish peace returned the war to a straightforward Anglo-Dutch struggle with Spain, though with the benevolent neutrality of Henry IV as well as James VI. With his victory over the English at the Blackwater (Yellow Ford) in August 1598, the earl of Tyrone appeared to be a significant military power in Ireland and on the strength of it offered to recognize Philip III as king. Yet for Spain the Netherlands remained the central concern and when at last a small expeditionary force was sent to Ireland in 1601, its primary purpose was to force Elizabeth into abandoning the Dutch. Only Robert Persons appears to have made the case for seeing Ireland as a springboard for the liberation of British Catholics as a whole.

So far as Britain itself was concerned the greatest single event of the period was the dynastic union of 1603. As Ralegh pointed out in his trial a year later the new Great Britain would occupy a potentially far stronger position in Europe than England alone had ever done. As such it marked a resolution of sorts of the previous Anglo-Scoto-

---

[8] Conyers Read, *Lord Burghley and Queen Elizabeth* (London, 1960), 456.

Hibernian relationship. The English claim to the crown of France was now redundant, though not abandoned in the post-Union royal style. It is tempting to say that the feudal-dynastic element had been removed from foreign policy, but there was to be a significant revival of dynastic policy under the Stewarts. In many respects 1603 marked a return to business as usual after the abnormal circumstances of the last fifty years.

Yet things were not the same as they had been in 1547, let alone 1502. The second half of the century had seen a far more dramatic change in England's position in the world than either Scotland's or Ireland's. This was to a considerable degree the effect of England's unusual prominence as the leading Protestant monarchy in Europe. Moreover, for all her failings and the frustrations of her policies, Elizabeth's international reputation soared in the last decades of her reign. In 1603 England's conception of itself was of a different order to what it had been before 1559, and this paradoxically made the actual implementation of union far more difficult then than it would have been earlier. It has been fashionable in recent years to mock the harking back to a mythical Elizabethan greatness, but the humiliation suffered over the comparatively paltry figure James VI and I cut on the European stage compared to the great queen was one of the political realities of early seventeenth-century England.

**Figure 10** Title page of the 1607 edition of William Camden's *Britannia*. Below an early representation of Britannia herself, Ceres and Neptune, with symbols of the fruits of both land and sea, support the map of Roman Britain, engraved on a silver platter, such as the earlier antiquary John Leland had promised to present to Henry VIII. It has handles and so can be carried out into the wider world. Ireland is literally marginalized and monarchy is not represented at all.

# Conclusion

Patrick Collinson

## I

Towards the end of the sixteenth century, a schoolmaster whose holidays were spent in amateur research into 'antiquities' published a book called *Britannia* (1586), soon to be translated into English as *Britain*. Both William Camden's book and its origins can tell us something about the sixteenth-century status of the island of Britain, containing the kingdoms of England and Scotland and the Principality of Wales, administratively if by no means culturally subsumed within England, and of that other island of Ireland, then as now uncomfortably related to its larger neighbour. We can also infer something about what the rest of Europe knew of these islands, which seems to have been not very much. Invited to say what they had heard about England on a quiz show, most continentals would have said that they had been told that there were no wolves to be found there and, after that, 'pass'.

But if continental Europe was not well-informed about Britain, the constituent parts of the British Isles had histories which had for long been intertwined with the continent. In the sixteenth century, the French connection was receding into England's past, but not in the imagination and ambition of Henry VIII, who tried to be Henry V reincarnate. Such dreams were not over even when, in 1558, Calais, the last English possession in France was lost. Henry's daughter Elizabeth was never reconciled to the loss, while for many reigns to come, kings of England would continue to claim in their formal style to be kings of France as well. By contrast, the 'Auld Alliance' of Scotland and France was a political reality, into the second half of the century. English interests, especially commercial interests, were closely bound up with those Low Countries across the North Sea which in the sixteenth century became the Spanish Netherlands, and, presently, in part, the independent United Provinces. Progressively, as the Protestant Reformation advanced and receded in much of Europe north of the Alps, England, which after some fluctuations had chosen the Protestant side in this conflict, followed momentous events across the Channel and North Sea with intense concern.

The emphasis in this book, and series, on the Britishness of our history should not therefore disguise the fact that late sixteenth-century England was more interested in continental Europe than in Scotland. Whereas, wrote the earl of Clarendon of the early seventeenth century, 'the whole [English] nation was solicitous to know what passed weekly in Germany and Poland and all other parts of Europe, no man ever inquired what was doing in Scotland, nor had that kingdom a place or mention in . . . any gazette.'[1] That, of course, did not prevent events in Scotland, and Ireland, from having a profound effect on what was to happen next, in seventeenth-century England.

Nor could Elizabethan England be indifferent to Scotland so long as Mary, queen of Scots, was alive and her son waiting in the wings. In Camden's other great work, his *Annals* of Elizabeth, there is a great deal of Scottish history, tightly interwoven with events in England. The indifference which Clarendon reported applied only to the decades in which Scotland had ceased to be a problem and before it became a problem again. From a Scottish point of view, England was always the problem. For the longest-serving of sixteenth-century English statesmen, William Cecil, Lord Burghley, English politics had to have a Scottish dimension. The security of the Protestant English state depended on what Cecil called 'perpetuity of a brotherly and national friendship betwixt the two realms', to which the only alternative was 'to be made one monarchy with England, as they both make but one isle divided from the rest of the world'.[2]

To return to *Britannia*: it was a Belgian geographer, Abraham Ortelius, who persuaded Camden to put Britain, literally, on the map. As Camden's biographer later wrote, for Ortelius and his friends

---

[1] Quoted in Jonathan Scott, *England's Troubles: Seventeenth-Century English Political Instability in European Context* (Cambridge, 2000), 27 n. 18.

[2] Stephen Alford, *The Early Elizabethan Polity: William Cecil and the British Succession Crisis, 1558–1569* (Cambridge, 1998), 57, 223.

'Britain was another world', and Camden was urged 'to restore antiquity to Britain, and Britain to his antiquity'.[3] What this meant was that Camden's book would tell the world that 'Britannia' was the name of a province of the Roman empire, and hence a place to be treated with respect, for the sixteenth century was obsessed with origins, whether mythical or otherwise. So Camden wrote in Latin, for a learned international readership, which tells us, if we needed to be told, that English was not yet a global language, not even a language of common currency in Europe, that it was understood by about as many as today understand Icelandic outside Iceland. As Princess Katherine told Henry V in Shakespeare's play, 'Your Majesty shall mock at me, I cannot speak your England'—and Henry's awful French was indeed marginally better than her English. It is significant if anachronistic that, according to Shakespeare, Henry wooed 'Kate' in his own language.

Celebrating what one of Camden's friends called 'the excellence of the English tongue', another schoolmaster, Richard Mulcaster, writing in 1582, thought that it mattered not a scrap that English was confined to one small island, and was not spoken in all parts even of that. (He meant Britain, including Scotland, and even so exaggerated, since English was used and understood in parts of Ireland and had been in that little England beyond the Channel, Calais.) Mulcaster boasted that 'though it go not beyond sea, it will serve on this side . . . Our state is no Empire to hope to enlarge it by commanding over [other] countries.'[4] In view of what was to happen to English in the centuries to follow, Mulcaster's apology for his own language is unconsciously ironical.

Camden was motivated by two strong urges: the love of old relics of the past, the the title deeds of Britain's very identity, an 'itch', we are told, 'that stuck so fast by him that he could not get rid of it'; and what he called 'the honour of his native country'. 'The glory of my country encouraged me to undertake it.'[5] We should not underestimate the fervent patriotism of the sixteenth century, even if in the form articulated by Camden it was a learned, elite commodity rather

---

[3] On Camden, Ortelius, and *Britannia*, Thomas Smith, 'Life of Camden', in Edmund Gibson's edition of *Britannia* (London, 1695), preface to *Britain* (London, 1610).

[4] Richard Mulcaster, *Elementarie* (London, 1582), 271.

[5] Smith's 'Life of Camden', preface to *Britain*.

than something genuinely popular, a distant cry from the patriotisms of, say, 1914, or of today's football 'fans'.

But what was Camden's 'country'? The full title of his book (to quote the first English edition of 1610) was a 'description of the most flourishing kingdoms, England, Scotland, and Ireland, and the islands adjoining'. Now Ireland was not, strictly speaking, part of 'Britain', or even according to Irish nationalists one of 'the British Isles', although some sixteenth-century maps were so captioned, while one map of Ireland on its own describes it as a British island. Many inhabitants of Ireland considered themselves to be English, as subjects of an English king who was also lord, and after 1541, king, of an Ireland 'annexed' to England. The handsome engraved title page of Camden's second edition of 1607, which consists of a map of Britain as it might have been in Roman times, illustrates these ambiguities, for it literally marginalizes Ireland, showing only the eastern half of an island never settled and civilized by Rome, while the map of Britain proper has no frontier separating England from Scotland. The poet and preacher John Donne was perhaps referring to Camden's title page when he told his congregation: 'Now it is a pleasant sight to look upon a Map of this Island, when it is all one.'[6]

So what did the sixteenth century mean by 'country', in Latin *patria*? England, of course, perhaps even a Britain which was not yet a political actuality, although by 1607 the two countries were semi-united under the same king, two crowns on one head, and James VI and I was, unsuccessfully, trying to persuade his English subjects to call themselves British, and their country Great Britain.

In Ireland, Gaelic lordships were also called 'patriae', as in 'patria O'Toole'. And in England 'country' could also mean one's native heath, for patriotism could be intensely local. *Britannia* was amongst other things a tour of England, county by county. In its English version it would be consulted not by Belgian geographers but by the English gentry, 'county' people, with a particular eye to their own shires. Camden both built on and stimulated a generation or two of locally patriotic antiquaries who were engaged in the rediscovery of their own country, beginning with the *Itineraries* of John Leland in the 1540s. Leland toured the whole of England, on foot, noticing, or

---

[6] *The Sermons of John Donne*, ed. E. M. Simpson and G. R. Potter (Berkeley, 1953), 221.

so he claimed, every remarkable natural and manmade feature. But most of the 'chorographers', as they called themselves, wrote about their own back yards: William Lambarde on Kent, Richard Carew on Cornwall, John Stow on London. Christopher Saxton's pioneering *Atlas*, which appeared a little before *Britannia* in 1579, remaining in use for two hundred years, consisted of both a large map of England, an England made up of 'coloured counties', and smaller maps of the individual counties themselves. When *Britannia* moved on from London, Camden's birthplace, he wrote: 'Now will I take my leave of my dear native country, and bid London adieu.'[7] National and local identities were fused and confused in Camden's Britain, an island to which, as it happens, he never bade adieu, not once leaving its shores, or travelling any farther north than Hadrian's Wall (which was beyond any point in the north of England reached by any of the Tudor monarchs), although he was a member of an international republic of learning and letters which transcended political frontiers.

Such was 'Britain' towards the end of the sixteenth century, a century when its various inhabitants rediscovered, even reinvented themselves in both space and time, and then began to imagine a new relationship to a much wider world. Three years after *Britannia*, Richard Hakluyt published his *Principall navigations, voiages and discoueries of the English nation*, anticipating an English, or British Empire, which did not yet exist, for in 1589 it was only the Spanish Empire on which the sun never set.

Local identities in sixteenth-century England, a landscape and society of towns as well as counties, were reinforced by the growth of the structures and functions of local administration. The numbers of gentry enrolled as Justices of the Peace increased with the laws and orders they were required to enforce, as did the occasions on which they sat together on the bench, in order of rank and seniority. Representation in Parliament became more highly valued and competitive. Political and administrative involvement was matched by intense social interaction, friendships and feuds, sporting occasions, marriages, not forgetting developing markets and industries. The magistrates in the towns were no less self-conscious, making statements about the pride and independence of their bailiwicks by erecting

[7] William Camden, *Britain* (1610), 437.

more stately public buildings and acquiring such trappings of display as silver processional maces.

All this happened above the heads of most people, but not beyond their concerns. The still more localized identity of the parish, both in town and country, was strengthened even as its independence was compromised by the demands of Tudor legislation, especially social legislation, which imposed new responsibilities, and constraints, on church wardens, constables and other parish officers, men (always men) without rank, but 'honest'. The opinion of the Elizabethan statesman and commentator Sir Thomas Smith that 'no account' was to be made of such people, 'but only to be ruled, not to rule other', proved to be more and more out of touch with reality.[8] It became a matter of pride, as well as a legal necessity, to care for the poor of the parish, mainly pensioners, but also to avoid by any means responsibility for other people's problems. My parish, right or wrong. These local repercussions of the process which historians rather grandly call 'state formation' had their counterparts in Wales, Scotland, and Ireland: in Wales a growing approximation to English ways, in Scotland a homegrown development towards greater 'civility', and the ever more intrusive business of the parochial bodies called 'kirk sessions', ministers and lay 'elders', who in their zeal for righteousness had scant respect for what are now called civil liberties; in Ireland a more violent process, destructive of traditional social and political ties and traditions.

The most important constituents of nationhood, or national self-consciousness, apart from the politics and laws defining and putting territorial limits on the state (not always, of course, coterminous with ethnic or linguistic identities), were a shared language, expressed in a written vernacular literature, and a shared religious identity. To take language first: if the sixteenth century witnessed the pretension to dominion of the English state throughout much of the British Isles, it was also the century which experienced what one historian of language has called 'the triumph of English'. But if we mean by 'English' the 'standard' form of the language, with 'received pronunciation', called in the sixteenth century (and not before) 'King's English', it was a language which only a minority habitually employed. England was

---

[8] *De Republica Anglorum by Sir Thomas Smith*, ed. Mary Dewar (Cambridge, 1982), 76–7.

composed of innumerable 'speech communities', geographical and occupational, which were by no means mutually comprehensible, and which tied those brought up in the mental worlds of these dialects to their often small and restricted neighbourhoods and discouraged spatial mobility. Travellers in Lincolnshire might be told: 'Yaw mun een goo thruft yon beck, then yaw's com to a new yate, then turr off to th'raight, o'er a brig that lays o'er a hoy doyke.' A stranger in Nottinghamshire was advised that his 'wy lig'd' by 'youn nooke', and he 'mun' go 'strit forth'.[9]

Something like standard English was emergent no later than the late fourteenth century and was used by the upper and educated classes, who nevertheless 'condescended' to the speech of the common people when in their company. If any individual is to be credited with the perfection of the English used by Shakespeare, then he was the Bible translator William Tyndale, whose New Testament of 1526, the first time that any part of the Bible had been printed in English, marked the most important of all milestones in our literary-linguistic history. (The better known 'Authorized' or 'King James' version of 1611 is simply Tyndale in rather more formal dress.) Tyndale, who hailed from the Forest of Dean in remotest Gloucestershire, where there were any number of localized dialects, but who was a highly trained linguist, expert in Latin, Greek, and Hebrew, must himself have been bilingual.

The dissemination of Tyndale's English, and its almost universal adoption by educated people, was only made possible by the printing press. In sixteenth-century England, the legitimate publishing industry was confined to London, and it is no accident that by 1589 George Puttenham was insisting on the literary use of 'our Southern English', the speech of London 'and the shires lying about London within sixty miles, and not much above' (which took in Oxford and Cambridge). 'Neither shall he follow the speech of a craftsman or carter, or other of the inferior sort.'[10] Richard Mulcaster, writing when Shakespeare was 18 years of age, and he had been schoolmaster to England's 'arch-poet', Edmund Spenser, believed that this form of English was equivalent to Greek in the age of Demosthenes, Latin in the time of Cicero:

---

[9] Adam Fox, *Oral and Literate Culture in England 1500–1700* (Oxford, 2000), 81–2.
[10] George Puttenham, 'Of Language', Bk. III, chap. 4 of *The Arte of English Poesie*, in *English Renaissance Literary Criticism*, ed. Brian Vickers (Oxford, 1999), 226.

sheer perfection. But both Mulcaster and Puttenham were acutely aware that language was fluid and unstable, the more 'primitive' forms the most 'pure'. Thirty thousand new words, mostly of Latin origin, entered the English language between 1570 and 1630, more than at any other time in history.

It was of the utmost importance for the cultural future of Wales that the Welsh acquired their own vernacular Bible, complete by 1588, with much the same significance for the Welsh language and literature as Tyndale had for English, and what might now be called a devolutionist potential. But it was no less significant that there was to be no translation of the Bible into Lowlands Scots, but rather the adoption of the English version prepared in Geneva in the late 1550s by Englishmen sharing the religious exile of the anglicized Scot, John Knox, and heavily indebted to Tyndale. This Bible was dedicated, significantly, to all the 'brethren of England, Scotland, Ireland etc.' and many of these Bibles would be imported into Scotland from London. This linguistic invasion diminished Scots as a language for educated people, and created a greater differentiation between the spoken and the printed language than obtained in at least south-eastern England.

These same generations witnessed the break-up of a classical Gaelic which had been common to western Scotland and Ireland, and the decay towards extinction of the Cornish language. In 1602 Richard Carew wrote that 'the English speech doth still encroach upon it and hath driven the same into the uttermost skirts of the shire.' 'Most of the inhabitants can speak no word of Cornish.'[11]

The convergence of English and Scottish high cultures was greatly accentuated by the religious changes which were the major events, or rather processes, of the sixteenth century in both kingdoms. England and Scotland were countries tranformed by the Protestant Reformation, in which Wales participated without much active dissent, but which had to be imposed, with very limited success, on Ireland. The circumstances of Reformation north and south of the border were different, a process carried forward by successive Tudor governments in England but to a great extent against and in spite of government, including the French interest, in Scotland, so that it amounted to a

---

[11] *Richard Carew of Antony: The Survey of Cornwall*, ed. F. E. Halliday (London, 1953), 127.

kind of national revolution. There were also differences in the forms of worship and belief adopted in the two countries, although they were not seen by many contemporaries to be insurmountable, so that a more or less shared religious faith distanced Britain from Catholic Europe and advanced the process of British integration.

Historians continue to disagree over the extent to which the English people took the new religion to heart and became more than what contemporaries called 'cold statute Protestants'. But it is now generally accepted that by the end of the century the English nation was Protestant at least in the sense that (except for a repressed minority) it was no longer Catholic, and even defined itself and its monarchy with the ideology and rhetoric of anti-Catholicism. The sense of an 'elect nation', modelled on biblical Israel, a nation beleaguered by more powerful monarchies but given a special God-given purpose for being, was greatly enhanced by this ideology, which was as nationalistic as it was religious. Scottish Protestants, too, were inclined to claim most favoured nation status (if England was Israel, surely Scotland was Judah, the smaller but purer of the Old Testament kingdoms?), but they were just as likely to invest a greater Britain with religious overtones. Britain was one Protestant island, in Shakespeare's words a 'precious stone set in the silver sea, which serves it in the office of a wall'. Admittedly Shakespeare called 'this blessed plot' England, not Britain, but only a united Britain enjoyed unbroken sea defences against a hostile world.[12] For generations to come, until called to order by late twentieth-century developments, English people would assume that 'England' and 'Britain' meant much the same thing.

## II

Once upon a time, students were taught that the Middle Ages ended and modern history began in 1485, when Henry Tudor at the Battle of Bosworth seized the crown of England by conquest from the usurper, Richard III. Nothing now seems that simple, and political and administrative historians emphasize not discontinuity but continuity

---

[12] Shakespeare, *Richard II*, II. i.

between England under the Yorkist kings and under the first of the Tudors. Henry VII meant the smack of firm government but nothing really novel, and if the medieval form and style of government gave way to something more 'modern', which it did only to a very limited extent, that happened later, in the reign of Henry VIII, and specifically in the 1530s, when there were so many significant changes that the leading Tudor historian of the last generation, Sir Geoffrey Elton, turned them into a 'revolution in government' which amounted to the birthpangs of the modern state. That suggestion remains controversial, even discredited, and to hunt for the beginnings of modernity in the sixteenth century may be futile. Quite contrary to what Elton required generations of students to believe, it was the functional weakness, not the strength, of English government under the Tudors which we ought to emphasize, especially if we want to make sense of what happened to the monarchy, and to the state, under their Stewart successors. A more recent historian has written of 'the absence of effective state-building in the sixteenth century' and of 'a weak post-medieval [rather than proto-modern] monarchy'.[13] This was only transformed into a recognizably modern, or early modern, military-fiscal state, capable of punching its weight in Europe and beyond, after the collapse of Stewart monarchy, with the aid of foreign intervention, in 1688–9.

But we can allow the long sixteenth century to begin in 1485, and to end in 1603, for these, the confining dates of the Tudor dynasty were all-important in giving shape to a history which was something more than just one damned thing after another.

Random events are fashioned into a meaningful history by those living through them, and equally by the generations which followed; and in the sixteenth century they were fashioned to a very limited extent by the interests and aspirations of nations, if nations could be said to have had such things, and overwhelmingly by dynasties, which is to say ruling families. The destinies of millions of subject peoples were everywhere determined both by the strategies and calculations of these families as they advanced their supposed interests through marriage and war, and even more by the biological accidents of fertility, infertility, and death, over which they had little or no control. Fifteenth-century England would have had a different history if

---

[13] Scott, *England's Troubles*, 68.

Edward III (king from 1327 to 1377) had not sired twelve children, including five sons who made it into adulthood, the family later developing a fatal faultline dividing its Lancastrian and Yorkist branches. And the sixteenth century would have been no less different if the Tudors, who through Henry VII's marriage to Elizabeth of York united and reconciled the Lancastrians and Yorkists, had not proved so infertile. When Henry died in 1509 he had only one legitimate son living. That son, Henry VIII, made no fewer than six marriages, five of them consummated, but these produced only three mature progeny, two of them girls, only one of whom married, and neither destined to be a mother. The only legitimate son, Henry's successor Edward VI, died in his teens. When his sister Elizabeth followed him and her sister Mary to her solitary grave in 1603, having lived longer than any other Tudor, it was the end of the line. Francis Bacon remarked, with wonder at the vagaries of human affairs, on those 'barren princes'.[14] The second half of the sixteenth century was dominated by uncertainty as to who was likely to fill the inevitable vacuum: a crisis as long as the Cold War in more recent memory, and with an equal potential for destructive conflict. For human nature abhors a vacuum, and was all too likely to fill it with civil war. Instead, and for as long as Elizabeth lived, the space was filled by politics of the kind described and analysed in John Guy's chapter.

If Henry VIII had fathered several sons, the history of the English state, and even more of the English Church, would not have been the same. One or more of those sons would surely have become archbishops, and in a Church still united with and obedient to Rome. But that was not to be. Henry's lack of a male heir was the precipitant, even the principal cause, of what really was a revolution: the unilateral declaration of independence from Rome of the English Church, declared and enacted by its Supreme Head, the king, in Parliament, and inseparable from a state now said to enjoy unlimited sovereignty, an 'empire'. The Church was much reduced in power and wealth and it was to be governed, under the crown, by middle-class bishops. None of that was bound to happen, for it is events, even accidents, which largely determine human affairs. 'Policy' is the fly on the wheel, kidding itself that it makes the world go round.

For the future of Britain, it mattered most that in 1500 Henry VII

<hr>

[14] *The Letters and the Life of Francis Bacon*, ed. J. Spedding, 3 (1868), 250.

had married his daughter Margaret to the king of Scots, James IV: more dynasticism. For it was the great-grandson of that marriage, almost precisely a century later, and in spite of an act of Parliament enforcing Henry VIII's will, which had excluded the Scottish line from the succession, who united the Scottish and English crowns as James VI and I. That this was not followed by a union of the two kingdoms, an event delayed until 1707, let alone of two nations, which remain distinct to this day, is evidence that this was a dynastic event. If there had been the will to do so, the English could no doubt have found ways and means of preventing James from inheriting their throne. They had done that with his mother, by the simple expedient of cutting off the head of Mary, queen of Scots. But if James's great-grandfather, James IV, had not consented, for reasons of transient policy, to marry his son to Margaret Tudor, there was no way that James VI could have become James I of England, and consequently king of Ireland, to that extent uniting the whole British Isles. And yet this was very much succession by default. As Sir Thomas More remarked in his book on Richard III, politics were but king's games, played upon 'scaffolds' (stages), and non-royal persons who attempted to change the plot were liable to get hurt, which, of course, was to happen to More himself.

# III

But as John Guy's contribution to this book suggests, More's sarcastic dictum about king's games did not contain the whole truth. At one level of political reality, sixteenth-century kingdoms were so many pieces of real estate, which could be inherited or otherwise lost or gained, aggregated and disaggregated, like other landed properties. Through a process which might now be called one of globalization, the future seemed to favour ever larger territorial portfolios, a Europe of empires rather than of sovereign nation states. When Philip II, usually said to be 'of Spain', but possessed of a collection of territories stretching from Sicily to Frisia, and of silver mines in America, married Queen Mary Tudor, it looked as if England would be subsumed within the Habsburg scheme of things, if not empire, much like a modern company falling victim to an aggressive takeover bid.

His contemporary Henry II of France, who in 1558 took possession of Calais, an incident in a war with the Habsburgs in which England had little interest, had other ideas. With his son and heir married to the young Scottish queen, Mary Stewart, and the French in military and naval command of Scotland and the waters around it, Henry boasted to the Sultan of Turkey, Suleiman the Magnificent, that he had every expectation of assuming control of the entire British Isles. It looked as if the future of England, and of Scotland, would be as satellites of one or other of the superpowers of the age.

That this was not to be depended upon a number of factors, including an ineluctable geography, sea rather than land frontiers, which in every century has tended to determine British history; and the mutual financial embarrassment of the two great powers of the mid-sixteenth century, who literally exhausted their credit with their international bankers. But what is of greater interest is that England was already more than a kingdom, and that its people, if they were definable, as they are to this day, as subjects of their monarchs, were also in a real sense citizens, members of a political society which was capable of imagining itself through its language, laws and public institutions, and of contributing to its own management. This, in a once famous phrase, was 'self-government at the king's command'. For as Sir John Fortescue described it in the fifteenth century, England was not a simple monarchy (the implication was, such as France), but a *regimen* (or *dominium*) *politicum et regale*. It was characterized not only by the institution of monarchy, for which it was not easy, or even possible, to envisage any alternative, but by a distinctive political culture.

This built-in ambiguity would be described in many ways in the long sixteenth century, and beyond. In 1559 John Aylmer wrote that it was a mistake to suppose that England was 'a mere monarchy'. Its constitution contained compatible elements of what the Greeks had defined as monarchy, oligarchy (or aristocracy), and democracy, and this was reflected in the English Parliament 'where you shall find these three estates'. Thomas Smith wrote at about the same time that Parliament 'representeth and hath the power of the whole realm, both the head and the body'. The monarch, we must always remember, was a member of the Parliament, one of its three constituent parts. What Parliament did was 'the prince's and the whole realm's deed'.[15] Aylmer's immediate purpose in developing this argument was to reassure anyone nervous about the government of a woman (Elizabeth) that within the English constitution she would not govern arbitrarily and unadvisedly. In 1610 Thomas Hedley said, in Parliament, that England enjoyed 'the blessings and benefits of an absolute monarchy and of a free estate'.[16] Anyone who finds that statement contradictory has not begun to understand the nature of government and politics in early modern England. In the mid-seventeenth century, the two halves of Hedley's equation were indeed to tear themselves asunder: a civil war waged against the king in the name of the king, but under the colours of Parliament. We look to the historians of that century to tell us whether that was something which was waiting to happen, even bound to happen.

But before those cataclysmic events, which led to the temporary extinction of both monarchy and Parliament, the end of all constitutional legality, it was the success of this balanced constitution which should impress us. This might appear to be in conflict with what has already been said about the functional weakness of the state in fiscal-military terms. According to the terms of a kind of civil contract, the country was unwilling to pay punitive, or even realistic, taxes, and the government was unable, or unwilling, to exact what the Gross National Product was capable of yielding, as only those same Civil War years were to show. In what have been called the 'predatory' 1540s, the crown helped itself to a larger share of the national income than at any other time until the 1690s. But these were the one-off fruits of the disendowment of the Church (mainly the dissolution of the monasteries), a windfall which was unrepeatable on the same scale. Emphatically, this was not a 'tax and spend' economy. It was apparently of some mutual benefit, to both the taxpayer and the government, that William Cecil Lord Burghley assessed his income for tax purposes at £133, when he was probably worth nearer £4,000. As Lord Treasurer, he *was* the government, so far as this matter was concerned.

It might appear to follow that there was a corresponding and chronic inability to pay for the defence of the realm. What was called

---

[15] John Aylmer, *An Harborowe for Faithfull and Trewe Subiectes* ('Strasborowe', *recte* London, 1559), sig. H3ʳ; Smith, *De Republica Anglorum*, 78–9.

[16] *Proceedings in Parliament 1610*, ii. *House of Commons*, ed. E. R. Foster (New Haven, 1966), 191.

the 'perfect militia' has sometimes seemed to be a sick joke, a ramshackle of 'musters' which Shakespeare hardly needed to parody in the satire of his *Henry IV* plays. However, if there was room for improvement in the department of recruitment, Simon Adams has argued in his chapter that the Elizabethan army, small though it may have been, was exceptionally well armed, and that England was already a leading player in the international arms trade. So far as war at sea was concerned, he writes of the Elizabethan navy's 'precocity', small ships equipped with formidable armament. Nevertheless, we are not talking about a great power, by the standards of the age, and this is not where we should look to find evidence of the success of the Tudor state.

But within the political economy of the kingdom, respect for the common law was practically a religion, the force of parliamentary statute irresistible. Some of the best evidence for this is to be found in the religious changes of the Reformation years. Under Edward VI, the great crosses which dominated the interior of all churches, flanked by images of Mary and John, were pulled down; under Mary, they were restored; under Elizabeth, taken down a second time. All of this cost local communities money. None of it could have been popular, with most people. But it was done. Today only one set of pre-Reformation 'rood imagery' survives in all of England and Wales. No less impressive, and in sharp contrast to the French experience, was the absence of homicidal violence on the streets of a country experiencing such drastic religious instability.

The sixteenth century witnessed an unprecedented expansion of the economic and social role of the state, especially in the creation of a national poor-relief system which was without parallel anywhere else in Europe. This is evidence of what Keith Wrightson has called 'the exceptional capacity of English government when it chose to act decisively', while Michael Braddick has written of 'an active and increasingly intrusive state apparatus'.[17]

But what was this 'state'? Are we even entitled to talk of a Tudor state? Not until the end of our period did contemporaries use the term as we would use it, to mean an impersonal public corporation,

---

[17] Keith Wrightson, *Earthly Necessities: Economic Lives in Early Modern Britain* (New Haven and London, 2000), 217; Michael Braddick, *State Formation in Early Modern England c.1550–1700* (Cambridge, 2000), 14.

existing apart from the monarchy. What we might regard as the revenues of the state, various kinds of taxation, were understood to
belong to the king personally, only in their administration different
from the income the king enjoyed from his private estates, and they
were not subject to any kind of public scrutiny or accountability. It
was up to the monarch whether to use his resources to wage war, or
build palaces, or reward his nobility. When Henry VIII found that he
had enough money in his coffers to afford it, he naturally went to war.
The disinclination of his daughter Elizabeth to wage war was directly
linked to financial stringency (our great cathedrals might have gone
the way of the abbeys to pay for two or three years of campaigning,
but fortunately they were spared), and one reason for that was political reluctance to be beholden to her subjects, as taxpayers, which
meant that not only subjects but the queen herself thought it
virtuous and advantageous to 'live of her own'.

There was the germ of our notion of the state in the curious legal
doctrine of 'the king's two bodies'. The monarch was possessed not
of one 'body' but of two. His (or, from 1553 to 1603 her) natural body
was subject to all the vagaries of human existence, physically and
intellectually empowered or limited, as the case might be. But the
king's public body never dies and is incapable of wrong, or of being
sued for wrongdoing. The king is dead. Long live the king. The point
of this doctrine was to emphasize the inseparability of these two
bodies, so that such personal incapacities as being a woman, or of the
wrong religion, were not a disqualification. The doctrine was not very
helpful when succession to the throne was a matter of great
uncertainty, as for the second half of the sixteenth century it always
was. Yet we may recognize in the notion of the king's body politic the
emergence of something like the idea of the modern self-
perpetuating state.

Service to that state, at every level, was what made and defined the
early modern English state, according to its latest historian, Michael
Braddick, who will not allow us to talk of deliberate 'state building',
of which there is no evidence, 'no architect or overall blueprint', but
who does permit 'state formation'. There was a state, but it consisted
in a burgeoning network of offices exercising political power, related
to the centre but not centrally located.

The two key words in the lectionary of sixteenth-century political
culture, putting on it what would now be called a distinctive 'spin',

were not 'state' but 'commonwealth' and 'counsel'. 'Commonwealth' was more or less interchangeable with the Latin *republica*, as in Thomas Smith's book which was called in Latin *De Republica Anglorum* but in English *Of the English Commonwealth*. We should not impose on this political culture the modern, anti-monarchist, implications of 'republic'. In the later seventeenth century, Algernon Sidney would insist that 'all monarchies in the world that are not purely barbarous and tyrannical, have ever been called Commonwealths'—which was as much as to say, republics.[18] England under the Tudors, and especially under the last of the Tudors, was, if you will, a monarchical republic.

That commonwealth was an expression strongly suggestive of matters of general and public concern is accentuated by some Tudor writers who were cautious about the 'socialist' implications of *Common* Wealth and preferred '*Public* Weal' (or 'weal public'), although this failed to catch on. It is significant that the term entered the language at a time of ineffective monarchical rule, in the mid-fifteenth century. For weak monarchy, or political instability at the top, was almost the condition for the existence and assertion of what is nowadays called a strong 'civil society'. Hence, in part, the especial prominence of 'commonwealth' ideas and values in the mid-sixteenth century, under the minority government of Edward VI.

But in the sixteenth century, the resonances of 'commonwealth' were greatly enriched by the more extensive appropriation of the political and intellectual language and legacy of ancient Greece and Rome. It became the weariest of all political commonplaces to repeat the Roman Cicero, himself following Plato. 'We are not born for ourselves alone, but our country claims a share of our being, and our friends a share.' Having quoted Cicero to this effect for the umpteenth time, a Member of the Elizabethan House of Commons declared: 'Mr Speaker, I do condemn him as . . . most unnatural and unworthy to live in any commonwealth that regardeth not his country, for which I intend to deal . . . since great necessity urgeth it.'[19] (The 'necessity' concerned the uncertain succession, something which touched the continuing interest of the 'commonwealth' more

---

[18] Scott, *England's Troubles*, 76.
[19] Cicero, *De officiis*, I. vii. 22; *Proceedings in the Parliaments of Elizabeth I*, i. 1558–1581, ed. T. E. Hartley (Leicester, 1981), 129.

than the monarch for the time being, who, in the nature of the case, would not be around to suffer the consequences of a contested succession.)

In Scotland, where the relation of the monarch to the nation was historically different, or was made to seem so by its leading sixteenth-century historian, George Buchanan, events sharpened the edge of what we may call monarchical republicanism. In 1567 Mary, queen of Scots, was forced to abdicate, in effect deposed, by a faction of the nobility, following the murder of her husband, Henry Darnley, an act of regicide in which the queen was held to have been complicit. Buchanan justified an act which had raised eyebrows throughout Europe, not only in his History of Scotland, *Rerum Scoticarum Historia*, published posthumously in 1582, but in the polemically motivated political treatise, *De iure regno apud Scotos*, which circulated widely in manuscript in international circles before being published in 1579.

Putting a sharp Scottish edge on the common stock of classical political theory, and especially on the distinction between true monarchy and tyranny, Buchanan insisted that monarchy was properly elective, with the negative consequence that tyrants like Mary Stewart could be removed by the political societies which had appointed them. As Cicero had written, the safety of the people was the ultimate law. Buchanan claimed the authority of two thousand years of Scottish history for this doctrine, and the precedents of no less than a dozen kings in the course of that (partly fictitious) history who had been deposed. He provoked a backlash, not least from his sometime pupil, James VI, who ordered the suppression of his writings and as king of England advanced a doctrine of divine right monarchy which was the antithesis of his tutor's anti-monarchism. From the English point of view, Buchanan was writing about the polity of what was still a foreign country. Nevertheless, his radical views were of great interest to some of England's citizens.

The indispensable glue which was supposed to hold in creative tension the principles and interests of monarchy and commonwealth was 'counsel', a concept extensively explored in this volume by John Guy. It was almost a definition of a tyrant that he was deaf to good counsel and surrounded himself with unprincipled flatterers who echoed his own selfish and foolish fantasies. The problem of counsel, which was how the monarch could be constrained to accept good advice, was at the heart of sixteenth-century politics, and was most notably spelled out in Thomas More's *Utopia*. That both the monarch and the commonwealth benefited from good counsel was not in doubt. What was contentious, not only in theory but in many of the practicalities of politics, was who controlled those whose function it was to give it.

In England from about 1540, the Council which, in one form or another, had always been associated with the monarchy in government, came to be called the Privy Council, a description emphasizing its physical proximity to the privacy of the king's own person and household. Kings appointed their councillors, and their power to fire as well as hire was not in dispute. As Elizabeth I reminded Mary, queen of Scots, on one occasion, her Councillors had been appointed by her and could be dismissed at will. (The Crown, through the Prime Minister, has this power over secretaries of state to this very day.) But in 1536, in the context of the Pilgrimage of Grace, the doctrine was asserted that the nobility had an inherited right to act as the crown's ministers and advisers. And while the Privy Council was a monarchical creation, it soon developed its own *esprit de corps,* and its own secretariat. In a paradoxical sense, Elizabeth's words to Mary Stewart were a recognition that in practice the Council did constitute, as it were, the magnetic pole of government. If on matters of high policy Councillors were supposed to advise the monarch individually, each standing in his place, as an administrative machine the Council exercised Cabinet-like, corporate powers. England was governed by the signatures appearing below Privy Council letters, some of them supplied by Councillors who may not have been present when the relevant decision had been taken. For many practical purposes, the 'Lords of the Council' constituted the government of the day.

Implicit in much of Elizabethan politics was a more radical position. Privy Councillors and other public men bore a relation to the Commonwealth and to God which might transcend their subservience to the monarch. And while members of the Privy Council had a special place in the economy of counsel, it was hard to deny the role of counsel to the high court of Parliament, which under the Tudors had been used, repeatedly, to alter the religion of the country, determine the succession, and to be party to many other major decisions. From many speeches made in the Elizabethan House of Commons, it is clear that, whether the queen liked it or not, and she didn't, some MPs believed that they had not only a responsibility but a right to offer counsel, and since they derived that claim from their representative function, that was as much as to claim that every Englishman had some claim to be heard, directly or by proxy, in matters which concerned him.

And here yet another Ciceronian maxim was always ready to hand. When a vessel faces shipwreck, everyone on board is bound to do what he can to save it from destruction. As Thomas Smith expressed it in his *Discourse of the Commonweal of this Realm of England* (1549): 'I cannot reckon my self a mere stranger to this matter; no more than a man that were in a ship which were in danger of wreck might say that, because he is not percase the master or pilot of the same, the danger thereof did pertain nothing to him.'[20] Monarchs like Elizabeth insisted, on the contrary, that matters of state, *arcana imperii*, belonged exclusively to them, and were to be discussed by their subjects only by invitation. And whether or not Parliament met, and for how long it sat, was entirely up to the monarch. This conflict of view and interest was another part of the legacy which the seventeenth century would inherit from the sixteenth.

---

# IV

The poet G. K. Chesterton once wrote of 'the people of England, that never have spoken yet', and in conclusion it is time to return to some of the concerns of some of the more ordinary people of the sixteenth century, the subject of Jim Sharpe's chapter, but focusing on England, in contrast to Sharpe's comprehensively British coverage. People were conscious of living through a time of change, and not only religious change, although such was the centrality of religion in the mentality of the time that changes which we might attribute to economics, or population growth, were often interpreted in moral and even religious terms. Someone said that it was 'merry world' ('Merry England' was an expression full of nostalgia for a religious world which was thought to have been lost) before the new religion came in, when you could still buy ten eggs for a penny. With only a little more

[20] *A Discourse of the Commonweal of this Realm of England*, ed. Mary Dewar (Charlottesville, 1969), 11.

sophistication, John Stow, the author of *A Survey of London* (1599), remembered how as a child he had walked every morning to the fields beside the Tower of London, land by the time he wrote all built over and 'developed', to buy a halfpenny-worth of milk, which was three pints in summer (a little more than a litre) and a quart in winter (a little less), 'always hot from the kine, as the same was milked and strained'. As a religious conservative, Stow was nostalgic for his own lost world, deeply regretting what we call privatization, the enclosure of what had been public spaces, and the passing away, as he believed, of the old values of charity and neighbourhood, when householders, on the religious festivals, used to invite their neighbours and passers by 'to sit and be merry with them', 'praising God for his benefits bestowed on them'.[21] London, after all, had trebled in size within this one man's lifetime, and this was perhaps the most momentous development of the entire sixteenth century for the future shape of English and British history.

The aspect of change of which there seems to have been the greatest public awareness was what contemporaries called 'dearth', not, as we might gather from that word, a shortage of food, but the inflation of prices, although the cause of inflation, accounted for by modern economic historians partly by an increase in the supply of money, but mainly by the pressure of an expanding population, was for them a mystery. In Smith's *Discourse of the Commonweal*, a maker of caps is made to say: 'I am fain to give my journeymen twopence in a day more than I was wont to do, and yet they say they cannot sufficiently live thereon.'[22] A merchant agreed. Various commodities from pins and knives to buttons and lace cost him one-third more than he would have paid seven years earlier.

People were aware that change brought benefits to some, difficulty if not privation to others. When the Essex clergyman William Harrison asked the old men living in his village what had altered in their lifetimes they specified three good things and three not so good. The three changes for the better were the arrival of chimneys, making the living space a smoke-free zone; the substitution of comfortable beds and pillows for the old sleeping arrangements of straw pallets and a

---

[21] John Stow, *A Survey of London*, ed. C. L. Kingsford (2 vols; Oxford, 1908), i. 126, 101.

[22] *A Discourse*, 17.

log of wood; and the replacement of wooden platters and spoons by pewter dishes and silver or tin spoons. The three things they identified as 'very grievous unto them' were the enhancing of rents, the insecurity suffered by many tenants, and 'usury', which we may define as falling victim to loan sharks.[23]

The winners in agrarian society were those who had security of tenure, paid reasonable rents if they were not actually freeholders, and who were able to take advantage of buoyant agricultural and other commodity prices. For a farmer with fifty acres, poor harvests were an advantage, since they meant higher grain prices. Such men (and their often comfortably off widows) are easily identified in surviving wills and inventories (with Harrison's county of Essex providing many good examples) where indeed we find feather beds, often complete with testers ('four posters'), other substantial furniture, carpets, and plenty of pewter ware. Farmers and tradesmen who could count on a surplus of income at the end of the year were able to educate their sons at grammar school, and even at university. The most prosperous of this class, below the rank of gentlemen, were the famous 'yeomen of England', whom social commentators at the time thought to be a dying breed. Thomas Wilson in an unpublished account of 'The State of England, Anno Dom. 1600' remembered that they had once been 'the glory of the Country', but believed them to be 'decayed'.[24] In fact we now know that the numbers of this 'middling sort' were on the increase, and in the exacerbated politics of the Civil War years they would be a force to be reckoned with.

This was a society in which the mean annual income of the richest of the nobility was more than £3,000, the wages of a labourer as little as thirty shillings: a ratio of 1,500:1. But the gap between haves and have-nots in the lower levels of society should not be exaggerated, and it was not as wide as it would be in the eighteenth and still more the nineteenth centuries. There were many social gradations rather than clear-cut class distinctions. In England's leading industry of cloth manufacture, for example, some 'clothiers' were already rich entrepreneurs, employing numbers of what one contemporary writer

[23] *The Description of England by William Harrison*, ed. Georges Edelen (Washington, DC and New York, 1994), 202.

[24] 'The State of England, Anno Dom. 1600 by Thomas Wilson', ed. F. J. Fisher, *Camden Miscellany* 16, Camden 3rd ser. 52 (1936), 18–19.

called 'work folks'. But others who styled themselves clothiers were no better off than many 'cloth workers' or 'weavers'.

Contemporaries spoke of those having 'ability' (financial sufficiency) and of 'the better sort', as distinct from 'the meaner sort'. These were substantial householders who were the leading men in their parishes. In 1596 there was a town meeting of those calling themselves 'the chief inhabitants' of a place in Berkshire (but administratively part of Wiltshire) called Swallowfield. These men considered themselves social equals, 'men of discretion', and they presumed to make orders to regulate the conduct of those beneath them in the social scale, 'such as be poor, and will malapertly compare with their betters'.[25] Whereas earlier in the sixteenth century men of this class could prove hostile to the gentry placed above them, as in the events in East Anglia in the summer of 1549 ('Kett's Rebellion'), when they briefly took things into their own hands, their grandsons seem to have been more conscious of the difference between property holders in general and those living more precariously, or below the poverty line. Unlike what happened in 1549, an attempt at direct action in Oxfordshire in 1596 failed to achieve critical mass and received no support from responsible social elements. Protestant doctrine, emphasizing order, obedience, and social discipline, will have had something to do with this, access to education too. But 'men of this class' (rather than 'sort') may be itself misleading. Arguably, there were no 'classes' in early modern society, or, if there were, the fluidity of social distinctions allowed for much upward, and downward, mobility. Some of the grandsons of the men of 1549 could have called themselves gentlemen. Others disappeared without trace.

Towards the end of the century, many villages were filling up from the bottom with the poor, especially in the exceptionally harsh economic climate which prevailed in the 1590s, a decade of poor harvests, low wages, and wartime taxation. Historians of the sixteenth century should not disguise the fact that its conclusion, its *fin de siècle*, was miserable. Desperate people, 'vagrants', were on the move and unregulated begging was on the increase. Householders, who were responsible for the relief of poverty, were frightened at the prospect of an uncontrollable tide engulfing their own communities, and

---

[25] Steve Hindle, 'Hierarchy and Community in the Elizabethan Parish: The Swallowfield Articles of 1596', *Historical Journal*, 42 (1999), 848–50.

they did their best to exclude incoming migrants, and even took steps to prevent the poor from breeding. Tough measures were taken against the mothers of illegitimate children and their offspring, and at Swallowfield the marriage of young people 'before they have a convenient house to live in' was prevented, which was actually against the law.[26]

The Elizabethan poor laws of 1597 and 1601, which built on the accumulated experience of many localities in preceding decades, was enlightened in the relief it provided for the deserving poor, those called at Swallowfield 'the honest poor, the blind, the sick, the lame and diseased persons'.[27] There was a discriminatory bias towards women, especially women of what would now be pensionable age, and children, some reluctance to relieve the poverty of men.

But the other side of this coin was a harsh and draconian attitude to the feckless poverty which was assumed to be voluntary and criminal. Although there were some local initiatives to 'set the poor on work', the phenomenon of systemic unemployment was scarcely acknowledged to exist, even when old industries were failing and markets closing. Whereas, in the first flush of the Protestant Reformation in the days of Edward VI, the 'commonwealth' values espoused by preachers and pamphleteers were unstinting in their criticism of the 'covetous' rich, insisting on a generous attitude to the poor 'without any regard', by the end of the sixteenth century clergymen were prominent in their verbal onslaught on the 'sturdy', idle poor, 'ulcers, scabs and vermin', 'mice, rats and polecats'. 'For those that can work and will not, let them starve', wrote one Essex preacher, a harsh rendering of St Paul's doctrine that if any would not work, neither should he eat.[28]

In his otherwise rose-tinted *Survey of Cornwall* (1602), Richard Carew reached the point where 'we must also spare a room in this Survey to the poor'. But it appeared that not much needed to be said on that subject. But for the shiploads of Irish immigrants (something for the British-minded historian to note!) there would not really have been a problem, and with so much shellfish on the beaches, no one in Cornwall had any excuse to starve. 'But let me lead you from these

---

[26] Hindle, 'Hierarchy and Community', 850.
[27] Ibid.
[28] Patrick Collinson, 'Puritanism and the Poor', in *Pragmatic Utopias, 1200–1630*, ed. R. Horrox and S. Rees-Jones (London, 2001).

unpleasing matters to . . . the Cornishmen's recreations, which consist principally in feasts and pastimes'—church ales, Cornish wrestling, a rough kind of football, miracle plays in the Cornish language, Merry England still alive and well in the far south-west.[29] In something of the same spirit, in the 250 words he devoted to the poor in *England under the Tudors*, Geoffrey Elton admitted that more might be said about the subject, 'but we must observe a proper proportion.' On balance, he believed that in that changing, developing, growing society, gains enormously outweighed losses. But Elton had the good grace to add: 'though this no doubt was small consolation to the losers'.[30] It is not from the point of view of the losers that history has been written, least of all the history of that glamorous, glittering Tudor age which was the sixteenth century.

[29] *The Survey of Cornwall*, 139–40.
[30] Elton, *England under the Tudors*, 2nd edn (London, 1974), 260–1.

# Further reading

## Introduction

The fashionable 'archipelagic' emphasis on Britain in the sixteenth and seventeenth centuries can be explored in three collections of essays: Steven G. Ellis and Sarah Barber (eds.), *Conquest & Union: Fashioning a British State 1485–1725* (London and New York, 1995); Brendan Bradshaw and John Morrill (eds.), *The British Problem, c.1534–1707: State Formation in the Atlantic Archipelago* (Basingstoke, 1996); and Brendan Bradshaw and Peter Roberts (eds.), *British Consciousness and Identity: The Making of Britain, 1533–1707* (Cambridge, 1998). Changing perspectives on English (rather than British) history in the sixteenth century can be traced through S. T. Bindoff, *Tudor England* (London, 1950); G. R. Elton, *England under the Tudors* (London, 1955; 2nd edn.; 1974); John Guy, *Tudor England* (Oxford, 1988); Penry Williams, *The Later Tudors: England 1547–1603* (Oxford, 1995); and Susan Brigden, *New Worlds, Lost Worlds: The Rule of the Tudors 1485–1603* (London, 2000), vol. V of the Penguin History of Britain, which excludes Scotland (as not under Tudor rule) but devotes considerable attention to Ireland. Wallace T. MacCaffrey has written a trilogy of books on Elizabethan politics: *The Shaping of the Elizabethan Regime* (Princeton, 1968); *Queen Elizabeth and the Making of Policy, 1572–1588* (Princeton, 1981); *Elizabeth I: War and Politics 1588–1603* (Princeton, 1992). For the outer limits of Tudor rule, see Steven G. Ellis, *Tudor Frontiers and Noble Power: The Making of the British State* (Oxford, 1995). G. R. Elton's claims for Thomas Cromwell and the 1530s were first made in *The Tudor Revolution in Government: Administrative Changes in the Reign of Henry VIII* (Cambridge, 1953) and defended and restated in many subsequent publications. Elton's broader agenda is defined by the primary documentation gathered and edited in his *The Tudor Constitution*, 2nd edn. (Cambridge, 1982). Newer approaches to Tudor politics, emphasising its intellectual and rhetorical dimensions, can be explored in two collections of essays: Dale Hoak (ed.), *Tudor Political Culture* (Cambridge, 1995) and John Guy (ed.), *Tudor Monarchy* (London, 1997). On the iconography of Tudor power, see John N. King, *Tudor Royal Iconography: Literature and Art in an Age of Religious Crisis* (Princeton, 1989). For the politics contained in canonical dramatic texts, see Greg Walker, *Plays of Persuasion: Drama and Politics at the Court of Henry VIII* (Cambridge, 1991) and *The Politics of Performance in Early Renaissance Drama* (Cambridge, 1998).

## Economy and society

The period is well served by a number of general introductions: among these are Joyce Youings, *Sixteenth-Century England* (London, 1984); Raymond Gillespie, *The Transformation of the Irish Economy, 1550–1700* (Dublin, 1991); S. G. E. Lythe, *The Economy of Scotland in its European Setting* (Edinburgh, 1960); and Ian D. Whyte, *Scottish Society in Transition c.1500-c.1760* (Basingstoke, 1997). No comparable overview exists for Wales, but there is much of value on social and economic matters in Glanmor Williams, *Recovery, Reorientation and Reformation: Wales c.1415–1642* (Oxford, 1987). More detailed studies include: W. G. Hoskins, *The Age of Plunder: King Henry's England 1500–1647* (London, 1976); David M. Palliser, *The Age of Elizabeth: England under the Tudors 1547–1603* (London, 1983); and A. J. S. Gibson and T. C. Smout, *Food and Wages in Scotland 1550–1780* (Cambridge, 1995). Agricultural matters are dealt with comprehensively, south of the border, in Joan Thirsk (ed.), *The Agrarian History of England and Wales*, IV, *1500–1640*, while a broad range of social and economic issues are covered in the various contributions to two collections of essays: on Ireland, Ciaran Brady and Raymond Gillespie (eds.), *Natives and Newcomers: Essays on the Making of Irish Colonial Society 1534–1641* (Dublin, 1986); and, on Scotland, R. A. Houston and I. D. Whyte (eds.), *Scottish Society 1500–1800* (Cambridge, 1989). Relationships between noblemen and their social inferiors are dealt with in Mary O'Dowd, 'Land and Lordship in Sixteenth and Seventeenth-Century Ireland', in Rosalind Mitchison and Peter Roebuck (eds.), *Economy and Society in Scotland and Ireland 1500–1939* (Edinburgh, 1988) and Jenny Wormald, *Lords and Men in Scotland: Bonds of Manrent, 1442–1603* (Edinburgh, 1985); while the themes of social relationships and socio-economic change loom large in the same author's *Court, Kirk and Community: Scotland 1470–1625* (London, 1981). Literacy receives a detailed but often criticized analysis in David Cressy, *Literacy and the Social Order: Reading and Writing in Tudor and Stuart England* (Cambridge, 1980). On women, several of the essays in Mary Prior (ed.), *Women in English Society, 1500–1800* (London, 1985) focus on the Tudor period, while how detailed work within this subject might develop is demonstrated in Katherine Warner Swett, 'Widowhood, Custom and Property in Early Modern Wales', *Welsh History Review*, vol. 18 (1996–7).

## The limits of power: the English Crown and the British Isles

Standard surveys of the 'Celtic' parts of the British Isles include: S. G. Ellis, *Ireland in the Age of the Tudors* (London, 1998); G. Williams, *Recovery, Reorientation and Reformation: Wales, c.1415–1642* (Oxford 1987); J. Wormald, *Court, Kirk and Community* (see above). C. Lennon, *Sixteenth-Century Ireland: The Incomplete Conquest* (Dublin, 1994); and M. Lynch, *Scotland: A*

New History (Edinburgh, 1992) are also especially good on particular themes and topics. For England's northern frontier, M. James, *Society, Politics and Culture: Studies in Early Modern England* (Cambridge, 1986), together with the last part of C. J. Neville, *Violence, Custom and Law: The Anglo-Scottish Border Lands in the Later Middle Ages* (Edinburgh, 1998), provide a balanced account of its general character and the particular administrative problems faced by the Tudors. For Scotland and Wales, J. Kirk, *Patterns of Reform: Continuity and Change in the Reformation Kirk* (Edinburgh, 1999) and G. Williams, *Wales and the Reformation* (Cardiff, 1997) provide good starting points in regard to the local impact of the Reformation movement. Other important aspects of government in the 'peripheral' kingdoms are addressed in B. Bradshaw, *The Irish Constitutional Revolution of the Sixteenth Century* (Cambridge, 1979); C. Brady, *The Chief Governors: The Rise and Fall of Reform Government in Tudor Ireland* (Cambridge, 1994); and J. Goodare, *State and Society in Early Modern Scotland* (Oxford, 1999). Recent calls for a holistic account of the British Isles, focusing more on state formation than nation building, have so far been answered in multi-authored volumes of essays: see Bradshaw and Morrill, and Ellis and Barber (under 'Introduction', above). J. Morrill (ed.), *The Oxford Illustrated History of Tudor and Stuart Britain* (Oxford, 1996) offers a wide-ranging survey.

## The change of religion

Short general surveys of the English story are provided in D. MacCulloch, 'The Reformation in England', in A. Pettegree (ed.), *The Early Reformation in Europe* (Cambridge, 1992) and D. MacCulloch, *The Later Reformation in England 1547–1603*, revised edn. (London, 2001). There is still much to be said for the account of the English Reformation to 1558 in A. G. Dickens, *The English Reformation*, revised edn. (London, 1990); to which C. Haigh, *English Reformations: Religion, Politics and Society under the Tudors* (Oxford, 1993) is conceived in part as a riposte. An essential perspective on the pre-Reformation English Church, and a catalogue of its destruction, is provided by E. Duffy, *The Stripping of the Altars: Traditional Religion in England c.1400–c.1580* (New Haven and London, 1992), while the building of a new Church is considered in D. MacCulloch, *Thomas Cranmer: A Life* (New Haven and London, 1996) and *Tudor Church Militant: Edward VI and the Protestant Reformation* (London, 1999). Amid Patrick Collinson's groundbreaking and prolific work on Puritanism and its place within the English Church, perhaps the most enjoyable introduction is *The Religion of Protestants: The Church in English Society, 1559–1625* (Oxford, 1983). Aspects of popular Protestantism are made visible in P. Collinson and J. Craig (eds.), *The Reformation in English Towns 1500–1640* (Basingstoke, 1998); C. W. Marsh, *Popular Religion in 16th Century England: Holding their Peace* (Basingstoke, 1998); and T. Watt,

*Cheap Print and Popular Piety* (Cambridge, 1991). The survival and reinvention of English Roman Catholicism is imaginatively discussed in J. Bossy, *The English Catholic Community 1570–1850* (London, 1975). A different perspective on popular belief is provided by K. Thomas, *Religion and the Decline of Magic* (London, 1971). Ireland may be approached through the majestic narrative and thematic treatment in T. W. Moody, F. X. Martin, and F. J. Byrne (eds.), *A New History of Ireland, iii. Early Modern Ireland, 1534–1691*, 2nd edn. (Oxford, 1991); with more detailed discussions in R. Gillespie, *Devoted People: Belief and Religion in Early Modern Ireland* (Manchester, 1997) and A. Ford, *The Protestant Reformation in Ireland, 1590–1641* (Dublin, 1997). Narratives of the Scottish Church in the sixteenth century are superbly catered for by I. B. Cowan, *The Scottish Reformation: Church and Society in Sixteenth Century Scotland* (London, 1982) and G. Donaldson, *The Scottish Reformation* (Cambridge, 1960). J. Kirk, *Patterns of Reform: Continuity and Change in the Reformation Kirk* (Edinburgh, 1989) offers some useful alternative discussion. G. Williams, *Wales and the Reformation* (Cardiff, 1997) is the magnificent culmination of a lifetime of original research and exposition.

## Monarchy and counsel: models of the state

J. W. Allen, *A History of Political Thought in the Sixteenth Century* (London, 1928) is still generally useful. For recent work on the Tudor monarchy, see the essays in John Guy's *The Tudor Monarchy* (under 'Introduction' above). Biographies of Tudor monarchs include, outstandingly, J. J. Scarisbrick, *Henry VIII* (London, 1968) and D. M. Loades, *Mary Tudor: A Life* (Oxford, 1989), with biographes of Elizabeth too numerous to mention, but none yet quite replacing J. E. Neale, *Queen Elizabeth* (London, 1934). For Sir John Fortescue, see A. Gross, *The Dissolution of the Lancastrian Kingship: Sir John Fortescue and the Crisis of Monarchy in Fifteenth-Century England* (Stamford, 1996); for the Scottish monarchy and Scottish political thought, J. H. Burns, *The True Law of Kingship: Concepts of Monarchy in Early-Modern Scotland* (Oxford, 1996) and R. A. Mason, *Kingship and the Commonweal: Political Thought in Renaissance and Reformation Scotland* (East Linton, 1998). For English interest in and designs on Scotland in the early Elizabethan period, see S. Alford, *The Early Elizabethan Polity: William Cecil and the British Succession Crisis, 1558–1569* (Cambridge, 1998). Aspects of the ideology of the Henrician Reformation are covered in V. M. Murphy, 'The Literature and Propaganda of Henry VIII's First Divorce', in D. MacCulloch (ed.), *The Reign of Henry VIII: Politics, Policy and Piety* (Basingstoke, 1995) and P. Tudor-Craig, 'Henry VIII and King David', in D. Williams (ed.), *Early Tudor England: Proceedings of the 1987 Harlaxton Symposium* (Woodbridge, 1989); critical commentators on the Tudor constitution in T. F. Mayer, *Thomas Starkey and the Commonweal: Humanist Politics and Religion in the Reign of*

*Henry VIII* (Cambridge, 1989) and J. A. Guy, *Christopher St. German on Chancery and Statute* (Selden Society; London, 1985). Useful essays on the resistance theories of the mid-sixteenth century are G. Bowler, 'Marian Protestants and the Idea of Violent Resistance to Tyranny', in P. G. Lake and M. Dowling (eds.), *Protestantism and the National Church in Sixteenth-Century England* (London, 1987)' and J. Dawson, 'Trumpeting Resistance: Christopher Goodman and John Knox', in R. A. Mason (ed.), *John Knox and the British Reformations* (Aldershot, 1998). The coexistence of different strands of classical scholarship and their political application in the latter part of this period and beyond are examined in M. Peltonen, *Classical Humanism and Republicanism in English Political Thought, 1570–1640* (Cambridge, 1995).

## The Renaissance in Britain

There is no shortage of introductions to the Renaissance in England, but among the best single-volume studies are: B. Ford (ed.), *The Cambridge Cultural History: Sixteenth Century Britain* (Cambridge, 1992); J. R. Hale, *England and the Italian Renaissance* (London, 1954); and George Holmes, *Renaissance* (London, 1996). More specialized in content are: J. W. Binns, *Intellectual Culture in Elizabethan and Jacobean England: The Latin Writings of the Age* (Leeds, 1990) and the essays in E. Chaney and P. Mack (eds.), *England and the Continental Renaissance: Essays in Honour of J. B. Trapp* (Woodbridge, 1990). On English poetry, see A. C. Spearing, *Medieval to Renaissance in English Poetry* (Cambridge, 1985); M. R. G. Spiller, *The Development of the Sonnet: An Introduction* (London, 1992), and E. Heale, *Wyatt, Surrey and Early Tudor Poetry* (London, 1998). On Shakespeare and the drama, Emrys Jones, *The Origins of Shakespeare* (Oxford, 1977) and Jonathan Bate, *Shakespeare and Ovid* (Oxford, 1993) are both excellent. The impact of the Reformation on English culture is sensitively discussed in Patrick Collinson, *The Birthpangs of Protestant England: Reformation and Cultural Change in the Sixteenth and Seventeenth Centuries* (Basingstoke, 1988); while Richard Helgerson, *Forms of Nationhood: The Elizabethan Writing of England* (Chicago, 1988) is the seminal study of 'Englishness' and the rethinking of history in the Elizabethan period. On Irish literature, Padraig Breathnach, 'The Chief's Poet', *Publications of the Royal Irish Academy*, 83 (1983) is useful; as are a number of essays in Moody, Martin, and Byrne (eds.), *A New History of Ireland* (see above). On Irish intellectual culture generally, see F. X. Martin, 'Ireland, the Renaissance, and the Counter-Reformation', *Topic*, 13 (1967) and John Sike, 'Irish Scholarship and the Renaissance, 1580–1675', *Studies in the Renaissance*, 21 (1973). On Welsh literature, H. I. Bell, *The Development of Welsh Poetry* (Oxford, 1936) is still valuable; as are the essays in R. Geraint Gruffydd (ed.), *A Guide to Welsh Literature, c.1530–1700* (Cardiff, 1977) and A. O. H. Jarman and Gwilym Rees Hughes (eds.), *A Guide to Welsh Literature,*

*1282–c.1550*, revised by Dafydd Johnston (Cardiff, 1997). Glanmor Williams and Robert Owen Jones (eds.), *The Celts and the Renaissance: Tradition and Innovation* (Cardiff, 1990) offers a trenchant analysis of the Renaissance in Wales more generally. For Scottish literature, R. D. S. Jack (ed.), *The History of Scottish Literature, i. Origins to 1660* (Aberdeen, 1988) provides a good introduction; and the contributors to J. Hadley Williams (ed.), *Stewart Style, 1513–1542: Essays on the Court of James V* (East Linton, 1996) bring their specialist knowledge to bear on the court culture of the first half of the century. D. Howard, *The Architectural History of Scotland: Scottish Architecture from the Reformation to the Restoration, 1560–1660* (Edinburgh, 1995) provides a splendid account of the architectural context.

## Britain, Europe, and the world

The classic survey of Tudor foreign policy, *Before the Armada: The Growth of English Foreign Policy 1485–1588* (London, 1966), has been revised in essay form by Simon Adams, 'England and the World under the Tudors', in Morrill, *The Oxford Illustrated History of Tudor and Stuart Britain* (see above), and in textbook form by Susan Doran, *England and Europe, 1495–1603*, 2nd edn. (London, 1996). For the reign of Henry VII, the established biography by S. B. Chrimes, *Henry VII*, paperback edn. (London, 1977) should be supplemented by Ian Arthurson, *The Perkin Warbeck Conspiracy 1491–1499* (Stroud, 1994). The foreign policy of Henry VIII is surveyed by David Potter in Diarmaid MacCulloch (ed.), *The Reign of Henry VIII* (Basingstoke, 1995). Scotland is not as well served, although the biographies in the Stewart Dynasty in Scotland series, Norman Macdougall, *James IV* (Edinburgh, 1989) and Jamie Cameron, *James V: The Personal Rule 1528–1542* (East Linton, 1998), are useful. The Anglo-Scots wars of the 1540s are now narrated in detail in Marcus Merriman, *The Rough Wooings: Mary Queen of Scots 1542–1551* (East Linton, 2000). G. D. Ramsay's two-part work, *The End of the Antwerp Mart: The City of London in International Politics at the Accession of Elizabeth Tudor* and *The Queen's Merchants and the Revolt of the Netherlands* (Manchester, 1975, 1986) provides the fullest account of the commercial dimensions of foreign policy in the first decade of Elizabeth's reign. For all its antiquity and flaws, Conyers Read, *Mr Secretary Walsingham and the Policy of Queen Elizabeth* (Oxford, 1925) remains the best-researched study of Elizabethan foreign policy in the 1570s and 1580s. R. B. Wernham, *After the Armada* and *The Return of the Armadas* (Oxford, 1984, 1994) are major narratives of the war years 1588–1603, based on a lifetime of work on the State Papers. Susan Doran, *Monarchy and Matrimony: The Courtships of Elizabeth I* (London, 1996) is the first detailed study of the diplomacy of Elizabeth's marriage negotiations. Three collections of essays provide the best introductions to their subjects: Michael Lynch (ed.), *Mary Stewart: Queen in Three Kingdoms*

(Oxford, 1988); M. J. Rodriguez-Salgado and Simon Adams (eds.), *England, Spain and the Gran Armada 1585–1604* (Edinburgh, 1991); and Nicholas Canny (ed.), *The Oxford History of the British Empire, i. The Origins of Empire* (Oxford, 1998). The discussion in this chapter of Elizabeth's policy towards the Netherlands is based on Simon Adams's forthcoming 'The Road to Nonsuch: The Netherlands in Elizabethan Policy 1575–85', part of which is summarized in 'The Decision to Intervene: England and the United Provinces 1584–1585', in José Martinez Millan (ed.), *Felipe II (1527–1598): Europe y la Monarquia Catolica* (Madrid, 1999).

## Conclusion

For many of the themes touched on in this Conclusion, see R. Helgerson, *Forms of Nationhood* (above). On William Camden, see Patrick Collinson, 'One of us? William Camden and the making of history', *Transactions of the Royal Historical Society*, 6th ser., 8 (1998). For the English language, high and low, see Brian Vickers (ed.), *English Renaissance Literary Criticism* (Oxford, 1999) and Adam Fox, *Oral and Literate Culture in England 1500–1700* (Oxford, 2000); and for Welsh, Geraint H. Jenkins (ed.), *The Welsh Language before the Industrial Revolution* (Cardiff, 1997). On the English state, and 'state formation', begin with S. J. Gunn, *Early Tudor Government, 1485–1558* (Basingstoke, 1995) and go on to M. J. Braddick, *State Formation in Early Modern England c.1550–1700* (Cambridge, 2000) and S. Hindle, *The State and Social Change in Early Modern England c.1550–1640* (London, 2000). Resistance to government is surveyed in A. Fletcher and D. MacCulloch (eds.), *Tudor Rebellions* (London, 1997). On Parliament, Jennifer Loach provides a general survey in *Parliament under the Tudors* (Oxford, 1991), G. R. Elton an in-depth study of the early Elizabethan parliaments in *The Parliament of England 1559–1581* (Cambridge, 1986). For the condition of the poor and relations with their betters in general, see Paul Slack, *Poverty and Policy in Tudor and Stuart England* (Harlow, 1988) and his *From Reformation to Improvement: Public Welfare in Early Modern England* (Oxford, 1999); and for the singular case of Swallowfield, Steve Hindle, 'Hierarchy and Community in the Elizabethan Parish: The Swallowfield Articles of 1596', *Historical Journal*, 42 (1999).

# Chronology

## General and dynastic

1485  Battle of Bosworth: death of Richard III and assumption of the crown by Henry Tudor as Henry VII

1486  Marriage of Henry VII to Elizabeth of York, uniting the houses of Lancaster and York

Battle of Stoke ends 'The Wars of the Roses'

1487  Lambert Simnel crowned 'Edward VI' in Christ Church Cathedral, Dublin; enters England and is defeated

1489  Henry VII's eldest son Arthur proclaimed Prince of Wales

1491  First appearance (in Ireland) of the pretender Perkin Warbeck

1502  Death of Arthur

1503  Marriage of Henry VII's elder daughter Margaret to James IV of Scotland, the first such marriage for two centuries; 'Treaty of Perpetual Peace' between England and Scotland

Death of John of Islay, last lord of the Isles

1509  Death of Henry VII and accession of Henry VIII

1513  Death of James IV of Scotland at the Battle of Flodden, succession of James V

Death of Gerald Fitzgerald, 8th earl of Kildare, deputy-lieutenant of Ireland

1520  The Emperor Charles V visits England and Henry VIII and King Francis I of France meet at the Field of the Cloth of Gold

1525  Death of Thomas Lord Dacre, warden-general of the English Marches towards Scotland (1511–25)

Death of Sir Rhys ap Thomas, justice and chamberlain of south Wales

Imperial troops defeat the French at Battle of Pavia; Francis I taken prisoner

1527  Sack of Rome by mutinous imperial troops

Henry VIII begins to negotiate with the Pope for an annulment of his marriage to Catherine of Aragon

1533  Henry marries Anne Boleyn; his marriage to Catherine of

Aragon declared void by Archbishop Thomas Cranmer; birth of Princess Elizabeth

1534    Second 'Treaty of Perpetual Peace' between England and Scotland

1536    Henry VIII executes Anne Boleyn, marries Jane Seymour

1537    Jane Seymour dies after giving birth to Prince Edward

Death of Henry Percy, 6th earl of Northumberland, warden of the East and Middle Marches

1538    Marriage of James V of Scotland to Mary of Lorraine (Mary of Guise)

1540    Henry VIII marries Anne of Cleves; the marriage declared void; Henry marries Catherine Howard

1542    Catherine Howard executed for adultery

Death of James V and accession of Mary Stewart, aged six days

1543    Under the terms of the Peace of Greenwich between England and Scotland, Edward is to marry Mary, but the treaty was later repudiated by the Scottish Parliament

1547    Henry VIII dies and is succeeded by Edward VI; Edward Seymour, earl of Hertford, duke of Somerset, becomes Lord Protector

Francis I dies and is succeeded by Henry II

Defeat of the Scots at the Battle of Pinkie

1553    Death of Edward VI and accession of Mary Tudor, after the abortive nine-day reign of Lady Jane Grey, 'Queen Jane'

1554    Mary marries Philip (later Philip II of Spain)

1558    Mary, queen of Scots, marries Francis, the French Dauphin

Mary Tudor dies and is succeeded by Elizabeth I

1559    Peace is concluded between Philip II, Henry II, and Elizabeth I, at Chateau Cambresis

Henry II is killed in a tournament and succeeded by Francis II

The Scottish regent, Mary of Guise, is deposed

1560    Francis II of France dies and is succeeded by his brother, Charles IX

1561    Mary, queen of Scots, returns to Scotland and begins her personal rule

1562    Elizabeth I almost dies of smallpox

1565    Marriage of Mary, queen of Scots, to Henry, Lord Darnley, styled king of Scotland

| | |
|---|---|
| 1566 | Murder in Edinburgh of Mary's musician and secretary, David Rizzio |
| | Birth of the future James VI of Scotland and I of England |
| 1567 | Murder of Darnley; Mary marries the earl of Bothwell, but is forced to abdicate |
| 1568 | Flight of Mary, queen of Scots, to England |
| 1569 | Rising of the northern earls in favour of Mary, queen of Scots, and the restoration of Catholicism |
| 1570 | Papal bull of excommunication and deposition against Elizabeth I |
| | Assassination of Scottish regent, earl of Moray; earl of Lennox becomes regent |
| 1571 | Ridolfi Plot to depose Elizabeth I |
| | Lennox is killed and is succeeded by earl of Mar |
| 1572 | Thomas Howard, duke of Norfolk, executed for conspiring with Mary, queen of Scots, against Elizabeth I |
| | Death of Mar; James, earl of Morton, becomes Scottish regent |
| | Massacre of St Bartholomew's Eve in France |
| 1574 | Charles IX of France dies and is succeeded by his brother, Henry III |
| 1578 | James VI begins his personal rule |
| 1579 | Climax of marriage negotiations between Elizabeth I and Francis, duke of Anjou; John Stubbs loses his right hand for his libel against the French marriage, *The Gaping Gulf* |
| 1582 | Raid of Ruthven; James VI in the hands of the English party in Scotland |
| 1583 | Throckmorton Plot to assassinate Elizabeth |
| 1584 | Assassination of William of Orange |
| 1585 | The beginning of English military intervention in the Netherlands under the earl of Leicester |
| 1586 | Babington Plot against Elizabeth; trial of Mary, queen of Scots |
| 1587 | Execution of Mary, queen of Scots |
| 1588 | The failure of the Gran Armada against England |
| 1589 | Death of Catherine de Medici, mother of three French kings |
| | Assassination of Henry III of France; Henry of Navarre (Henry IV) claims the crown |

| 1593 | Conversion of Henry IV to Roman Catholicism |
| 1594 | Beginning of Nine Years War in Ireland |
| 1598 | Death of Philip II of Spain |
| 1601 | Execution of the earl of Essex for attempted *coup d'état* |
| 1603 | Death of Elizabeth I and accession of James VI of Scotland as James I of England |

## Ecclesiastical and religious

| 1492 | See of Glasgow elevated to become Scotland's second archbishopric |
| 1494 | University of Aberdeen founded |
| 1507 | Aberdeen Breviary published: ordered to replace Sarum liturgical books in Scotland |
| 1517 | (31 Oct.) Martin Luther announces disputation on indulgences, Wittenberg (Germany) |
| 1518 | Thomas Wolsey made papal legate *a latere* in England |
| 1521 | Henry VIII writes *Assertio septem sacramentorum* against Luther and is awarded the title of 'Defender of the Faith' by the Pope |
| 1525 | First portion of William Tyndale's English translation of the New Testament published, Cologne |
| 1526 | Complete New Testament of Tyndale's translation published, Worms |
| | Carmelite friary founded in Edinburgh: last pre-Reformation monastic foundation in Britain |
| 1529 | Blackfriars trial of Henry VIII's Aragon marriage annulment ends without result |
| 1533 | Thomas Cranmer appointed archbishop of Canterbury |
| | Act in Restraint of Appeals |
| 1535 | Henry VIII orders the compiling of the *Valor Ecclesiasticus*, a comprehensive valuation of the wealth of the Church of England |
| | Publication of the first complete Bible in English |
| 1536 | Lincolnshire Rising and Pilgrimage of Grace; second Pilgrimage rebellion crushed, winter 1537 |
| | Royal Injunctions require systematic religious instruction |
| | The Ten Articles, a statement of theological orthodoxy for England with Lutheran elements |

| | |
|---|---|
| 1537 | Bishops Book or 'The Institution of a Christen Man', further defining orthodoxy in the Church of England but not authorized by Henry VIII |
| | First general official order for the provision of English Bibles in England and Wales |
| | Irish Reformation Parliament meets in Dublin |
| 1538 | It becomes compulsory for all parishes in England to keep registers of births, marriages, and deaths |
| | Destruction of the shrine of Thomas a Becket at Canterbury, and of other shrines and relics |
| | 'Form of the Beads' issued by Archbishop George Browne of Dublin |
| 1539 | Publication in England of the officially authorized 'Great Bible' |
| | The Act of Six Articles signals a conservative religious backlash in England |
| 1540 | Dissolution of English and Welsh monasteries complete; six monasteries saved as new (secular) cathedrals |
| 1543 | Reading of the vernacular Bible restricted in England; restricted reading of vernacular Bible first allowed in Scotland |
| | The 'King's Book' (*A necessary doctrine and erudition for any Christian man*) redefines English theology in a conservative direction |
| 1545 | First Jesuit mission to Ireland |
| 1546 | Cardinal David Beaton murdered by evangelicals, St Andrews |
| 1547 | Legislation orders closure of all chantries, England and Wales |
| | Heresy laws abolished in England |
| | Promulgation in England of the *Book of Homilies*, conveying unambiguously Protestant doctrine |
| 1549 | (Summer) First English Prayer Book made compulsory; Western Rising; Kett's Rebellion or 'camping time' |
| | (Oct.) Fall of Protector Somerset |
| 1552 | Second English Prayer Book |
| | Archbishop John Hamilton's Scots Catechism |
| | John Bale appointed bishop of Ossory |
| 1553 | Forty-Two Articles of Religion of the Church of England |
| | The *Reformatio Legum Ecclesiasticarum* (a replacement for the existing canon law) presented to Parliament but not enacted |

1554     (30 Nov.) Cardinal Reginald Pole reconciles England to the see of Rome

1555     Mary I's English government begins the burning of heretics, following restoration of the heresy laws; Bishops Hugh Latimer and Nicholas Ridley are burned at the stake in Oxford

1556     Archbishop Cranmer is burned at the stake in Oxford

1557     Parliament in Dublin repeals Henrician and Edwardian reform statutes

1559     Elizabethan Settlement of Religion (Act of Uniformity with a revised Prayer Book, Act of Supremacy); followed in Irish Parliament

        Matthew Parker becomes archbishop of Canterbury

1560     Publication, in Geneva, of the Geneva Bible

        Scottish national revolution: Protestant Kirk created

        Parliament in Dublin passes Acts of Supremacy and Uniformity

1561     First *Book of Discipline* establishes the constitution of the Reformed Kirk in Scotland

1563     John Foxe publishes the first English version of *Actes and Monuments* (the 'Book of Martyrs')

        Thirty-Nine Articles of the Church of England formulated by Convocation of Canterbury

1566     Archbishop Matthew Parker's *Advertisements*, imposing uniformity in clerical attire

1567     Calvinist Book of Common Order translated into Gaelic by John Carswell, *Foirm na n-Urrnuidheadh*

1568     Publication in England of the Bishops Bible

        English Catholic college founded at Douai

1570     Papal bull '*Regnans in excelsis*', excommunicating Elizabeth I

        Second and greatly enlarged edition of Foxe's *Actes and Monuments*

1572     Publication of the radical Puritan manifesto, *An admonition to the Parliament*

        Death of John Knox

1574     First Roman Catholic missionary priest arrives in England

1575     Death of Archbishop Parker and appointment of Edmund Grindal

| | |
|---|---|
| 1576 | First printing in England of the Geneva Bible |
| 1577 | Clash between Archbishop Grindal and Elizabeth I over prophesyings leads to Grindal's house arrest |
| 1578 | English college moves from Douai to Rheims |
| 1579 | Foundation of English college at Rome |
| | Nicholas Sander, papal legate, lands near Dingle, south-west Ireland |
| 1580 | Arrival in England of the Jesuits, Edmund Campion and Robert Persons |
| 1581 | First drastic legislation against Roman Catholic recusancy in England |
| 1582 | Publication of the Rheims (Catholic) version of the New Testament |
| | College of Edinburgh founded |
| 1583 | John Whitgift becomes archbishop of Canterbury and mounts onslaught on puritan nonconformity |
| | The last edition of Foxe's *Actes and Monuments* to be published in the author's lifetime. |
| 1584 | 'Black Acts' in Scotland drive hard-line Presbyterian nobility and ministers into English exile |
| 1587 | A presbyterian 'Bill and Book' introduced into the House of Commons; an abortive attempt to establish Presbyterianism in England |
| 1588 | William Morgan's complete Welsh Bible published |
| | The 'Marprelate Tracts' attempt to overthrow episcopacy in England with the weapon of ridicule |
| 1591 | Trial of English Presbyterian leadership in Star Chamber |
| 1593 | English Parliament passes laws against Protestant Separatists; execution of separatist leaders, Henry Barrow and John Greenwood |
| | First part of Richard Hooker's *Laws of Ecclesiastical Polity* published |
| | Marischal College Aberdeen (independent university) founded |
| 1594 | Trinity College Dublin founded |
| 1603 | Gaelic translation of the Book of Common Prayer published |

## Economic and social

1496    *Intercursus Magnus*, a comprehensive commercial treaty with the Netherlands

1497    Monopoly for trade with Antwerp granted to Merchant Adventurers

1503    Scottish legislation limiting the right to beg

c.1507–8    First printing press in Edinburgh

1517    First of Thomas Wolsey's enclosure commissions

1523    First edition of John Fitzherbert's *Book of husbandry*

1542    Debasement of the English coinage begins, with implications for foreign exchange rates and the cloth industry

1548    Protector Somerset sets up an enclosure commission under John Hales

1549    Major peasant uprisings in England

        Sir Thomas Smith writes *A discourse of the commonweal of this realm of England* (not published until 1581)

1551    Devaluation of the English coinage, causing a trading recession and a sharp drop in cloth production

1553    Muscovy Company founded

1557    First edition of Thomas Tusser's *A hundreth good pointes of husbandrie*

1560    Reform and stabilization of the English currency

1563    Statute of Artificers regulates conditions of employment and apprenticeship in England

        Witchcraft acts in England and Scotland

        Plague in London and Edinburgh

1564    Trade war between England and Spain (affecting mainly trade with the Netherlands); English merchants leave Antwerp for Emden

1571    Royal Exchange opens in London

1574    Reginald Scot publishes *A perfite platforme of a hoppe garden*, the first treatise on the growing of hops

1576    Plague in Norwich

1579    Comprehensive Scottish Poor Law

1581    Formation of Levant or Turkey Company

1584    Sack of Antwerp, ending its commercial dominance

1584–5    Severe plague in Scotland

| 1586 | English Privy Council issues Book of Orders regulating the response of local JPs to poverty, disease, etc., a policy repeated in crisis years until 1630s |
| 1586–7 | Bad harvests throughout Britain |
| 1590–1 | Major witch-hunt in Scotland |
| 1596 | Abortive popular rising in Oxfordshire |
| 1596–8 | Bad harvests throughout Britain |
| 1597 | Scottish Act of Parliament transfers administration of poor relief in rural areas to kirk sessions |
| 1598 | Major English Poor Law, extended in 1601 |
| 1600 | East India Company founded |

## Cultural

| 1515–30 | Hampton Court built |
| 1516 | The Latin text of Sir Thomas More's *Utopia* printed |
| 1519 | Death of John Colet |
| 1522 | Death of Gavin Douglas |
| 1527 | Death of Tudor Aled |
| | Hector Boece's *Scottum Historiae* printed in Paris |
| 1529 | Death of John Skelton |
| 1531 | John Bellenden's English translation of Boece's *Scottum Historiae* printed in Edinburgh |
| 1532 | First edition of the Complete Works of Geoffrey Chaucer (ed. William Thynne) |
| c.1532 | Maghnus Ó Domhnaill's *Life* of St Colum Cille completed |
| 1534 | *Ordinances for the Government of Ireland*, first pamphlet printed for Ireland |
| 1535 | Death of Robert Jones |
| 1536 | Formal abolition of Welsh law |
| 1537 | Reworking of Falkland Palace begins |
| 1538 | John Bale's *Three Laws, John the Baptist's Preaching*, and *God's Promises* printed |
| 1539 | Work begins on Nonsuch Palace |
| 1540 | Original version of Sir David Lindsay's *Ane Satyre of the Thrie Estaitis* performed |
| | Reworking of Stirling Castle begins |

| 1542 | First edition of Edward Hall's *Union of the Two Noble and Illustre Families . . .* printed |
| 1545 | Death of John Taverner |
| 1550 | William Salibury's Welsh primer printed<br>Birth of William Schaw |
| 1551 | Printing press established in Dublin to print the First Book of Common Prayer |
| 1553 | *Gammer Gurton's Needle* and *Respublica* performed |
| 1554 | John Foxe's *Commentarii rerum in Ecclesia gestarum*, earliest Latin version of his (later) *Actes and Monuments*, published at Strasbourg |
| 1555 | Death of Sir David Lindsay |
| 1559 | John Foxe's *Rerum in Ecclesia gestarum*, the second version of what was to become his *Actes and Monuments*, published at Basle<br>First edition of the *Mirror for Magistrates* |
| 1562 | Norton and Sackville's *Gorboduc* performed |
| 1563 | Birth of John Dowland |
| 1564 | Birth of William Shakespeare and Christopher Marlowe |
| 1567 | First moves to suppress the York cycle of mystery plays<br>Arthur Golding's translation of Ovid's *Metamorphoses* printed |
| 1570 | Publication of Roger Ascham's *The Schoolmaster* |
| 1571 | John Kearney's *Aibidil Gaoidhilge & Caiticiosma*, first Gaelic book printed in Ireland |
| 1573 | Sir John Prys's *Historiae Brytannicae Defensio* printed posthumously |
| 1575 | Last performance of the Chester cycle of religious plays |
| 1576 | James Burbage builds The Theatre |
| 1577 | First edition of Raphael Holinshed's *Chronicles* printed |
| 1579 | Publication of Christopher Saxton's *Atlas*<br>Thomas North's translation of Plutarch's *Lives* printed |
| 1580 | The last attempt to stage the York cycle fails |
| c.1580 | Sir Philip Sidney writes the first version of *Arcadia* ('The Old Arcadia') |
| 1581 | *Ten Tragedies* of Seneca printed |

| | |
|---|---|
| 1582 | Richard Mulcaster publishes his *Elementarie ... which entreateth of right writing of our English tung* |
| | Death of George Buchanan, in the year that his *Rerum Scoticarum historia* is printed |
| 1583 | Birth of Orlando Gibbons |
| 1584 | David Powel's *Historie of Cambria now called Wales* completed |
| 1585 | James VI's *Essayes of a Prentise* printed |
| | Death of Thomas Tallis |
| 1586 | First edition of William Camden's *Britannia* |
| | Death of Sir Philip Sidney |
| 1587 | Publication of John Knox's *History of the Reformation in Scotland* |
| | Second, enlarged, edition of Holinshed's *Chronicles* |
| | The first books of Edmund Spenser's *Faerie Queene* printed (complete edition, 1596) |
| 1588 | Work begins on Wollaton Hall, Nottinghamshire |
| 1589 | George Puttenham's *Arte of English Poesie* printed |
| 1590 | Work begins on Hardwick Hall, Derbyshire |
| | Marlowe's *Tamburlaine the Great* printed |
| | Shakespeare begins work on the three parts of *Henry VI* |
| | Fulke Greville publishes Sidney's *New Arcadia* |
| 1591 | Sidney's *Astrophil and Stella* printed |
| c.1591 | Shakespeare's *Richard III* written |
| 1593 | Death of Christopher Marlowe |
| | Shakespeare's *Venus and Adonis* printed |
| 1594 | Death of Thomas Kyd |
| 1595 | Sidney's *Apology for Poetry* printed |
| | Shakespeare's *Richard II* written |
| 1596 | Death of William Maitland of Lethington |
| 1597 | Thomas Morley's *Plain and easy introduction to practical music* printed |
| | Shakespeare's *Henry IV, Part I* performed |
| 1598 | Marlowe's *Hero and Leander* published posthumously |
| 1599 | Shakespeare's *Henry V* written |
| c.1600 | Shakespeare's *Hamlet* written |

## Politics, the state, and the international scene

1489 Murder of Henry Percy, 4th earl of Northumberland; rebellion in Yorkshire

   Council for Wales and the Marches established and located at Ludlow

1494 Sir Edward Poynings appointed governor of Ireland; Poynings's Law

1497 Cornish rebellion

1504 Battle of Knockdoe

1507 Book of Rates

1511 Thomas Lord Dacre appointed warden-general of the English Marches towards Scotland

1513 The beginning of the rise, and rise, of Thomas Wolsey

   Machiavelli writes *The Prince* (published 1532)

   English victories in France ('the Battle of the Spurs') and Scotland (Flodden); English troops occupy Tournai (until 1518)

*c.*1513–19 Thomas More writes *The History of King Richard III*

1516 Publication of Thomas More's *Utopia* at Louvain

1518 Treaty of London makes peace between England, the Empire, France, Spain, and the Pope: Wolsey's finest hour

1521 Attainder and execution of Edward Stafford, 3rd duke of Buckingham, for allegedly seeking the succession to the crown

1522 England goes to war against France

1525 Failure of the 'Amicable Grant', a scheme, mainly of Wolsey's devising, to finance an invasion of France

   Regional councils for Wales and the north of England re-established at Ludlow and Sheriff Hutton

   Treaty of the More: peace with France

1529 Treaty of Cambrai, making peace between the Empire, France, and England

   Wolsey falls from office and power

   Sir Thomas More appointed Lord Chancellor

   The so-called Reformation Parliament meets (in seven sessions to 1537)

*c.*1529–35 Thomas Starkey writes *A Dialogue between Reginald Pole and Thomas Lupset*

1530    Henry VIII is shown the manuscript of *Collectanea satis copiosa*

1531    Publication of Christopher St German's *A Little Treatise Called the New Additions*

Publication of Sir Thomas Elyot's *The Book Named the Governor*

1532    Sir Thomas More resigns as Lord Chancellor

Border conflict between England and Scotland concerning the 'Debateable Lands'

Thomas Cromwell established as first minister

1533    Parliament passes the Act in Restraint of Appeals: 'this realm of England is an Empire'

1534    The Act of Supremacy ends all papal jurisdiction in England and acknowledges and enforces the supremacy of the king as head of the Church

Cicero's *De officiis* translated by Robert Whittinton

Publication of Edward Foxe's *Of the True Difference between Royal and Ecclesiastical Power*

Reorganization of government in the borderlands: rebellion and attainder of Thomas Fitzgerald ('Silken Thomas'), 10th earl of Kildare; trial and acquittal of William Lord Dacre

1535    Siege and capture of Maynooth castle; Kildare surrenders (executed 1537), signalling a major change in English policy towards Ireland

Execution of Sir Thomas More and Bishop John Fisher

Publication of Stephen Gardiner's *An Oration of True Obedience*

Publication of German's *An Answer to a Letter*

1536    Start of a parliamentary process (culminating in the Act of Union of 1543) which incorporates Wales into England, turning the Welsh marcher lordships into counties and providing for parliamentary representation

Dissolution of the smaller monasteries

Rebellion in the north, known as the 'Pilgrimage of Grace'

1539    Dissolution of the greater monasteries undertaken

1540    Execution of Thomas Cromwell

War with France

Emergence of the new-style Privy Council

1541    An Act of Parliament makes Ireland a kingdom, annexed to England

Henry VIII's progress to York

| | |
|---|---|
| 1542 | A policy of 'surrender and regrant' brings the Gaelic Irish lords into a new and feudal relationship to the king |
| | The Scots invade England and are defeated at Solway Moss, precipitating the death of James V |
| 1543 | Treaty of Mutual Aid |
| | War with France |
| 1544 | Capture of Boulogne |
| | English sack of Edinburgh and the 'Rough Wooing' |
| 1550 | Treaty of Boulogne between England and France |
| | Resumption, survey, and leasing of Leix-Offaly for plantation |
| 1551 | Treaty of Norham between England and Scotland |
| 1554 | Publication of Sir Thomas Wilson's *Art of Rhetoric* |
| | Mary of Lorraine (or of Guise) becomes governor of Scotland |
| 1555 | Wyatt's Rebellion against Queen Mary's Spanish marriage |
| 1556 | Publication of Nicholas Grimald's translation of Cicero's *De officiis* |
| | John Ponet's *Short Treatise of Politike Pouuer* published at Strasbourg |
| 1557 | Battle of St. Quentin; Spaniards defeat French and English take part in siege |
| | Leix and Offaly shired as Queen's and King's Counties |
| 1558 | Surrender of Calais |
| | John Knox's *First Blast of the Trumpet against the Monstrous Regiment of Women* and Christopher Goodman's *How Superior Powers O[u]ght to be Obey[e]d of their Subjects* published at Geneva |
| | Book of Rates |
| | Militia Act, the basis of local defence for centuries to come |
| 1559 | John Aylmer's *An Harborowe for Faithfull and Trewe Subiectes* published at London |
| 1560 | Treaty of Edinburgh |
| | Death of Amy Robsart, wife of Lord Robert Dudley (earl of Leicester) |
| 1562–3 | English intervention in the first War of Religion in France, at Le Havre ('Newhaven') |
| 1565 | Last private battle of Tudor nobles at Affane, Co. Wexford |

| | |
|---|---|
| 1566 | Jean Bodin publishes his *Method for the easy understanding of history* at Paris |
| 1568 | John Hawkins's third voyage to the Caribbean |
| 1569 | Rising of the northern earls |
| | Regional council for Connaught established |
| | Publication of Sir Thomas Wilson's *Three Orations of Demosthenes* |
| 1569–73 | Second embargo on English trade with Netherlands and Spain |
| 1570 | Regional council for Munster established; projects for the plantation of east Ulster |
| 1571 | William Cecil created Lord Burghley (lord treasurer, 1572) |
| 1575 | Elizabeth offered countship of Holland and Zealand |
| 1576 | Spanish Fury at Antwerp |
| 1577–80 | Francis Drake's voyage of circumnavigation |
| 1578 | Massacre of Mullaghmast, Co. Kildare |
| 1579 | Revolt of Gerald Fitzgerald, 14th earl of Desmond (suppressed 1583) |
| | George Buchanan publishes his *De jure regni apud Scotos*, dedicated to James VI |
| | Fitzmaurice expedition to Ireland |
| 1580 | Bastiano San Giuseppi's force lands at Smerwick, south-west Ireland; massacre of Smerwick |
| 1583 | Publication of Sir Thomas Smith's *De Republica Anglorum* |
| 1584 | Bond of Association in England |
| | Commission for the Composition of Connaught |
| 1585 | Treaties of Nonsuch; English intervention in the Netherlands |
| | Scheme for the plantation of Munster |
| 1585–6 | Sir Francis Drake's West Indies voyage |
| 1586 | Elizabeth's annual subsidy for James VI |
| 1587 | Political fallout from execution of Mary, queen of Scots, includes Star Chamber trial and punishment of Secretary of State William Davison |
| 1591 | English expeditionary force sent to Brittany |
| | Cawdrey's Case (Court of King's Bench) |
| | Sir Henry Savile publishes his translation of the first four books of Tacitus' *Histories*, with the life of Agricola |

| | |
|---|---|
| 1594 | Joost Lips's *Six Books of Politics* translated into English |
| 1595 | Ulster confederacy defeats English army at Clontibret |
| 1596 | Robert Cecil becomes Secretary of State (his father Burghley dies, 1598) |
| | Attack on Cadiz |
| 1597 | Failure of further Spanish naval expeditions against England |
| 1598 | Tyrone defeats English army at the battle of the Yellow Ford; Munster plantation overthrown |
| | James VI's *The trew law of free monarchies* published at Edinburgh |
| | Complete text of Aristotle's *Politics*, translated from the French edition by Louis Leroy |
| | Publication of Richard Greneway's translation of Tacitus' *Annals* |
| | Robert Devereux, earl of Essex, appointed governor of Ireland; makes unfavourable treaty with Tyrone |
| | First printing of James VI's *Basilikon Doron* in an issue of seven copies, for private distribution |
| 1600 | Charles Blount, Lord Mountjoy, succeeds Essex as governor of Ireland |
| 1601 | Spanish army under Don Juan del Aguila lands at Kinsale, south-west Ireland |
| 1603 | Tyrone surrenders to Mountjoy at Mellifont; Tudor conquest of Ireland complete |
| | *The trew law of free monarchies* and *Basilikon Doron* reprinted in London |

# Glossary

*ad fontes*: 'from the source': a rallying cry for humanist scholars anxious to return to authentic texts and inspiration.

*arcana imperii*: secrets of state, held by monarchs and monarchists to be beyond the capacity, or responsibility, of subjects.

**Archpriest** (or **Appellant**) **Controversy**: in 1598 a running dispute among the English Catholic clergy over the influence of the Society of Jesus came to a head with the papal appointment of George Blackwell, a priest sympathetic to the Jesuits, as Archpriest or head of the mission to England. The published *Appeal* against Blackwell initiated a pamphlet war (hence the Appellant Controversy), in which Elizabeth's government discreetly assisted the Appellants.

**attainder**: forfeiture of real and personal property, together with corruption of the 'blood', normally the consequence of a sentence of death in respect of treason.

**Augmentations, Court of**: the department of state set up after the Dissolution of the Monasteries, administering ex-monastic property, handling sales, and paying pensions to the ex-religious; later subsumed within the Court of Exchequer.

**Auld Alliance**: the name commonly given by Scots to their traditional ties with the French crown. England was the *auld inemie*.

**bastard feudalism**: the name originally coined by the Revd Charles Plummer for the late medieval practice by which lords attracted the political support of neighbouring gentry by granting them fees and offices.

**Bond of Association**: an oath, or bond, entered into by the bulk of the English 'political nation' in the autumn of 1584, promising to wreak vengeance on anyone (by implication Mary, queen of Scots, and her abettors) threatening the life of Queen Elizabeth.

**Border surnames**: the semi-autonomous clans or kinship groups, addicted to *reiving* (cattle rustling) and robbery, who inhabited the upland regions of the Anglo-Scottish Marches. They acted together, collectively sought vengeance for injuries, and often accepted joint responsibility for their misdeeds.

*brehon* **law**: the customary system of law and legal practice in use among the Gaelic peoples of Ireland and Scotland, and increasingly supplanted by English and Scottish common law from the later sixteenth century.

**breviary**: liturgical book containing the cycle of hymns, readings, and prayers to be used in the offices (non-eucharistic services) of the Western Church.

Caesaropapalism(ist): the doctrine according to which the earthly monarch is both pope and king ('emperor') in his own dominions; asserted in England by Henry VIII, who was therefore a 'Caesaropapalist'.

canon law: the legal system of the Western Church; formalized mainly by the Roman bureaucracy from the twelfth century, but deriving many principles from the law of the Roman empire.

celibacy: abstention from marriage or sexual relations; required of monks and nuns, and came to be expected of all other clergy in the Western Church, from the twelfth to the sixteenth centuries.

chantry: an endowment to celebrate masses, involving prayer for souls departed, to speed them through Purgatory (Latin *cantare* = to sing). Chapels might be provided for the celebration of the mass ('chantry chapels').

chorography (and hence 'chorographers'): the art of delineating and describing, in maps and prose, a geographical region; considered to be distinct from the science of geography, in that it exercised the eye and the imagination rather than the calculating brain.

classical orders: the rules of proportion and design governing classical architecture, relating specifically to columns, their capitals and bases, divided into three principal styles: Doric, Ionic, and Corinthian.

colloquy: a conference: in particular the discussions on theology between various religious groupings during the Reformation.

commonwealth: a term which can be traced from the fifteenth-century reign of Henry VI, more or less equivalent to our 'state' and, in Latin, to *republica*, but also expressive of certain socio-political values, especially as reinforced in the sixteenth century by classical humanism.

*conciliarism(ist)*: a constitutional principle originally worked out by ecclesiastical lawyers and opposed to definitions of the Church as a simple papal monarchy. The Church consists of Head and Members, and in certain circumstances the Head is subject to the whole body, represented in a General Council. An idea readily applicable and adaptable to secular monarchies.

*Convocation(s)*: the synods of the two ecclesiastical provinces of Canterbury and York, summoned only when Parliament was summoned, capable of legislating for the Church, but of interest to the crown primarily as the source of ecclesiastical taxation.

copyhold: a customary form of land tenure entailing fixed and, therefore, in inflationary conditions, low rents, deriving its name from the copy made of the arrangement in the court roll of the manor; increasingly replaced by forms of leasehold, which were more advantageous for the landlord.

**counsel:** advice given to the monarch, especially, but not exclusively, by the King's Council, from about 1540 the '**Privy Council**' (q.v.).

**Debateable Land:** a disputed parcel of land in the Anglo-Scottish West Marches north of Carlisle, which was claimed by both kingdoms and eventually partitioned between the two in 1552.

**Demission of Mary Stewart:** on 24 July 1567, Mary Stewart signed a letter of demission or abdication in favour of her son James VI, which she later repudiated on the ground that she had done so under duress. Since until 1587 James's title rested on the demission, its legitimacy became a major constitutional issue.

**diocese:** late Roman administrative unit: term borrowed by the Church for the area governed by a bishop, usually taking its name from the city where his throne is situated.

**Divine right monarchy:** a monarchy which considered itself to be subject to no other power than that of God, not limited by the pope, and domestically subject only to voluntary and moral, not legal and political constraints.

**Englishry:** the areas inhabited by English settlers in Ireland and Wales and in which English law, language, and administrative structures were used.

**esquire:** an English social rank enjoyed by gentlemen who could claim to be 'armigerous', that is, entitled to a coat of arms; one notch lower in the social scale than a knight.

**evangelical:** from the Greek *evangelion* ('good news', or the Gospel: hence the whole message of the Bible), often used in a British context to describe early Protestant reformers and their theologies.

**Exchequer:** the principal medieval and Tudor 'court', or department of state, concerned with financial administration, remodelled in the mid-sixteenth century.

*fin amour:* refined or 'courtly' love: shorthand term for the ideals and practices of courtship and conduct exemplified in medieval romance literature and amorous lyrics.

**First Fruits and Tenths, Court of:** the department of state, later subsumed within the Exchequer, which handled the fiscal yield of the taxes for which the clergy were liable under an Act of Parliament of 1535: in principle the whole of the first year's revenues of a benefice, and thereafter a tenth of the annual income.

**franchises and liberties:** areas in which subjects exercised quasi-regal administrative and judicial powers.

**friar:** members of a religious community distinguished from earlier monasticism. Orders of friars evolved to meet the new challenges facing the Western Church during the twelfth century. Though living in community, they had an active ministry in the world at large.

**Gaedhil** and **Gaill**: the Gaelic names for the peoples, native and settler respectively, of Ireland and Scotland.

**Geraldine League**: an alliance of leading Gaelic lords organized in 1538, nominally to obtain the restoration of the earl of Kildare, but also to oppose the Reformation. The League was defeated in August 1539, but did not finally dissolve until 1541.

**gild** (or **guild**): medieval voluntary organization bound by oath and membership levy with common purposes; rapidly expanding from *c*.1300, they supplemented the parish system in local organization.

**glebe**: land forming part of the endowment to support a parish priest, in effect owned by him while he was in office.

**Gothic**: the form of architecture dominant in the high medieval period, characterized by high pointed arches, ribbed vaulting, and elaborate surface decoration.

**Great Enterprise**: Cardinal Wolsey's description of the joint invasion of France planned by Henry VIII and Charles V between 1520 and 1522. On their victory the allies proposed to partition France between them and depose Francis I in favour of Henry VIII.

**Hanseatic League**: association of north German mercantile cities promoting and regulating their overseas trade.

**Holland and Zealand, States of**: on 19 July 1572, the States of the province of Holland assembled themselves of their own volition and agreed to support William of Orange against the duke of Alba. After uniting with Zealand in 1575 (the Union of Dordrecht), they offered to recognize Elizabeth as count of Holland, effectively repudiating Philip II.

**Huguenot**: the nickname for French Protestants. Although it became widespread in the early 1560s, its origin is still debated. According to one theory it was derived from Eygenot, a party in Geneva that in the 1520s supported breaking with Savoy and joining the Swiss Confederation.

**Justices of the Peace**: commissioners appointed by the English crown in royal shires to administer justice (especially in their **quarter sessions**) and to enforce an ever-widening body of social and economic legislation. In England their numbers grew fivefold in the course of the century. From 1536 commissions of the peace were appointed for the new Welsh shires, and increasingly also for counties in Ireland.

**kern** (from Gaelic *ceithirn*): unarmoured Gaelic footmen, equipped with sword, bow or javelin.

**Kirk session:** the term used in the Reformed Church in Scotland for a congregational assembly or court composed of ministers and lay ruling 'elders', which exercised the 'discipline' emphasized in Calvinist church order, and many of the functions retained by the bishops in episcopal churches: the essence of 'Presbyterianism'.

**legate:** representative of the pope. In pre-Reformation England, the archbishop of Canterbury was automatically *legatus natus* ('legate born'). A special envoy with papal powers bypassing normal arrangements was legate *a latere* ('on the side').

**letter of marque:** a commission granted by the admiralty of a legitimate government to a private individual, licensing the seizure of specified shipping, and thus defining him as a privateer rather than a pirate.

*ligue, ligueur* (**royalist–***ligueur* **debates**): the *ligue* or Catholic League was a popular association to defend the Church in France, formed initially in 1576. The more famous *ligue* emerged in 1584 under the leadership of the duke of Guise, to resist the accession of the king of Navarre (Henry IV), and formed a core of resistance to him until his abjuration (conversion) in 1594. The extensive pamphlet war between the *ligue* and its royalist opponents, in which the royalists claimed that the *ligue* was dominated by the Jesuits, was closely followed in England.

**Lollardy:** late medieval religious dissident grouping taking its inspiration from the teachings of the Oxford philosopher John Wyclif (*c*.1330–1384).

**Lords of the Congregation:** a political alliance of the Protestant Scottish nobility, committing them to the protection of the new religion. A shadowy first band had been made in 1557. The more famous second band (with a slightly different membership) was signed on 31 May 1559 and led the resistance to the regent Mary of Guise in 1559–60. Although the duke of Chatellerault became its figurehead, its effective leader was Mary Stewart's half brother the Lord James Stewart, later earl of Moray.

**madrigal:** a short, secular song in parts for a number of singers, usually sung unaccompanied. The form was popular in England from the late 1580s.

*manræd* or *manrent* (**bond of**): literally 'counsel of men', the military service available to a lord from his tenants and connection, under a contractual bond.

**March:** the typical frontier or border region of the Middle Ages, in which commonly the population was heavily militarized and subject to a special system of **march law**, governing cross-border relations. So by extension **marchland**, and **marcher lord(ship)**, especially of Wales. The Anglo-Scottish border region was traditionally divided on both sides of the border into the **East, Middle**, and **West Marches**.

**Mass:** name used from the fourth century in the Western Church for the Eucharist or Holy Communion; taken from the puzzling last words of the Latin rite '*Ite missa est*' ('Go, it is sent').

**Metropolitan:** the title of a bishop (styled archbishop) exercising powers over other diocesan bishops, in a province composed of dioceses.

**militia:** local defence forces 'mustered' under the terms of parliamentary militia statutes.

**motet:** a short, sacred song, generally in Latin, sung primarily during church services.

**Nine Years War:** the name commonly given to the final phase of the Elizabethan conquest of Ireland during which Hugh O'Neill, earl of Tyrone, led an Ulster confederacy against English encroachment in that province.

**nuncio:** the official representative of the papacy, either at a foreign court on a permanent basis, or on a particular mission. Nuncios were normally clerics and various powers of dispensation and appointment were delegated to them.

**Old English:** the name eventually adopted by the descendants of the medieval English settlers in Ireland to distinguish themselves from the New English, those settlers who came to Ireland from 1534 onwards.

**Pale:** a medieval term for a defensive zone surrounding a fortress. In 1500 there were three, each guarding one of England's land frontiers. The Dublin Pale was the largest in extent (hence the term 'beyond the Pale'), followed by Calais and Berwick-upon-Tweed.

**Pilgrimage of Grace:** the general name given to a series of uprisings in the north of England in 1536 and 1537. The main risings were in Lincolnshire and Yorkshire, with subsidiary risings in other northern counties. The rebel grievances were a mixture of religious, political, and socio-economic matters.

**plantation:** a colonial settlement, in the sixteenth century mainly in Ireland.

**pluralism:** the practice of holding more than one ecclesiastical office at the same time; often regarded as an abuse if both offices involved the pastoral care of a congregation (cure of souls).

**polyphonic:** music, and especially church music, composed for a number of voices, or parts.

**Poynings's Law:** the statute of the Irish Parliament, passed in 1494, by which no Parliament could meet in Ireland and no bill be introduced there without the prior consent of the king and council in England, certified under the great seal of England.

**praemunire:** an offence, originally defined in fourteenth-century English legislation, reactived in the sixteenth century, which made legally *ultra vires* appeals against English law to a foreign (i.e. papal) jurisdiction.

**predestination**: a decision by God about the fate of individuals in the afterlife, regardless of their moral conduct. In its ultimate logical extension, known as 'double predestination', God is seen as electing some to salvation and 'reprobating' the rest to damnation. Predestinarian doctrine, stressed by Augustine of Hippo (354–430), is particularly associated with Reformed theologians like John Calvin.

**prerogative**: what belongs to the monarch as inherent right, exercised in making proclamations, conducting foreign relations, and (according to James I) in imposing customs duties on certain internationally traded commodities: as *arcana imperii* (q.v.), not discussable.

**Presbyterians**: a term somewhat loosely applied to English and Scottish Protestants (often in England called '**Puritans**' (q.v.)) who denied the superiority of bishops and denounced the hierarchical constitution of the traditional Church, insisting on the equality of ministers (presbyters) and local churches; not until the following century clearly distinguished by the top-down authority of 'presbyteries' and synods from the more radically devolved ecclesiology of the Independents (or Congregationalists).

**Privy Council**: the King's Council as remodelled in 1540. While the title emphasizes its political and even physical proximity to the monarch, the Privy Council acquired and developed its own secretariat and method of keeping records of its executive actions.

**Proctors**: delegates or representatives. Proctors of the Irish clergy had a place in the Irish Parliament.

**Puritans**: a derogatory and stigmatizing term often somewhat indiscriminately applied by their enemies in later sixteenth-century England to those who favoured a 'further reformation' of the Church, or who were merely more conspicuous and vocal in their religious profession and behaviour.

**recusancy**: in general, this means refusal (Latin *recuso*, I refuse) to obey government orders, but (from Edward VI's reign) it became the term for the specific refusal to attend services of the Church of England, mostly by Roman Catholics, but also by puritan separatists ('sectary recusants').

*regimen* (or *dominium*) *politicum et regale*: an expression coined in the fifteenth century by Sir John Fortescue to make the constitutional point that England was not a 'simple' monarchy but what would later be called a 'mixed polity', the 'political' element contained mainly in Parliament.

**rhetoric**: the art of persuasive discourse, and the formal rules governing it, applying to speeches on all occasions, sermons, and correspondence, an art highly valued in the sixteenth century.

**rood:** the popular term for the Cross, especially applied to the large cross, flanked by images of Mary and John, which before the Reformation was erected on the 'rood beam' above the 'rood screen', separating the nave of the church from the chancel.

**Royal Supremacy:** the doctrine, embodied in the Act of Supremacy (1534), that the king by virtue of his regality, was in his own dominions, head of the Church of Christ on earth. By the Elizabethan Act of Supremacy (1559), Elizabeth I was accorded the title of Supreme Governor (surviving to this day), which, as one contemporary wrote, 'amounts to the same thing'.

**Salic Law:** by the sixteenth century, the barring of the descent of the crown of France to a woman or through the female line was claimed to be of great antiquity, dating back to the Salic Franks, and a fundamental law of France. In fact it was 'discovered' in the mid-fourteenth century, when it was employed to repudiate Edward III's claims to the throne through his mother.

**Sarum Use:** local traditions in Christian worship are called Uses, and are named after the cathedral which developed them: in this case Salisbury ('Sarum'), the most widely employed Use in the pre-Reformation English Church.

**Schmalkaldic League:** an alliance of princes and free cities of the Holy Roman Empire formed in the Saxon town of Schmalkalden in December 1530 to defend the Lutheran Confession of Augsburg. During the 1530s it engaged in a series of negotiations with Henry VIII, which ultimately collapsed because Henry would not accept the Augsburg Confession.

**seminaries:** colleges to train clergy, generally of the Roman Catholic Church; hence 'seminarists', a common and derogatory term for Catholic clergy entering Protestant England from seminaries on the continent.

**serf** (also **villein, native, betagh**): an unfree peasant, commonly of non-English descent, who was bound to a lord or manor.

**shrievalty:** the office discharged by sheriffs. Each shire or county had a sheriff appointed annually to collect royal revenues, serve writs, and arrest those who disturbed the peace.

*studia humanitatis*: the 'humanist' curriculum, based upon grammar, rhetoric, poetry, history, and moral philosophy.

**surrender and regrant:** the modern name for the process whereby Henry VIII and his successors regularized titles by Gaelic law to land.

**suzerain:** in feudal law, the overlord who has no earthly superior, the effective end of the feudal chain. Suzerainty carried with it the basic feudal rights of homage, forfeiture (for disloyalty), wardship, and escheat (reversion of a fief if the feudal inferior died without heirs). In the sixteenth century the English crown revived the claim to suzerainty over Scotland.

**three-field system:** a pattern of arable farming typical of nucleated settlements in lowland Britain. The land was distributed in three open fields with strip cultivation and one of the fields regularly lying fallow.

**tithe:** one-tenth of the produce of a parish was supposed to be handed over to the parish priest, or whoever possessed his right, although many local definitions and customs evolved in response to particular circumstances; known in Scotland as 'teinds'.

**Treaty of Greenwich:** the treaty between England and Scotland in July 1543 which proposed a union of the English and Scottish kingdoms through the eventual marriage of Henry VIII's heir, Prince Edward, and the infant Mary, queen of Scots. The treaty was later repudiated by the Scots.

**Union of the Crowns:** the union, in 1603, of the crowns of England and Scotland, when James VI of Scotland acceded to the English crown as the closest descendant by blood of the deceased Queen Elizabeth. He was the great-grandson of Henry VII.

**vicar apostolic:** in 1591 the papacy decided that a full Irish hierarchy could no longer be maintained, and commissioned priests entitled vicars apostolic to carry out quasi-episcopal functions in Irish dioceses.

**warden:** the principal royal officer in the Anglo-Scottish border region, appointed by English and Scottish kings respectively to organize the defence of the **Marches** (q.v.), and having jurisdiction over the king's subjects there in their **warden courts**, in which **march law** (q.v.) was enforced.

**yeoman:** an English farmer cultivating enough land to enable him to enjoy a surplus, and a social status higher than smaller 'husbandmen', but inferior to the gentry; the sixteenth century idealized the military and other capabilities of the *yeomen* or *yeomanry* of England.

# Genealogy

## The Royal Houses of England (1485–1603) and Scotland (1473–1603)

John of Gaunt (3rd son of Edward III),   m.   (3) Katherine Swynford
Duke of Lancaster                                      (d. 1403)
(d. 1399)

John Beaufort,   m.   Margaret Holland
Marquess of Somerset            (d. 1439)
(d. 1410)

John, Duke of Somerset   m.   Margaret of Bletso
(d. 1444)                                    (d. 1482)

Edmund Tudor,   m.   Margaret Beaufort
Earl of Richmond            (d. 1509)
(d. 1456)

Elizabeth of York   m.   **HENRY VII**
(daughter of Edward IV)       (1485–1509)
(d. 1503)

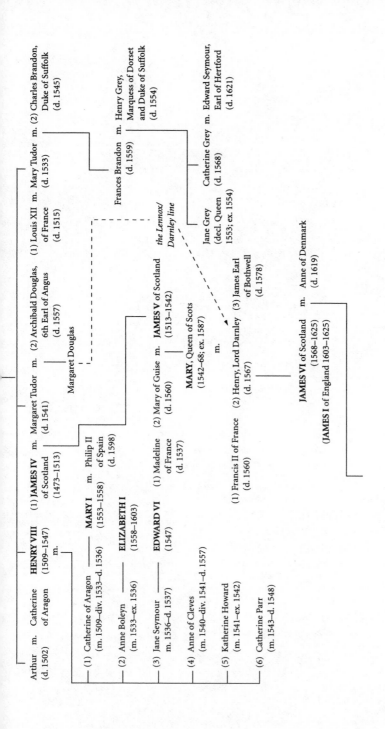

# Maps

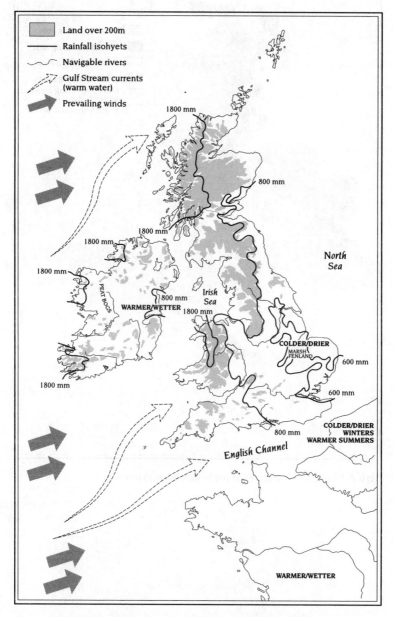

**Map 1** Physical geography of the British Isles, indicating land over 200m and rainfall isohyets

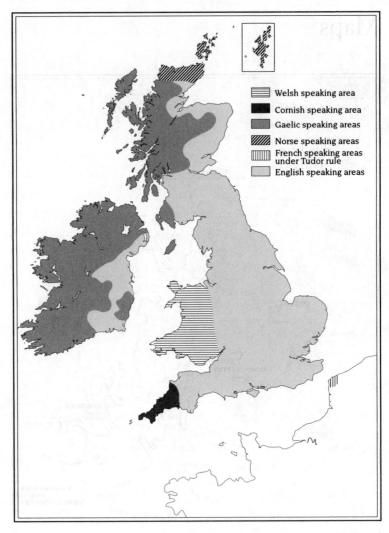

**Map 2** Linguistic boundaries of the British Isles, *c*.1500

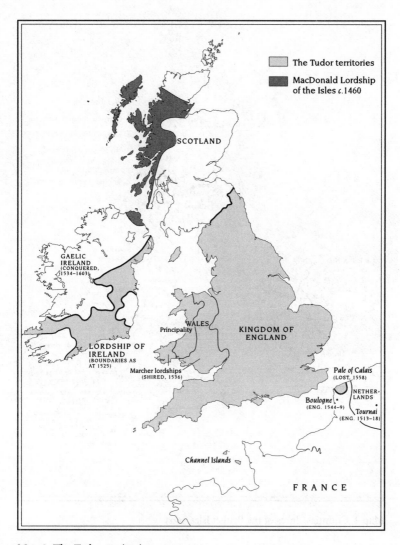

The Tudor territories

MacDonald Lordship
of the Isles *c.*1460

SCOTLAND

GAELIC
IRELAND
(CONQUERED,
1534–1603)

WALES
Principality

KINGDOM OF
ENGLAND

LORDSHIP OF
IRELAND
(BOUNDARIES AS
AT 1525)

Marcher lordships
(SHIRED, 1536)

Pale of Calais
(LOST, 1558)

NETHER-
LANDS

Boulogne
(ENG. 1544–9)

Tournai
(ENG. 1513–18)

Channel Islands

FRANCE

**Map 3** The Tudor territories, *c.*1525

**Map 4** Counties/shires of the British Isles, 1603

**Key for map 4**

*Scottish Counties*
1 Aberdeen
2 Argyll
3 Ayr
4 Banff
5 Berwick
6 Bute
6a Caithness
7 Clackmannan
7a Kinross
8 Cromarty
8a Nairn
9 Dumbarton
10 Dumfries
11 Edinburgh
12 Elgin
13 Fife
14 Forfar
15 Haddington
16 Inverness
17 Kincardine
18 Kirkcudbright
19 Lanark
20 Linlithgow
21 Orkneys & Shetlands
22 Peebles
23 Perth
24 Renfrew
25 Ross
26 Roxburgh
27 Selkirk
28 Stirling
29 Sutherland
30 Wigtown

*Irish Counties*
1 Antrim (1560)
2 Armagh (1585)
3 Carlow
4 Cavan (1579)
5 Clare (1560)
6 Coleraine (1585)
7 Cork
8 Donegal (1585)
9 Down (1560)
10 Dublin
11 Fermanagh (1585)
12 Galway (1569)
13 Kerry
14 Kildare
15 Kilkenny
16 King's County (1557)
17 Leitrim (1585)
18 Limerick
19 Longford (1571)
20 Louth
21 Mayo (1576)
22 Meath
23 Monaghan (1585)
24 Queen's County (1557)
25 Roscommon (1569)
26 Sligo (1576)
27 Tipperary
28 Tyrone (1585)
29 Waterford
30 Westmeath (1542)
31 Wexford
32 Wicklow (1560)

*English Counties*
1 Bedford
2 Berkshire
3 Buckingham
4 Cambridge
5 Cheshire
6 Cornwall
7 Cumberland
8 Derby
9 Devon
10 Dorset
11 Durham
12 Essex
13 Gloucester
14 Hampshire
15 Hereford
16 Hertford
17 Huntingdon
18 Kent
19 Lancashire
20 Leicester
21 Lincoln
22 Middlesex
23 Monmouth (1536)
24 Norfolk
25 Northampton
26 Northumberland
27 Nottingham
28 Oxford
29 Rutland
30 Shropshire
31 Somerset
32 Stafford
33 Suffolk
34 Surrey
35 Sussex
36 Warwick
37 Westmorland
38 Wiltshire
39 Worcester
40 Yorkshire

*Welsh Counties*
41 Anglesey
42 Brecknock (1536)
43 Cardigan
44 Carmarthen
45 Carnarvon
46 Denbigh (1536)
47 Flint
48 Glamorgan
49 Merioneth
50 Montgomery (1536)
51 Pembroke
53 Radnor (1536)

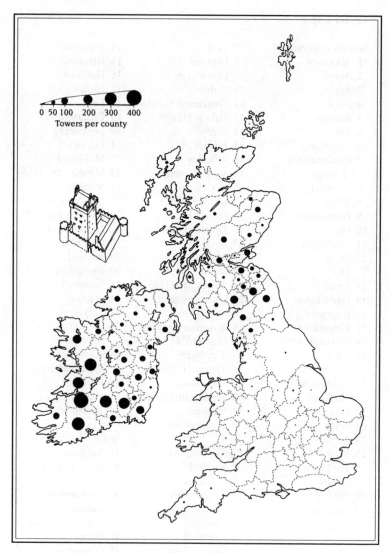

**Map 5** Towerhouses, fourteenth to seventeenth centuries

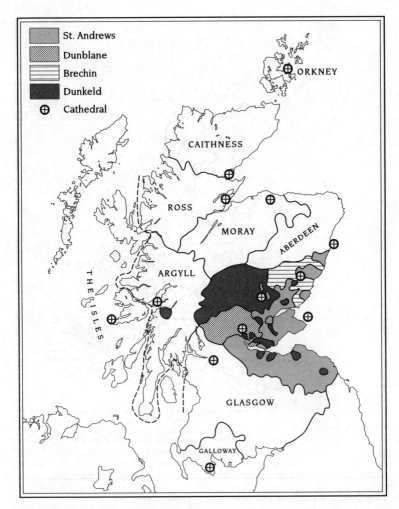

**Map 6** The Scottish dioceses and cathedrals in 1560

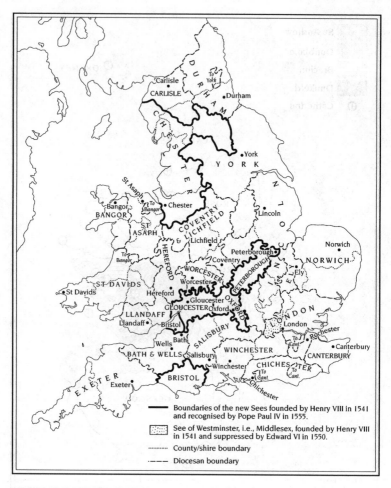

**Map 7** Sees of England and Wales after 1541 and 1555

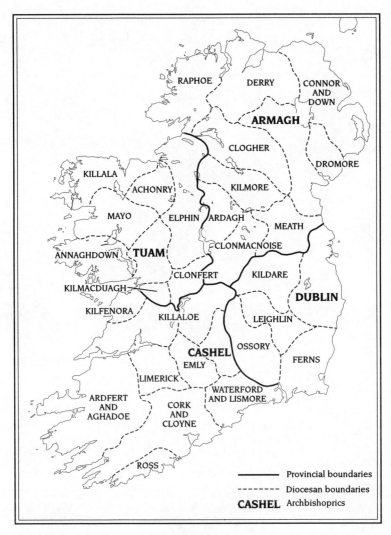

**Map 8** Dioceses in Reformation Ireland

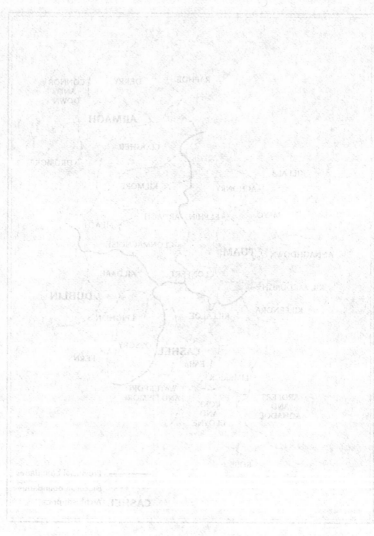

# Index